Disability Interactions

Creating Inclusive Innovations

Synthesis Lectures on Human-Centered Informatics

Editor

John M. Carroll, *Penn State University*

Human-Centered Informatics (HCI) is the intersection of the cultural, the social, the cognitive, and the aesthetic with computing and information technology. It encompasses a huge range of issues, theories, technologies, designs, tools, environments, and human experiences in knowledge work, recreation and leisure activity, teaching and learning, and the potpourri of everyday life. The series publishes state-of-the-art syntheses, case studies, and tutorials in key areas. It shares the focus of leading international conferences in HCI.

Disability Interactions: Creating Inclusive Innovations
Catherine Holloway and Giulia Barbareschi

ISBN: 978-3-031-03749-8 Paperback
ISBN: 978-3-031-03759-7 PDF
ISBN: 978-3-031-03769-6 Hardcover

DOI 10.1007/978-3-031-03759-7

A Publication in the Springer series
SYNTHESIS LECTURES ON HUMAN-CENTERED INFORMATICS
Lecture #53
Series Editor: John M. Carroll, Penn State University

Series ISSN 1946-7680 Print 1946-7699 Electronic

Disability Interactions

Creating Inclusive Innovations

Catherine Holloway and Giulia Barbareschi
University College London

SYNTHESIS LECTURES ON HUMAN-CENTERED INFORMATICS #53

ABSTRACT

Disability interactions (DIX) is a new approach to combining cross-disciplinary methods and theories from Human Computer Interaction (HCI), disability studies, assistive technology, and social development to co-create new technologies, experiences, and ways of working with disabled people. DIX focuses on the interactions people have with their technologies and the interactions which result because of technology use. A central theme of the approach is to tackle complex issues where disability problems are part of a system that does not have a simple solution. Therefore, DIX pushes researchers and practitioners to take a challenge-based approach, which enables both applied and basic research to happen alongside one another. DIX complements other frameworks and approaches that have been developed within HCI research and beyond. Traditional accessibility approaches are likely to focus on specific aspects of technology design and use without considering how features of large-scale assistive technology systems might influence the experiences of people with disabilities. DIX aims to embrace complexity from the start, to better translate the work of accessibility and assistive technology research into the real world. DIX also has a stronger focus on user-centered and participatory approaches across the whole value chain of technology, ensuring we design with the full system of technology in mind (from conceptualization and development to large-scale distribution and access). DIX also helps to acknowledge that solutions and approaches are often non-binary and that technologies and interactions that deliver value to disabled people in one situation can become a hindrance in a different context. Therefore, it offers a more nuanced guide to designing within the disability space, which expands the more traditional problem-solving approaches to designing for accessibility. This book explores why such a novel approach is needed and gives case studies of applications highlighting how different areas of focus—from education to health to work to global development—can benefit from applying a DIX perspective. We conclude with some lessons learned and a look ahead to the next 60 years of DIX.

KEYWORDS

disability, assistive technology, accessibility, human computer interaction

Contents

Preface

When we look back at it, this book has probably been in the making since we started working together in 2014, almost seven years ago, and maybe even before that. The two of us have undoubtedly much in common, but we also come from very different backgrounds. Giulia is an Italian physiotherapist, turned baker, turned medical device scientist, turned assistive technology researcher with a focus on international development. Cathy is an Irish bartender, turned industrial engineer, turned transport accessibility researcher, turned HCI professor with an interest in social innovation. Neither of us has what you would call a traditional or straightforward background, and both of us have, over the years, interacted with many amazing researchers, practitioners, activists, academics, politicians, UN agents, clinicians, and of course people with disabilities in different corners of the world. As we worked in between and across different fields we often found ourselves explaining *"why disability inclusion is so important for creating a better and fairer world for everyone," "why assistive technology is a key aspect of disability inclusion," "why innovation is so crucial to assistive technology,"* and *"why we need to work together to achieve meaningful change."* We have had many discussions—especially with the GDI Hub co-founders and Directors Victoria Austin and Iian McKinnon—about how we answer these questions and realize a fairer world. These conversations have fueled and helped to clarify our thinking. In this book, we make our best effort to discuss these matters in a comprehensive and structured way for the HCI community (as both of us are occasionally prone to rambling about things we are passionate about).

What we have observed over the years is that disability and assistive technology research and practice draw on a variety of domains, ranging from human–computer interaction and clinical sciences to disability studies and global development. In many of these fields people often seem to speak different languages, use different approaches, and measure success in different ways. Yet, we always felt that the ultimate goal of disability justice and inclusion is something that most of share, and that there is so much that can be learned and gained from integrating the perspectives that comes from all these different fields. The scope of the Disability Interactions approach presented in this book is exactly this. Although much of the focus is on Accessible and Assistive Technology and the interactions that take place between people with disabilities and the technologies that they use (and sometimes also the ones that they do not use), we look at them as part of complex socio-economic systems working on a global scale. Through this we hope to show you how, although ensuring that people with disabilities worldwide can access technology that answers their needs is indeed a complex problem, by collaborating with stakeholders across the value chain and drawing from the strengths of different disciplines we can make positive strives toward that goal.

If you are passionate about disability and technology and if you believe that as researchers, practitioners, developers, designers, teachers, and students we can work toward building a fairer and more inclusive world then this book is for you. We hope you enjoy it and that you join us in this journey with your unique wisdom and skills.

Acknowledgments

This book might feature just our names, but it truly would never have seen the light without the wisdom and help of many who have supported us along the journey. First and foremost, we would like to express our sincere gratitude to our editor Diane Cerra for her support and her work across all stages of this book—from its inception through to the actual copy you are reading now. We are also grateful to Dafne Zuleima Morgado Ramirez and Yvonne Rogers who gave us detailed feedback and advice on some sections of the book that had proven to be the hardest for us to pin down. Many thanks also to the wonderful reviewers who provided us with invaluable feedback at various stages of proposals and book drafts. We want to especially thank all the experts and the organizations who have authored the many case studies you find in this book. Their invaluable work provides depth and grounding to the ideas we present across the various chapters. Another huge thanks goes to Jason Wilsher-Mills who agreed to let us use his beautiful art for our book cover; this book would not look nearly as cool without it. We also want to acknowledge our GDI Hub, AT2030, and UCLIC families and extended families—the wonderful colleagues, collaborators, and research participants that have worked with us throughout the last seven years and even before that—whose unique contribution, wisdom, and enthusiasm helped us develop our ideas and conduct the research that is the backbone of this book. Thank you also to the funders of our research, especially the Engineering and Physical Sciences Research Council and UKAID.

Thank you to Jo who managed to keep one of us sane over the years, and by consequence the other one as well.

Finally, a special thanks to Vicki, Benen, and Barney; without their encouragement and support we could hardly manage our day-to-day lives, never mind authoring a book.

We dedicate this book to Barney who died tragically after it was finished, and just before it was published. He was a source of daily inspiration and love.

CASE STUDIES:

We gratefully acknowledge the contributions of all the researchers, designers, experts, and organizations that have authored the case studies found in the chapters of this book.

- **Tigmanshu Bhatnager, Global Disability Innovation Hub** — "Tacilia, Designing Interactive Technology for Blind Students" (Chapter 3)

- **Ben Oldfrey, Global Disability Innovation Hub** — "Local Production Opportunities for Assistive Technology" (Chapter 3)

- **Youngjun Cho, Global Disability Innovation Hub** — "Glance at a Future Technology: Artificial Intelligence-powered Physiological Computing for Better Quality of Life" (Chapter 3)

- **Jake Honeywill and Nancy Mbugua, Motivation UK & Motivation Africa** — "Motivation InnovATe Wheelchairs, Reimagining Wheelchair Bespoke Wheelchair Manufacturing Through Technology" (Chapter 3)

- **Supriya Dey and Amit Prakash, Vision Empower & Centre for Accessibility in the Global South** — "Creating Accessible STEM Content and Making it Available at Scale Through Subodha" (Chapter 3)

- **Manohar Swaminathan and Supriya Dey, Microsoft Research India & Vision** — "Computational Thinking for Children in Schools for the Blind" (Chapter 4)

- **Suparna Biswas, Kilimanjaro Blind Trust Africa** — "Enabling Access to Quality, Inclusive Education for Learners with Visual Impairment in Africa" (Chapter 5)

- **Dafne Zuleima Morgado Ramirez, Global Disability Innovation Hub** — "Neurodiversity and Disability, Reflections" (Chapter 5)

- **Jamie Danemayer, Global Disability Innovation Hub AT2030** —"Measuring Need through Population Health Data and Screening Tools" (Chapter 6)

- **Sujatha Srinivasan, Indian Institute of Technology Madras** — "The NeoFly-Neo-Bolt System, Enabling Seamless Indoor-Outdoor Mobility for Wheelchair Users" (Chapter 6)

- **Richard Cave, UCL and Adecco** — "Google Euphonia, Supporting People with Impaired Speech to be Better Understood" (Chapter 7)

Terminology

Before we begin the book, we want to acknowledge the complexities of terminology within the space of disability.

Terminology, how we describe people with disabilities, or disabled people, is contested, complex, and reflects a history of stigmatization and marginalization. There are layers to the debate concerning disability terminology. At the highest level there is a tension between geographies and groups who prefer "person-first" language. This language acknowledges that people are people first whether or not they have a disability. The aim of person-first language is to level the playing field and ensure people with disabilities are recognized first and foremost as people. Therefore, whether speaking about people with or without disabilities, we as scholars should stipulate the population. However, we tend not to do this and instead tend only to use person-first language when referring to disability [136]. This can have the unintended effect of introducing a bias [136].

Within the United Nations and within specific geographies such as the United States and across the continent of Africa, person-first language is passionately defended and used. However, in the United Kingdom of Great Britain and Northern Ireland, things are perceived differently. Here, identity-first language is much preferred, and "disabled people" is the term of choice of the community. There are three reasons for this. The first is simple—it claims the identity of the person, as being a disabled person is integral to the individual and their culture and not a thing which can be separated from the person [73]. Second, it reclaims the power of the term; this is especially true of certain sub-groups within the umbrella term of "disability," e.g., autistic and d/Deaf communities. Finally, we come to grammar and the common principle of having positive pronouns before a noun [206]. When speaking of anything positive we state it first—for example intelligent people. We would not say "people with intelligence" for example, and as Dame Tanni Grey-Thompson once tweeted—"Yes. I'm not keen on person with a disability. Makes it sound like I have a choice. I'm not a person with Welshness" [383].

The history of the Disability Rights movement which you will see in Chapter 1 helped to move society from a medical model of disability—where the problem sat at the level of impairment and the person, to the social model of disability—where the problem was one of interaction and design. People were excluded from society not because of an impairment but in how we had designed society which excluded their participation. This shift, as you will see, was essential, monumental, and is still ongoing. In addition, language is an important part of the Disability Rights struggle. It is beyond the scope of this book to fully unpack this struggle, but it is important that as interaction designers we are fully aware of our use of language and the power it holds to either further the inclusion agenda or prevent progress. It may well be that language will further evolve, and that words will change their meaning over time as people's attitudes change and society evolves, and so we present the glossary below as a good starting point. The good news is that the terms referring to the technology people use are less contested and more forgiving to mistakes. We would urge all researchers to work with disabled people and their groups when planning their studies and deciding on language choices.

With regards to technology, the following terminology is used in this book. First, we use Accessibility and Assistive Technology (AAT) to refer to the intersection of disability and technology that covers specific technology developed for people with disabilities and accessible technologies which have been inclusively designed. We use this as a collective term, when we are talking about the broad area which encompasses accessibility and assistive technology.

We specifically refer to accessible technology when we mean digital, mostly software, and interfaces which have been designed to be usable by as many people as possible. Accessible technology is mostly designed under the ethos of universal design (sometimes called inclusive design), which is the design process which ensures as many people as possible can use a technology or access a place without the need for a specialized adaptation.

Assistive technology (AT) is a type of specialized adaptation which in HCI is often used to refer to products or interfaces which have been adapted for a person with disabilities. Within the domain of Health, assistive technology has a particular meaning and refers to not only an assistive product (examples of which include wheelchairs, hearing aids or communication aids) but also the policy, provision, trained personnel, and service through which a user is given an assistive product and trained to use the product. We use the two versions of AT within this book depending on whether we are talking within the Health or HCI domains and hope the specific definition is clear at the time for the reader. Understanding the differences between the two definitions is important for a nuanced understanding and therefore better future collaboration with our Health colleagues.

Finally, we have used the term Global South throughout the book to recognize those countries which lie geographically to the South of the equator and are often operating with fewer economical resources, due to a variety of historical and socio-political reasons. We understand that others might use the term developing countries or majority world and while there is not scope here to debate the nuances, we have adopted Global South as the most meaningful and respected term. We recognize there is a wide variety of socio-economic and environmental differences within the geography covered by "Global South."

CHAPTER 1

History of Disability Interactions

This chapter aims to give an historical overview of the field of disability interactions and to bring to the reader's attention some of the most pivotal moments of accessibility and assisstive technology (AT) research in the context of human-computer interaction (HCI). It is not meant as a systematic review and is not by any means exhaustive. More systematic reviews have been conducted previously, including topic-specific critical literature reviews such as those related to neurodivergence conducted by Spiel and colleagues in 2019 and 2021 [362, 363] or the comprehensive systematic review recently carried out by Mack et al. [236]. Here, instead, we look to set the argument for what has been achieved in Accessibility and AT and what is left to do.

1.1 INITIAL INTERACTIONS: OLDER HISTORY WITH NOVEL IDEAS

The history of the connections between the field of HCI and the areas of Disability, AT, and Accessibility[1] is rich and diverse. Engineers and computer scientists worked on the development of the first motorized wheelchairs and Alternative and Augmentative communication devices from as early as 1916 and 1960, respectively. However, it was not until the mid-1970s that researchers began to fully concentrate on how people with disabilities used these devices in everyday life. Some of the earliest work in this area focused on the usability of Augmented and Assistive Communication (AAC) devices to enable individuals with Cerebral Palsy, who could not communicate verbally and were unable to use a typewriter, to articulate speech using simplified interfaces with sliders and switches [112, 402].

The first publication in this area at the *Conference on Human Factors in Computing Systems of the Association for Computing and Machinery*, ubiquitously known as CHI, one of the oldest and most important venues for publication of HCI work, was called "Human Interface Design and the Handicapped User" [76]. This paper was written in support of a panel discussion, planned for the CHI conference in 1986, that primarily aimed to provide attendees and readers with a broad overview of disability. The paper presented connections between the different types of impairments that were associated with specific conditions and the types of AT that helped facilitate computer access. A second aim of the paper was to highlight how the decisions that designers and researchers made during the development of computer systems impacted accessibility for people with disabilities [76]. Interestingly, panelists expressed some incredibly progressive and visionary recommendations,

---

[1] The terms disability research, assistive technology research, and accessibility research are used interchangeably within this chapter.

such as advocating for universally accessible hardware and software, rather than relying on customized solutions. Customization and specialist interfaces were seen as impractical and not economically viable on a large scale [76]. Furthermore, panelists highlighted how improved accessibility for persons with disabilities often means improved accessibility for all. For example, an alternative to a traditional keyboard was seen as potentially beneficial not only for a person with a physical disability, but also a busy business executive who finds the traditional input method slow and clunky [76].

In many ways, this panel discussion sums up many of the arguments put forward in this book. We are simply elaborating the argument further and looking again at the problem space. Since the panel there has been much which has advanced, and yet, still much to do. Despite the clarity displayed at the panel, the union between designing for users with disabilities and universal design did not converge immediately. For many years, disability and AT remained a relative niche area of interest among HCI researchers and practitioners. Much of the work focused on strictly controlled lab-based studies that aimed to evaluate bespoke solutions for individuals with specific impairments, usually physical and visual impairments [121, 409]. Although often motivated by a desire to help and using methods that are scientifically sound especially for exploring specific isolated research questions, they were conducted before the influence of in-the-wild studies that allowed for more context and depth to be studied to complement the strict lab-based scientific rigor. Therefore, they failed to be transformational in their impact, but rather developed incremental successes. As noted by Gilnert and York [140], the research at the intersection of HCI and disability was simply too scarce and the effort of promoting "design for disability" was incorrectly seen as not cost-effective for most developers and manufacturers. Furthermore, when we look back at those early research studies, it is easy to see how, in line with the main AT trends of the time, disability was strictly seen through the lens of the medical model with access challenges solely depicted as being linked to personal functional limitations with scarce consideration for the social dynamics that reinforced exclusionary practices [247]. This of course had important implications for HCI research and practice as disability was described as a problem caused by a functional impairment that should be somehow corrected or bridged by technological means [247].

The passing of the American with Disabilities Act in 1990 partially contributed to an increased interest in the areas of disability, AT, and accessibility in HCI research [155, 67, 401]. It is worth noting that much of the interest generated in HCI following the introduction of the ADA in the United States, and similar legislation in Europe and Australia in the 1990s, was rather narrowly focused on issues related to computer accessibility in relation to work [155]. Nonetheless, this increase in interest led to the production of important documents for designers, engineers, and developers stating the importance of computer accessibility and providing guidelines for the development of accessible systems [403]. Moreover, and more specific to the HCI community, this led in 1994 to the launch of the First International ACM Conference on Assistive Technologies, commonly known as ASSETS (the conference changed its name in 2004 and became *the International ACM SIGACCESS Conference on Computers and Accessibility*).

The launch of the, then bi-annual, ASSETS conference represents a turning point for the HCI community as it indicates that the fields of disability, accessibility, and AT had gained sufficient interest to deserve the creation of a dedicated venue for publication and discussion. However, many of the problems outlined earlier in relation to a very medicalized and functional vision of disability, combined with a prominent focus on the development of bespoke and individualized solutions, which were unlikely to scale, were still largely present [237].

1.2 UNIVERSAL DESIGN AND INTERACTIONS FOR VARYING ABILITY

As ASSETS began its life, so did the movement of the concept of Universal Design (UD) begin to take root in HCI. UD was defined in the late 1990s by Ronald L. Mace as "The design of products and environments to be usable by all people, to the greatest extent possible, without the need for adaptation or specialized design" [106]. This definition and the movement which followed had several important implications, but two are particularly notable.

The first is UD stipulation for designers, researchers, engineers, and product developers to include the needs of all potential users, including users with disabilities, from the beginning of the design process [302]. In this light, accessibility needs to be built into any product, application, or program from the beginning and should never be considered as an afterthought [ibid.]. This was a huge shift from the prevailing wisdom of the time which was still developing inaccessible mainstream products, which then relied on AT or specialized adaptations as a retrofitted bridge to make the original product accessible. However, this meant that the additional technologies and adaptations were outside of the main product maintenance life cycle, necessitating separate updates to the AT as and when the main product was updated. This is highlighted by Stephanidis et al. [302] who describes this design process as "reactive." A proactive approach to UD was described as a potential solution that targeted the root of inaccessibility. The second important consequence of the rise of UD was to present accessibility as a mainstream issue, rather than something that only affected or concerned a small group of people. In part, this was linked to the fact that UD surfaced multiple needs from multiple user groups, which previously have been segregated into niche problems or areas. UD pushed developers to collate these different access needs together, and see them as a comprehensive complex problem, rather than a collection of smaller and fragmented issues [369]. When clustering together all the people who had various kinds of access needs as a single, if diverse, group they suddenly appeared as a much larger user base!

Case Study: Web Accessibility

The UD movement defined a clear series of general design principles that could be distilled into guidelines and recommendations that could guide researchers and designers throughout the development of new interfaces, programs, and technologies. Perhaps the most notable example of universal accessibility guidelines is the Web Content Accessibility Guidelines (WCAG), originally established in 1999 by the Web Accessibility Initiative (WAI) of the World Wide Web Consortium (W3C). The scope of the WCAG was to provide specific standards enabling developers to ensure that the websites and applications they created were accessible. One of the major strengths of the WCAG is that they do not just provide developers with broad and fuzzy suggestions, but they are an actionable framework that is both technical and specific, and features supporting documentation with instructions and techniques for testing the accessibility of a system. As highlighted by Abascal, this attention to both high-level principles and more concrete guidelines and methods brought by the rise of UD helped to create more unity in the field of accessibility and AT within HCI, moving away from the "patchwork of adaptations" that characterized earlier efforts [465].

However, web accessibility is still not a given and much of the Internet remains inaccessible or poorly accessible to many users, especially visually impaired users who access the Internet through screen readers.

UD supporters in many ways, adopted, reinforced, and helped to mainstream some of the arguments made by pioneers in the HCI and accessibility discourse. Specifically, by highlighting how any user, even one who does not identify as having a disability, could be impaired by environmental factors or temporary circumstances, and would benefit from more accessible interfaces [44]. Poignantly, the title of a panel hosted at the CHI conference in 1996, which featured prominent academics, industry researchers, and disability activists was "Everyone Has Special Needs" and panelists discussed several scenarios in which accessible interfaces could be beneficial to people without disabilities [44]. Only in more recent years researchers have in fact started to better explore this area and developed studies that look at the potential of interfaces developed for people with disabilities to support users without disabilities facing different types of situational impairments [48, 251].

It is worth noticing however, that UD and AT were (and are) not seen as opposing concepts, but as complementary ones [44]. UD did not argue for a single solution that could accommodate for the needs of all people but for flexible and complementary solutions that could be suitable for different users and different contexts of use [ibid.]. This push toward flexible systems that can adapt to different users, instead of the previous mindset that focused on providing users with adaptations so that they could interact with an inflexible system, reached a turning point in 2011 when Wobbrock and colleagues [433] proposed the concept of ability-based design.

The first defining attribute of this novel approach was, as the name suggests, a shift of focus from what the person could not do to what they could do (from "disability" to "ability") [433]. According to the authors, ability, like height, money, age, or power, is a continuous rather than discrete scale and it is dependent on the characteristics of the context as much as on the characteristics of the individual [230]. This reframing of the interaction between individuals and systems is much more inclusive and egalitarian at its core and builds on some of the most important visions expressed by accessibility scholars and advocates over the years [44, 76]. One could, for example, possibly argue against the statement by Bergman et al. that "everyone has special needs" [44], however, it is near impossible to rebuke the notion that everyone has abilities. This is an important inflection point in our thinking as a community. Wobbrock and colleagues [433] plot factors that limit one's ability to use technologies along two axes: location and duration (Figure 1.1). The former ranges between "from within," an intrinsic factor that is always present regardless of the context, and "from without," an extrinsic limitation that is removed or disappears as the context changes. The duration aspect instead ranged between "Ephemeral" factors that may only last seconds to "Enduring" factors that would affect the person for decades [ibid.]. As argued by the authors, although transitory or situational impairments are by no means equated to the experiences associated with longer term impairments, they might benefit from similar design approaches [ibid.].

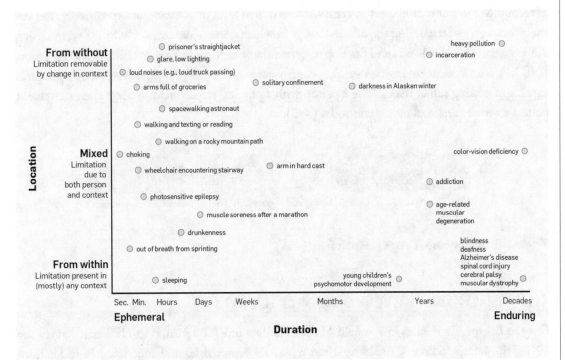

Figure 1.1: Factors that limit one's ability to use technologies along two axes: location and duration. From [433], used with permission.

The second defining attribute of the ability-based design approach is the focus on developing systems that are inherently able to adapt to the abilities of the user, without the need for external tools to mediate the interaction (see Figure 1.2). This idea for systems which are both modular and adaptable successfully tackles issues of high cost, cumbersome maintenance, and fragmented complexity which were linked to more traditional AT research [102]. At the same time, the clear articulation of a system that could implement multiple modular solutions in response to varying user needs serves to dispel a criticism often directed at UD, that of pursuing "one-size-fits-all" approaches [302]. Instead, ability-based design systems would proactively assess the performance of the users and characteristics of the context, and adapt its interface in accordance with the situational needs of the person [433].

A notable example that illustrates how ability-based design works in practice is SmartTouch, an adaptive touch-based interactive technique that is able to analyze how users interact with a touch screen and identify their intended point of contact based on the different touch behaviors that they use (which often involve different parts of the hand) [273]. The adaptability of this approach is essential for many people who have reduced upper limb dexterity as they might not be able to comply with common requirements of most touch screen interfaces which rely on accurate and consistent finger-based touch input [273]. Instead of focusing on way in which external pieces of technology might enable users to achieve the required level of accuracy and consistency, the authors focus on understanding the different ways in which users make contact with the screen using different parts of their hands and develop a system that adapts to their own abilities and behaviors [ibid.]. A second example is when gaming controls are used to map to the movements a person is capable of making rather than asking a person with a physical impairment to adapt their movement patters to what is needed by the controller [433].

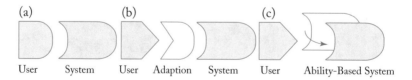

Figure 1.2: Ability-based design diagram from [433].

1.3   LOOKING BEYOND FUNCTIONALITY

Despite the great advances in the field of Accessibility and AT research in HCI made since the 1970s, the interpretation of disability often remained centered around functional considerations related to what people with disabilities could not (or could) do [230]. This is further linked to the fact that researchers and practitioners often evaluate AT based on the relative functional advantage that they provide to the individual [15] However, research that looked at the relationship that people developed with their assistive devices and the reasons that affected their decision to discontinue use and abandon these technologies, showed that personal and social factors played an important role [294, 314, 349]. In a pivotal paper that sought to understand how the use of AT by people with disabilities was affected by the social context, Shinohara and Wobbrock [350] conducted an interview study involving 20 participants with different disabilities. From their analysis it emerged that concerns around stigma associated with AT could lead to outright refusal to use a device such a white cane or a hearing aid as it would mark the person as different, making their disability the most prominent feature about themselves. Technological devices were often associated with reduced fear of stigma, but the aesthetic appeal of these devices could have significant implications on how comfortable participants felt using them in social settings [ibid.]. Furthermore, the use of AT was surrounded by two main misperceptions which caused significant social friction between people with and without disabilities: the belief that AT would functionally eliminate disability and that, consequently, people with disabilities would be completely helpless without AT [350]. These misperceptions were guided by the incorrect assumption that challenges associated with functional impairments would lead to a continuous need for assistance, coupled with an overestimation of what AT can actually do. Together, these beliefs reinforce each other and contribute to a problematic view of the relationship between persons with disabilities and their AT. Ultimately, the findings from this study highlighted how social *acceptance* might be a more important and comprehensive goal for AT than functional outcomes alone [350].

The exploration of the social implication of AT design and use has gained increased relevance in the last decade. For example, further work from Shinohara and Wobbrock [351] looked at how the visibility and use of assistive devices shaped both how people with disabilities perceived themselves and were perceived by others, generating feelings of self-efficacy, self-confidence, or self-consciousness [351]. The testimonies collected through this four-week diary study involving both people with and without disabilities showed how the functional advantage granted by a successful interaction with an AT could boost feelings of self-efficacy, whereas failure or breakdown of AT caused people to draw unwanted attention and feel self-conscious, which was seen as particularly problematic in work situations [351].

Attracting attention to one's AT is not always seen as problematic by users, but what is important is that the person is able to decide what image of themselves they feel comfortable and proud of, and then are able and empowered to project this. For example, when Profita and colleagues [307] analyzed an online community of users of cochlear implants and their families they found that many people liked to customize their devices in ways that increased their visibility. The scope of many of these customizations was to allow the wearer to express their own identity and creativity, creating objects that could appear desirable rather than stigmatizing, and celebrating anything from meaningful life events, sports teams, or one's sense of style [ibid.]. In a follow-up study conducted in 2018 [308], the authors conducted a series of interviews to better understand the motivations that drove users to customize their cochlear implants. Responses from participants highlighted how individuals often had multiple and complex reasons for wanting to modify their devices in a way that made them both more visible and personal. Whereas some were more motivated by the willingness to demonstrate agency and express themselves, others wanted to attract attention to their device to increase awareness around deafness and hearing loss or signal to others that they might need to adapt their communication as they were interacting with a person who was deaf or hard of hearing [ibid.]. Similarly, in a study involving 14 adults with upper limb loss, Bennett et al. [39] explored how prosthetic devices influenced the development of their sense of identity both as individuals and as part of larger communities allowing them to leverage their own bodies as an "intimate laboratory" for aesthetic exploration.

These studies, and many others which have investigated the multifaceted interaction between people with disabilities, AT and society at large, highlight the complexity in the conceptualization of disability which should NEVER be reduced to a solely functional dimension [40, 62, 177, 389]. In this context, HCI and accessibility research need better frameworks and theoretical grounding to ensure that studies focusing on AT remain aware of this complexity and question their goals and outcomes as much as the methods leveraged to engage with participants. An influential example of this relatively recent movement is the article published in 2010 by Mankoff and colleagues [247]. In this paper, the authors highlight how the field of Disability Studies and the one of AT often share the ultimate goals of increasing understanding of disability and developing solutions that could help tackle issues that are relevant to people with disabilities [247]. However, the field of AT is often plagued by ableist and paternalistic rhetoric that, despite the inherent drive to "do good," could often reinforce unbalanced power dynamics and generate negative unintended consequences [247]. Authors argue that a closer link with the field of Disabilities Studies could help AT and accessibility research to gain a more nuanced understanding of the role of technology in can play, both positively and negatively, in the lives of people with disabilities moving beyond simplistic functional considerations and encompassing crucial societal and cultural aspects [247]. Unfortunately, accessibility research that actively engages with the field of Disability Studies is still rare and more recently scholars working at the intersection of HCI and disability through the lens of participation, social justice, and intersectionality have called for the development of a Critical Disability manifesto in HCI that could serve as a theoretical ground for future research in the space [364].

This acknowledgment of the increased complexity of disability has also been pursued by Frauenberger [350], who proposed the use of critical realism to better understand the experience of disability, guiding both the development and the evaluation of AT. Interpreting disability using an interactional lens allows researchers to capture the different layers that shape the experience of the individual including physical, biological, psychological, psychosocial, and emotional, socioeconomic, cultural, and normative dimensions [131]. This non-reductionist critical approach could also foster increased reflection on the methods used for research promoting ethical reflections and moving the goals of AT from the resolution of problems toward the promotion of wellbeing in a way that preserves the agency of participants [ibid.]. Similar considerations that strongly argue for the use of participatory methods to avoid the risk of oversimplification and reductionist misconceptions in AT and accessibility research were also made by Spiel et al. [361] and Bennett et al. [41]. Both authors highlight how empathy-building exercises led by researchers and designers have the tendency to reduce the experiences of people with disabilities to simplistic vignettes that fail to truly capture the experience of the individual and silence the voice of people with disabilities in favor of the interpretation of the more powerful researcher [41, 361].

Disabled scholars and advocates have also highlighted how these unbalanced and oppressive power dynamics that silence the voice of people with disabilities are often perpetrated in both the HCI and AT research communities and the work that they produce. Ymous and colleagues [438] describe the systematic dismissal of people with disabilities, including scholars with disabilities themselves, as experts of their own lived experience as epistemic violence. Moreover, through the testimonies of researchers working across different domains of HCI, accessibility, and AT presented by Williams [427], we can see how intersectional identities can create even more complex and marginalized experiences when different elements such as race, gender, religion, and professional roles are taken into account. To increase accountability among researchers, Williams and Gilbert [425] argue for the need to explore both the positive and negative implications of the technologies that are conceptualized and developed and the methods used to engage (or not engage) people with disabilities in their development. Ultimately, even though accessibility and AT research strive to promote positive change in the world, they need to acknowledge their own potential to cause harm by perpetrating discriminatory and paternalistic narrative about disability.

What we are seeing, in essence, is an emergence of a more interdisciplinary approach to disability within HCI, with a closer connection to disciplines like disability studies, which allows us to develop a more nuanced and therefore deeper understanding of disability to help guide our design process. We will return to this need for interdisciplinary working, but first conclude our introduction with a question: As experiential and contextual factors play such an important role in the relationship between individuals with disabilities and their ATs, it is worth asking: What happens when the environmental, societal, and cultural context are significantly different?

1.4   IS ACCESSIBILITY RESEARCH TRULY GLOBAL?

The large majority of the 1 billion people with disabilities in the world live in the Global South [449]. It is worth asking how this fact plays out or is indeed present in the available research in AT HCI and accessibility. Are we capturing people's experiences in these contexts and how does this reflect in the development of new solutions that are contextually appropriate? Although in the last few years, research in the field of accessibility and AT has begun to grow, combining forces with the HCI for development work, the number of relevant studies is, unfortunately, still scarce [265]. The ethnographic study conducted by Jones and Pal [197] with AT users from Sierra Leone shows how people leveraged AT and ICT to promote an image of themselves as competent and technically savvy in contrast to the stereotypical label of people with disabilities as "helpless" from members of the community.

In several studies, participants with different disabilities highlighted how both the inaccessibility of the environment and discriminatory beliefs surrounding disability in their society create insurmountable barriers that can be impossible to navigate without AT and the presence of a strong social network [31, 35, 197]. At the same time, the multi-city study conducted by Pal et al. [289] shows how access to both Information and Communication Technologies (ICT) and ATs can be incredibly more complicated for people with disabilities in the Global South, regardless of the presence of appropriate high-level policy frameworks in most countries. The reasons for this limited accessibility are varied and encompass individual, environmental, and societal factors ranging from cost of devices and perceived benefit associated with them, to infrastructural weaknesses such as lack of electricity or language barriers [289].

In many of these studies, stigma emerges as one of the most insidious and pervasive barriers that surround not only access and use of assistive devices, but the experience of disability as a whole [32, 212, 213, 289]. Despite their functional benefits, ATs can become a mark of disability that attracts unwanted attention on the individual, going as far as completely overshadowing one's identity [32] or becoming the cause of abuse and discrimination [212]. The poor quality of many of the devices available to individuals and their inappropriateness to both the environmental and cultural contexts often creates additional issues from both a functional and social point of view [274]. In contrast, the development of assistive products and services that enable people with disabilities to express themselves and feel empowered not only by the device itself, but by the service provision model that accompanies the product is key to evoke feelings of agency and ownership of the AT [34]. Interestingly, these considerations are not only relevant to the users of ATs, but also to the service providers that are essential for the successful delivery of these products [34].

Finally, the social infrastructure of the individual seems to play a much more relevant role in how people with disabilities in the Global South access and use AATs compared to the Global North (areas laying North of the Equator) [31, 35, 289]. This can play out in two ways. First, we see mediated interactions which are not as common in the Global South act as facilitators to AAT. This was demonstrated in a recent study in Kenya which showed how friends, family members, or other members of the community who acted as supporters or intermediaries were essential to enable successful interactions between technology and people with disabilities living in the informal settlement of Kibera in Kenya [31, 35]. Second, due to the multiple physical and social challenges faced by people with disabilities in the Global South, technology use can be more transformative.

For example, people with visual impairment in India [406] found technology could unlock the possibility of widening one's social sphere, engaging with others in a way that would otherwise be extremely challenging [406].

1.5   WHERE DO WE GO FROM HERE?

Throughout this chapter we briefly explored the evolving relationship between AT and HCI from the initial encounters largely driven by narrowly focused technological pursuits that aimed to tackle specific functional issues that researchers associated with disability, to more cohesive and global efforts to capture the nuanced experience of disability through active and equal collaboration with people with disabilities. What is noteworthy is how well the evolution which has taken place—accelerated by UD and later advanced by ability-based design—builds on and toward the vision set by the first CHI panel on this topic. In the next chapter we build further. By taking a more critical approach to the assessment of how far we have come, we hope to help build the argument toward why we think a new framework for Disability Interactions could help to drive an even more impactful research agenda.

CHAPTER 2

Why We Need a Disability Interactions Approach

2.1 WHY A NEW APPROACH?

After having read the first chapter of this book, you might have started to ask yourself the following question: With so many theories, conceptualizations, and frameworks cutting across the fields of disability, AT, and HCI, do we really need a new one? (If you are a student this probably translates into something along the lines of "With the tens of papers and publications I already need to read for my course, why should I add this book to the pile?") We believe there is a need for a conversation on the role HCI has in tackling the wider problems facing people with disabilities. In many instances, HCI researchers will be a part of much wider teams delivering projects, both big and small. We are looking to bring together strands of emerging research from Disability Studies to HCI for Development, to start a conversation about how we develop a more impactful research agenda for AT and accessibility research. This chapter is a part of that discussion. It will set the foundations for Chapter 3, when we will look at some dimensions along which we can measure this wider agenda of disability interaction and introduce tools to help develop more integrated working across disciplines and teams seeking to leverage technology for disability inclusion. The reasons for our belief in a re-focused energy are several and we will attempt to summarize them in this chapter. However, the first thing to note is that Disability Interaction does not aim to be in opposition or even to surpass other approaches and frameworks. In fact, it couldn't and wouldn't exist without them. Disability Interactions strives to bring together and build on concepts such as Universal Design [96], Ability-Based-Design [433], Critical Realism [131], and Living Disability Theory [177].

2.2 ISSUES OF SCALE

HCI has had a tremendous impact on increasing the understanding of how people with disabilities use existing technologies in different contexts from the workplace [63], to classrooms [261], public transport [82], and their own homes [3]. At the same time, HCI and accessibility researchers have worked hard to find novel and disruptive ways to engage with people with disabilities in the design of new bespoke technologies that can address challenges encountered in everyday life [158, 277, 311, 420]. Although extremely valuable, these technologies can suffer from the problem of scale, which transcends all of HCI research [328].

HCI is difficult to scale. This is highlighted by Rosenberg [328], who describes well the dilemma: "How a seed is carried on a breeze, how a bird flies, and how a 747 aircraft moves across the globe are simply not the same, even though all three are technically examples of flight in motion. The demands of scale change everything!" Scale can be described across three dimensions: with respect to the number of users, the diversity of setting and contexts, or the interaction of multiple technology ecosystems [328]. We look at each in turn with respect to AAT.

2.2.1   GOING BEYOND SMALL-SCALE STUDIES

Solutions designed with a small group of users or for a specific context do not necessarily behave in the same way when deployed in different settings or adopted by a larger number of users. Incorrect assumptions about the consistency of technological systems at different scales can be generally referred to as a Scaling Fallacy [75]. It is worth remembering that scale is only partially an issue of number of users or devices, but more generally one of complexity. Brown et al. [66] describe three types of scale in relation to HCI that contribute to increasing complexity: the number of users of a particular technology, the different contexts of use in which a technology can be used and deployed, and the interactions between different systems and technologies. According to Brown and colleagues [ibid.], many of the HCI methods and approaches don't enable us to deal with these concerns satisfactorily as practical studies are limited in the number of users that can be recruited. This leads to an approach where technologies are often studied one at the time and in a particular context, and layers of interactions between technologies across multiple systems are rarely explored.

In the context of disability inclusion, accessibility research, and assistive technologies, scale is critical to ensuring that all people with disabilities have full access to their human rights and can lead fulfilling lives [107]. People with disabilities represent 15% of the population [449], and most people will live some part of their life with one or more disabilities, as they age or acquire an injury during the course of their life. We will therefore all interact as a person with a disability with technology at some point in our lives and, depending on our individual circumstances—including personal preferences, habits, and the social and environmental factors—our needs and desires from our interactions with technology will vary. This again brings to light the need for adaptability at a user level and across systems which we saw argued in Chapter 1.

Case Study: Accessibility Mapping

A perfect example of how scale can create challenges for researchers working on disability and technology is represented by the difficulties encountered around accessibility mapping. Many accessibility assessments for sidewalks and various urban spaces are routinely carried out through in-person auditing done by professionals or, less commonly, by private individuals using specially designed reporting tools [164]. An auditor will physically show up to a street and tick on a checklist aspects of the street which are accessible, or not, as the case may be. Systems such as the Pedestrian Environment Review Software (PERS) are used for these purposes [393]. However, most of these strategies, which work well on small areas, or in regard to very specific accessibility issues relevant to a particular group of users, encounter significant challenges (namely cost and number of trained personnel) when they need to be scaled to larger geographical areas or used by groups of users with diverse access needs [109]. In the 2019 forum on Universal Interactions, Froehlich and colleagues [132] outlined five Grand Challenges in Accessible Maps. These challenges encompass diverse aspects including data collection, data management, modeling, accessibility of maps produced, and user foci [ibid.]. All of them can be attributed to the complexity that originates from the need to scale either in relation to the need to collect increasingly large amounts of data to categorize and map extended geographical areas, or to provide information to an expanding group of users in a way that is both relevant and accessible to them. Take, for example, data collection, where we don't yet have a reliable or open collection method, and we are unclear even who might collect the data or how to categories transient problems that might be linked to situational impairments which occur alongside, or in addition to, pre-existing impairments (e.g., the noise created by roadworks might cause hearing difficulties for all pedestrian, but its impact would be different for a person who relies on echolocation when navigating). For the blind and partially sighted community, an open standard has been produced to try and overcome some of these issues, ensuring universal delivery of information to users. However, even with this there is a lack of uptake of solutions. Mapping solutions for those on wheels—mostly developed for wheelchair users, but useful for anyone who likes step-free routes and access—have issues of sufficient data. Relying on user-led mapping, using a citizen-science approach is in effect only getting us so far, this is even the case when we use already collected data, e.g., AXS map use of Google maps to classify sections of street infrastructure. We attempted to overcome some of these challenges by developing a sort of fit-bit for wheelchair users which could classify street conditions automatically as well as capturing push style of the user to help solve two problems: (1) personalized both automatic accessibility mapping; and (2) wheelchair user fitness and upper limb health [86]. However, despite good technical advances and user acceptance, we found it difficult to advance the solution beyond the prototype stage. Something which is a frequent challenge to new technologies in this space. Finally, as highlighted by Hamraie [161], even when public and shared spaces are compliant with accessibility guidelines this does not guarantee "collective access," especially for those individuals who fall outside the disability categorization adopted by most legal frameworks. Leveraging digital tools for capturing and presenting accessibility data is important. However, we also need a critical examination of dominant sociospatial practices that govern politics of access and exclusion [ibid.]. Ultimately, collective action guided by the lived experiences of people with disabilities and other marginalized groups is essential to understand what we mean by accessibility and how we can move beyond observing and critiquing the existing built environment to promoting architectures of inclusion and pursue disability justice through the creation of spaces that are truly accessible to all [161, 162].

2.2.2   SETTINGS AND CONTEXTS

Technologies that aim to scale also need to consider how different contexts of use can have an impact on what devices and practices might be considered acceptable, practical, or even feasible by users. Although these considerations are relevant for any type of technology, they become particularly important in the context of disability where people are often subject to stigma and discrimination and therefore are sensitive to how they are viewed and perceived. In the context of countries where disability is more normalized and accepted, we see people with disabilities using AT as a means of expression. For example, we see prosthetic limbs being designed for children which are themed as superheroes (see Chapter 3 for more). However, in research in Uganda for example where we still see evidence of stigmatization of people with disabilities, we find people rejecting more functional limbs in favor of limbs which are non-functional but which look more like an anatomical limb [29, 205]. The more general point here is that the use of AT significantly affects the way in which people with disabilities perceive themselves and are perceived by others which has consequences in relation to disability stigma [126]. The study by Branham and Kane [62] shows how people with visual impairments and their sighted companions modify their behaviors and strategies to manage accessibility, often to their own detriment, when outsiders are present so as not to upset other people's sensibilities. For example, participants reported being unable to use adhesive tactile markers to allow for independent use of washing machines and dryers which were shared among building's residents as neighbors stated that it would deface the equipment. Similarly, the visually impaired users participating in the study by Abdolrahmani et al. [1] clearly stated that they would immediately disengage with a device that would fail or cause errors that might result in social embarrassment or lead to a negative portrayal of their own independence. Technology failures that result in negative social consequences could lead to lack of trust in the device or even full discontinuation of use [ibid.].

Large-scale systems that are used by millions of people are usually affected by multiple tensions originating from the conflicting priorities among different groups of users or between users and service providers. These tensions can often have negative consequences for minority groups of users, such as people with disabilities. These consequences can cause dilemmas for companies and designers. Take, for example, the case of TikTok and the recent uprising caused when the company made the decision to censor the voices of people with disabilities to prevent them from being the subject of cyberbullying [450]. Users with disabilities create content on popular platforms such as TikTok for a variety of reasons that range from the desire to debunk myths surrounding disability to logging personal reflections or gamifying their experiences of rehabilitation to motivate others [116]. However, TikTok found people with disabilities to be the subject of bullying due to their "physical or mental condition," and so limited the number of times their content could be shared, preventing people with disabilities from going viral. TikTok insisted the measures were temporary and would like all users to celebrate their uniqueness. However, even with good intentions of preventing bullying, which of course TikTok has the responsibility to control and moderate, the ultimate approach was one which limited freedom of speech and of visibility of people with disabilities, thereby punishing the people who were doing no harm apart from challenging social norms. It is not clear if users with disability were consulted before the decision. One would assume not, as it would be hard to think of a policy such as this being co-designed with the people it was aiming to protect.

At the same time, platforms such as TikTok have also enabled content creators with disabilities who are likely to be excluded from most mainstream media to showcase their creativity, engage with broad audiences and find their own communities [451, 452]. Despite top-down ableist practices reinforced by shadow banning algorithms, bottom-up collective practices of resistance implemented by content creators with disabilities and their audience still make the platform incredibly popular within the disability community. The friction between the interests of the company looking to find easy ways to prevent cyberbullying, and the demand of people with disabilities to remain visible to re-write social narratives is a poignant example of how conflict can arise in large-scale systems when the priorities of providers and users are not aligned.

2.2.3   MULTIPLE TECHNOLOGY ECOSYSTEMS

According to Brown, Bødker, and Höök [66], HCI has the tendency to look at the components of a system, rather than at the whole ecology, and therefore the authors ask if: "the innovative systems we study today are perhaps like jigsaw-puzzle pieces, the significance of which will not be apparent until other parts of the puzzle are adopted. How then can we understand a single piece, without access to the whole puzzle?" Within AAT this is specifically important for a number of reasons.

First of all, many people with disabilities will have multiple needs and require multiple technologies which need to integrate as seamlessly as possible. However, integration between ATs

Figure 2.1: Blister pavement.

is often problematic even within the same device. For example, many applications to support urban navigation for people with visual impairments are only geared toward indoor or outdoor navigation. Transitioning between environments often creates challenges for people as they are required to switch between different applications that do not perfectly align [293]. Second, many people with disabilities experience fluctuating capabilities due to a multitude of factors ranging from their underlying medical conditions, successful rehabilitation, tiredness, or due to external factors. Therefore, AAT users are often plugged into multiple ecologies and will need to adapt their mode of interaction over time according to both personal and external circumstances [177]. As highlighted by Hofmann et al. [177], "by designing AT one impairment at a time, we may make the problems we need to solve more tractable, but inflexibility may create new ones in the process." This is true at multiple levels, not only when considering the interactions between multiple technologies used by a single individual, but also when analyzing larger ecosystems where the needs of different people with disabilities might be in conflict. A poignant example of these accessibility conflicts is represented by the tactile pavement that can be found at many crossroads in the UK; see Figure 2.1. These "blistered pavements" are used to help people with visual impairment to identify and navigate the crossroads more safely. However, previous studies by Newton et al. [280] have shown that the irregular surface can create problems for wheelchair users and people with reduced mobility. Overall, we acknowledge that achieving perfect and universal integration between multiple technology ecosystems at both individual and collective level might be impossible. However, we argue that researchers and technology developers should strive to identify where frictions between different systems might arise and which strategies could be used to negotiate them.

2.3 DISABILITY INCLUSION AS A WICKED PROBLEM

Designing AAT allows us to explore a wide range of disability interactions. This can occur at different scales—at an individual level we can understand how people interact with technology, at a higher level we can explore how technology allows for activities and therefore mediates interactions across communities and in places. We do this in part toward the aim of inclusion of people with disabilities and equality of experience, and of life for all people regardless of their abilities. However, we live in a very divided world and so often our technology or advances will not help toward the wider agenda of disability inclusion. You could argue that this doesn't matter, or at least is far beyond the remit of HCI researchers. This is a valid position, and no one would doubt or indeed could contradict that with each piece of research which enables a better understanding of disability interactions and any level, there is advancement of the vision to make technology inclusive and usable by all. However, here, we argue for a different position. We argue that if we understand more about the complexity inherent in designing for the full ecosystem in which people with disabilities operate, then we will be able to better design technologies which can scale and reach people who need them.

When setting out the Disability Interactions Manifesto, one of the first principles is to acknowledge that disability inclusion is a wicked problem [178]. This means that, when designing a new disability interaction, the aim of the technology in itself might be intended as positive. Yet, its application could have a perversely negative impact [178]. These negative consequences could be directly linked to the technology itself such as the case for one of the examples presented by Williams and Gilbert where a smartwatch that aims to detect higher stress level in autistic wearers and suggest strategies for emotional regulation designed by caregivers might lead to the wearers to feel coerced into suppressing their own emotions [425].On the other hand, indirect negative consequences might occur if as a community we skew our research toward one population or another and thereby defocus attention from other areas or populations [73, 94, 95, 136, 206]. Of course, we can't do everything, but we can be more aware researchers which can help us make more informed decision. Specifically, we can look to measure the value our interventions.

We start our argument at the level of the accessibility of the ACM SIGCHI, which one might think is a rather complex but not "wicked" task; and it might seem surprising that in a recent review of efforts to make the ACM SIGCHI community accessible, it was found it had all the hallmarks of a wicked problem [246]. However, this was indeed what the review found and acts as a good introduction into the nature of wicked problems. Making SIGCHI accessible was found to involve modifying a complex multi-stakeholder system in which there can never be a single one-size-fits-all conference types and venues option [246]. Moreover, there was found to be a conceptual mismatch between the SIGCHI community who is designing the accessibility of the system and users, namely, conference organizers. In essence, a well-meaning activity, the development of a report to identify accessibility barriers and opportunities for inclusion had the effect of causing more issues and was found to merely scratch the surface of concerns of both conference attendees and conference organizers, without being able to identify clear pathways to inclusion which were implementable across the spectrum of SIGCHI events and within the resources available to conference organizers [246]. For example, the report was unable to highlight examples of resources providing concrete advice and good practices that could guide both organizers and attendants facing accessibility issues. Moreover, the report identified some of the tensions existing between disabled conference attendees who need accessibility measures to be put in place to be able to participate in conferences that impact their careers and the conference organizers who are required to run successful conferences that are inclusive toward people with access needs while balancing budgets which are both uncertain and limited [ibid.]. Ultimately, Mankoff raised the point that in order for proposed changes to be both effective in increasing accessibility and actionable when organizing a conference, there needs to be a better understanding and alignment between the accessibility community which will design these measures and the conference organizers who will need to implement them. The analysis concludes that "well-meaning change is not enough. Well-designed change is the bar we should strive to reach" [246].

Wicked problems are defined by ten distinguishing properties. The first is a lack of definitive formulation of the problem statement—disability inclusion is still not fully understood. We do not know how to increase positive disability interactions across systems for people with varying levels of abilities; hence, we do not really know what success looks like. For example, what would it mean to identify the issue of inclusive education for children with disabilities? Within HCI perhaps, we focus our attention purely on technologies to aid inclusive education for this population. And perhaps we narrow our geographic focus to North America, Europe, or East Africa. However, what we might not know is how different schools in a district are funded, what is the quality of teachers in each school, what is the home environment of all children, or what level of stigma is faced by children with disabilities within a particular community. All these factors will confound our study.

In fact, as we delve into understanding the issue, we will in fact only further define the problem within the wider system, while also probably solving a small part of the jigsaw. We will, for example, gain better insight into how we can help increase coding education in primary school across the UK among visually impaired pupils [269]. Alternatively, we can choose to focus on how ATs can support visually impaired students enrolled in higher education institutions in Tanzania [215]. However, the wider issue of inclusive education will remain unsolved, only slightly further illuminated.

This brings us to the second property of a wicked problem: they have no stopping rule, as "the process for solving the problem is identical with the process of understanding its nature" [317]. The additional eight properties cover the issues of solution finding, noting there is no ultimate test for a solution to a wicked problem (4), and that any solution cannot be defined as good or bad (3). Due to their contextual issues, wicked problems are one-shot operations with no ability to test alternative theories (5); moreover, there are no exhaustively describable set of solutions (6) making every wicked problem unique (7).

Another key aspect that is often overlooked is that each wicked problem is a symptom of another wicked problem (8). The compounding nature of disability and poverty is a perfect example of this. Poverty and disability have shown to be closely linked issues, especially in the Global South [49]. People with disabilities are more likely to encounter barriers in accessing education and job opportunities due to a complex series of barriers that range from the inaccessibility of the built environment, the lack of access to AT and the stigma and discriminatory practices perpetrated by society [49]. This significantly limits their opportunity to earn a sufficient income, increasing the chance of poverty [ibid.]. In turn, people who are poor are more likely to experience worse health outcomes which significantly increase the chances to develop chronic conditions or acquire a disability [233]. The intersecting nature of poverty and disability creates a vicious circle of wicked problems that are incredibly complex and hard to tackle. As a result, this leads to multiple interpretations or lenses through which to view each wicked problem (9). Finally, the solver of a wicked problem has no right to be wrong (10). The decisions about which solutions should be promoted or implemented to support disability inclusion have a tremendous impact not only on the lives of people with disabilities, but of society as a whole. Therefore, research in this space should be led by a drive to empower people with disabilities, cultivating a sense of responsibility about the consequences not just of our results, but our methods and intentions as well.

2.4   ASSISTIVE TECHNOLOGY AS PART OF A SYSTEM

The WHO pays a lot of attention to the detail of the definition of AT as being more than a product but something which encompasses a whole system of delivery. In this definition they emphasize the need for products to be given through services which are appropriate. However, as we have seen 90% of people who need AT do not have access to them. And so even when we design wonderful products, the benefits they afford are not fully realized by the people we would like to use them, for they cannot gain access to the device. Much of the research carried out in HCI around AT focuses on the physical and digital products used by persons with disabilities [350, 442, 446]. Significant attention is of course dedicated to users, and AT is seen as a piece of a much larger puzzle of abilities, human infrastructures, environmental factors, and social conventions [38, 242, 421]. However, there are relatively fewer studies, and less attention, paid to the multiple factors that determine how people with disabilities are provided with or acquire AT.

Beyond HCI, researchers have described ATs as part of a complex system of factors ranging from national and international policies to provision systems, users, and providers. In fact, the World Health Organization (WHO) [419] defines AT as "an umbrella term covering the systems and services related to the delivery of assistive products and services." Khasnabis, Mirza, and MacLachlan [210] coined the term Assistive Technology systems which they defined as "the development and application of organized knowledge, skills, procedures and policies relevant to the provision, use and assessment of assistive products." Assistive products, the technology itself, is only a portion of this much more complex system that determines if persons with disabilities are able to access these technologies, what they have access to, how these devices are used in real life, and why.

To ensure that research and practice cover all relevant aspects necessary to promote access to assistive products for people with disabilities, the Global Cooperation on Assistive Technology (GATE) has proposed a 5P framework that encompass the key elements of AT systems: People, Products, Policy, Personnel, and Provision [417]. As shown in Figure 2.2, the central part of the framework revolves around the involvement of people with disabilities and their families. The assistive products themselves, the provision mechanisms that enable procurement and supply and the relevant personnel which is key to assessment, fitting, training, and follow-up of AT are depicted as interlinked with each other. Finally, the wider national and international policies are seen as surrounding all the previous aspects as they would regulate fundamental aspects to AT access such as national financing strategies for assistive products and services, health and welfare insurance programs, and the adoption of national and international standards and guidelines AT systems [ibid.]. Two additional P's which are not included in the picture but have been suggested for inclusion in the framework are Place and Pace [179]. The first one highlights the need to consider how the environment and sociocultural contexts of individual affect how ATs are procured, accessed and used [179]. Finally, Pace speaks to the need to incorporate time dimensions in our understanding of AT systems. This is seen as essential not only because the AT needs of individuals with disabilities are likely to change overtime (both across the lifetime and within a single day as individual capabilities are, by their own nature, fluid and affected by contextual factors), but also to understand the pace at which AT services operate, which might be different depending on the country [179].

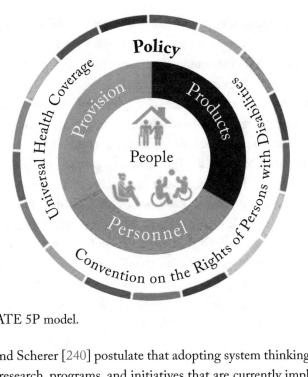

Figure 2.2: WHO GATE 5P model.

MacLachlan and Scherer [240] postulate that adopting system thinking would enable better connection between research, programs, and initiatives that are currently implemented in the field of AT, promoting impact and sustainability overtime. According to the authors, systems thinking is characterized by distinctive advantages such as: "Forest Thinking," described as the ability to distinguish between individual trees, while being conscious of the relationships that create wooded areas; "Dynamic Thinking," which enables to see how the patterns of relationships change overtime and depending on the context; and "Loop Thinking," which allows for the observation of cause-effect relationships as reciprocal and iterative [240]. They also emphasize the need for researchers and practitioners to disregard disciplinary boundaries and abandon the tendency to simplify AT related challenges to explainable "problems" that can be tackled by simple solutions [240]. The inherent complexity of the disability and AT fields can appear overwhelming at first. However, viewed another way it is an opportunity. We have the opportunity to realize greater impact when working across disciplines and within the wider AT ecosystems, rather than only focusing on product-level interactions.

For example, McGookin, Robertson, and Brewster [254] developed a tangible user interface that enables visually impaired learners to access graph and chart-based data. This technology has huge potential for inclusive education at different levels, as the teaching of many subjects heavily relies on the use of graphs and charts that are inaccessible to visually impaired students. However, without expanding from the initial user studies and applying system thinking to understand how this technology could be integrated in the curricula, how teachers can learn to employ it in the classroom, how schools can have access to funding necessary to unlock the procurement of these devices, and how national policies can incorporate new technologies into frameworks for inclusive education, the Tangible Graph Builder would not make any significant difference to the educational experience of a visually impaired student.

Even when focusing on assistive products alone, we should move beyond mere technological considerations and interaction analysis to understand broader barriers to implementation such as awareness of users and providers, availability of devices, accessibility of products (from a physical and economic point of view), acceptability (in relation to culture, age, gender, and situation), and adaptability. MacLachlan et al. [238] proposes a progressive approach to address the AT system gap, see Figure 2.3, to ensure that research and practice can truly make a difference on the level of access to AT and the impact that it has on the lives of people with disabilities. Ultimately, only by increasing awareness of AT can we hope to increase demand toward improved availability. In turn, improving availability will reduce cost and promote affordability. Mainstreaming the need for AT can also help to ensure more and more products are made accessible and technologies become better able to adapt to different situations. Differentiation is also essential to support the development of technologies that are acceptable to users with different profiles. As our learning progresses from this increasing development, the quality of available products will also improve and increased use will help with further refinement.

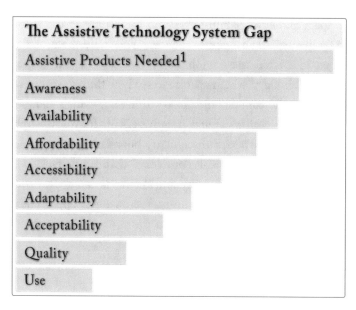

Figure 2.3: Progressive approach to address the AT system gap (image from [238]).

2.5   CAPTURING COMPLEXITY AS A KEY AIM

At the start of this chapter, we posed the question "With so many theories, conceptualizations and frameworks cutting across the fields of disability, AT and HCI, do we really need a new one?" Throughout this chapter we presented you with three reasons why we believe that there is the need for a new approach that could help to bring together insights from research and practice across different areas and disciplines to ensure that the work that we do can really translate into real world impact for people with disabilities. Ultimately, all three reasons concerning Issues of Scale, Disability Inclusion as a wicked problem, and Accessibility and Assistive Technology as part of a system highlight the need to better capture the complexity of AT beyond traditional technological aspects and issues around the interactions between users with disabilities and the technologies we hope to design and promote. The real world in which AT is deployed is incredibly complicated, and while understanding all the implications pertaining to the technologies research and development would be impossible, we nonetheless should aim to be mindful of them. In the next chapter we will present the DIX approach and explain its different facets that attempt to account for the complexity surrounding disability, AT, and accessibility research.

CHAPTER 3

The Disability Interaction (DIX) Approach

The Disability Interactions manifesto, which appeared in the *Interactions* magazine in 2019, was the first attempt at describing a new agenda for developing technology for people with disabilities. In it, a wider vision for disability and HCI was explored. This vision built on the established concepts of ability-based design and accessibility and looked a little wider at the power of social movements and the possibilities for radically different approaches to designing technology which aims to target all aspects of disability inclusion. In essence, it sought to push the boundaries of HCI research beyond the abilities of people with disabilities, toward full acceptance of people and their technology in society. This new space incorporated a little of Computer Supported Cooperative Work and Social Computing (CSCW) and much of the HCI for Development (HCI4D) agenda. The manifesto laid out five principles upon which we could build an expanded vision of disability inclusion, thus enabling what was termed: disability interactions.

The DIX manifesto was a sort of call to action. It asked more questions than it answered. It asked, for example, how we overcome the societal stigma faced by people with disabilities, how we make our disability-related research and practice more relevant to people in the Global South, and how we can better design future technologies with people with disabilities. These are big questions, and they are only partially explored in the manifesto, in part because of space, but mostly because the concepts we were proposing were still maturing. Since writing the manifesto, and in only two years, much has happened within the HCI disability-related community and at the Global Disability Innovation Hub (GDI Hub). GDI Hub is research and practice center which has both a not-for-profit section and an academic research center, which is led by University College London's Department for Computer Science. Since the manifesto was written, GDI Hub has expanded to having projects in 35 countries with 70 partners, delivering projects across a portfolio of £50m. GDI Hub has reached 21 million people and with UCL leads the World Health Organization's Collaborating Center on Assistive Technology. Throughout our work across projects and collaboration with many partners we have evolved our thinking on Disability Interactions.

In this chapter we unpack the concept of Disability Interactions in more detail, we update the principles first proposed in the manifesto, and we connect into the learnings from the HCI community over the past two years to develop dimensions of DIX which can be used to measure components of DIX projects. We also draw on learnings from a large program called AT2030 which GDI Hub has been leading since the time of writing the Manifesto.

The aim of AT2030 is to test "what works" in getting assistive technology to people globally. In the four months prior to being awarded the grant the GDI Hub team had been developing a consortium, conducting a scoping review, and doing deep-dive research in a number of African countries, including Uganda and Kenya. What we uncovered was a series of systemic failures which cut across governmental departments of: Health, Education, Labor, and Social Welfare, and ICT. Many of the problems we identified went far beyond the scope of HCI alone, and problems which in many cases were individually known, but perhaps lacking an interconnected view prior to our work. They tended toward the wicked side of problem statements and felt impossible to tackle, even with the £20m of funding which was allocated to the program. However, through partnerships and perseverance, design thinking and co-design, we have slowly uncovered larger bits of the jigsaw of what is preventing disability inclusion. Along the way, we have learned how to conduct applied research (which answers questions but also creates new ones), and how to better work in interdisciplinary teams. We have also discovered just how hard it is to accomplish certain goals and promote positive change, and where HCI is best placed to put its efforts. Combined with learnings from the wider HCI community over the past two years, such as the reflections on ableism in HCI [438] and the recent systematic review of accessibility in CHI [237] and reflections in ASSETS [177], we present here a refined vision for DIX, which we hope is detailed enough to be actionable and therefore further refined in future years by the HCI community. We start by explaining the updated principles of DIX Framework.

3.1   THE DIX FRAMEWORK: AN OVERVIEW

The Principles of DIX act as lenses through which to set the intentions for work in this space; they help to influence the approach and overall methodology projects which aim to better understand technology-mediated disability interactions at the user, community, or even country or international level. There are six principles of DIX and these are shown in Figure 3.1. Each of the six principles contributes to the discussion and conceptualization of the whole DIX Framework.

Alongside these principles are given individual dimensions of DIX. These are represented in the inner circle of Figure 3.1. The dimensions are more measurable and precise and can be used to design, implement, and evaluate relevant research and projects. Each dimension has associated theory, methods and tools which can be used to measure how far along each dimensions a specific project is. These are explained later, but first we give an overview and definition of what each element of the framework is.

Figure 3.1: Disability interactions principles (outer purple ring) and disability interaction dimensions (inner yellow ring).

3.1.1   DIX PRINCIPLES: AN OVERVIEW

The DIX principles act as guides to help us frame each DIX program and project.

- **Disability inclusion is a wicked problem:** Wicked problems can *seem* impossible to solve as factors are difficult to define, remain in flux, and can be unmeasurable; disability inclusion is complex involving inclusive education, healthcare, employment, communities, and more; it is also linked to poverty. DIX acknowledges this complexity when designing disability interactions

- **Applied and Basic Research Combined (ABC):** We apply Shneiderman's ABC approach as a principle. Applied research is defined as a mission-driven approach resulting in practical solutions and guidelines; the goal is to examine complex interactions between multiple variables using realistic scenarios. Basic research is defined as curiosity-driven, employs reductionist models to identify universal principles and relies on simplifications and idealizations to secure fundamental knowledge. Combined, they can tackle "immense" (and possibly even wicked) problems.

- **Co-Created Solutions across a wide range of actors:** Within DIX we aim co-create products and approaches in collaboration with both the people who will use the technology within given contexts, and the people and systems who enable (or prevent) this use.

- **Radically Different Interactions:** We seek to utilize advantages in technology to create radically new ways for people with disabilities to interact with technology, with people and across environments with the aim of enabling new experiences.

- **Value and Usefulness:** Usefulness of a device is linked to measuring the value of a particular "thing" to the user and to society more broadly. The usefulness in question is of the device not the person using the device. When measuring usefulness, we are measuring how easily and well a technology enables a person to do something. We are measuring the value placed by society and the user on the technology, in essence building a case for its inclusion within society and helping to create pathways to its diffusion.

- **Open and Scalable:** Technology designed for DIX is open. This does not necessarily mean open-source, although of course open-source technology is developed using an open approach. What we emphasize is that technology should be developed and deployed in an open manner, rather than a hidden one, open to collaborations to make it better and more available to everyone who might benefit from it. Wherever possible we look for opportunities to scale solutions to increase their reach.

3.1.2   DISABILITY INCLUSION IS A WICKED PROBLEM

A wicked problem is defined by Horst Rittel [317] through the ten characteristics of urban planning which have been explored in Chapter 2. These ten principles lay out how a wicked problem is unique, complex, with elements which overlap with other problems and therefore have multiple possible solutions. In essence, they can *seem* impossible to solve as individual factors are difficult to define, remain in flux and can be unmeasurable. Poverty, education, and healthcare are good examples of wicked problems that are present at global level [453]. The Interaction Design Foundation offers a good primer on wicked problems for HCI researchers [453]. In this paper the authors develop the link between design thinking and wicked problems which was first proposed by Richard Buchanan [69] and propose a combination of systems thinking and agile methodologies to help approach wicked problems [ibid.].

There are many examples of disability-related research being defined as wicked problems, from inclusive education [14] to care [301] to the earlier example in Chapter 2 of the inclusion of AccessSIGCHI. However, it would appear there are few published examples of how wicked problems have been solved or attempted to be solved by the HCI community. This, however, may simply be due to a lack of acknowledgment that we are designing with societal impact and in complex interdisciplinary ways—the fact we shy away from the label of wicked problems doesn't mean we are not actually solving them. To explain this point, let us look a little closer at Buchanan's initial paper [69] in 1992. On page 16, he claims wicked problems are complex and interdisciplinary and have indeterminate scope, due to a multitude of causes and user needs. To solve them, recursive attempts are needed which adapted to the changing needs of individuals and society within a given culture and with the available (possible) technology [69]. HCI is therefore very well positioned to answer the call of wicked problem solving, as many of our problems start from these fuzzy definitions, and through a series of user-centered design methods we are able to put some structure toward a number of possible solutions which can be developed; these then are iterated and tested, redesigned and tested again, until a final design is chosen. It is not the only possible solution, but it is one which satisfies the best possible sub-set of the user needs, with the resources that are available. The critical step is therefore to acknowledge the complexity of the problem and its orientation toward solving a societal problem.

Within HCI we are seeing an evolving attempt to solve the wicked nature of inclusion through the AccessSIGCHI. This has started with the acknowledgment of the complex nature of the problem [246] and a desire to hear from the diverse array of users of HCI conferences: from researchers with disabilities to organizers, of both large conferences and small [ibid.]. From here, if we were to apply the thinking from the Interaction Design Foundation [453], we would begin to break down the problem into nodes and links then visualize our AccessSIGCHI map and collaborate with all users to develop solutions, and iterate [ibid.]. Given AccessSIGCHI is a volunteer organization it might also be necessary to dedicate financial resource to this problem to help the volunteers and leaders realize ideas that emerge.

When speaking of wicked problems, we want to exercise caution, as they can appear negative, unsolvable, and huge. Disability inclusion is highly complex and, depending on your personality type, can appear impossible or simply very hard. We like to take the glass half full approach and look at wicked problems as highly complex, but solvable design spaces where HCI researchers can maximize their contribution to society. So, rather than make it seem impossible to do anything, it pushes us to do better. What happens if we don't acknowledge the complexity of disability? By not acknowledging the complexity of the identities of people with disability globally, we have over simplified problems to discrete blocks, often focusing on an impairment, therefore solving a problem, but not necessarily in the real (and social) context in which the problem itself occurs [247, 364]. Unfortunately, accessibility research is peppered with examples of well-meaning ableism and oversimplification, which often result from an ableist mentality. Ableism can (and does) affect everyone as it a "system that places value on people's bodies and minds based on societally constructed ideas of normalcy, intelligence, excellence and productivity" [381]. The constructed ideas, which we are often unaware to possess, "are deeply rooted in anti-Blackness, eugenics, colonialism, and capitalism" [381], thereby making them complex to overcome [177]. When it comes to accessibility and AT research, Shew argues that ableism or, as she redefines it technoableieism, pushes us toward the imagination, design, and development of new technologies that we perceive as empowering, but that might just reinforce stereotypes of which type of bodies and minds are worthy of being pursued [346]. For example, exoskeletons are often seen by many people without disabilities as revolutionary technologies that will enable persons with reduced mobility to complete multiple tasks independently. However, many members of the disabled community have eyed these technologies with distrust as they reinforce stereotypes that help to promote walking as the only valid form of locomotion, relegating wheelchair as a sub-par choice [ibid.]. Williams [424] highlights how our ableist tendencies might push us even further toward establishing hierarchies that delegitimatize and devalue the expression of agency when it needs the intermediation of technology to be expressed. The example she brings is the one of AAC users and non-speaking people, who frequently see their ability to communicate being represented as less valid and somehow altered by technological or human intermediaries which affects its veracity [ibid.]. By accepting that we are all affected by these social norms, which are interwoven into the societies we live, we can acknowledge and seek to overcome them in our research projects. This will help in creating more meaningful design requirements, more comprehensive and impactful insights, and hopefully a better quality and disability-inclusive agenda.

Within DIX the concept of wicked problems is an overarching lens through which we look at all other principles. We will now move onto Applied and Basic Research Combined.

3.1.3   APPLIED AND BASIC RESEARCH COMBINED

In the DIX Manifesto a brief mention is made to Shneiderman's assessment that Applied and Basic Research Combined—a new type of ABC of research agenda—is necessary for research to be able to work on and more rapidly advanced solutions for what are termed "immense problems" [352]. Shneiderman argues that we are designing and researching in a new context, one which combines: immense problems, new technologies, and raised ambitions. In setting out this new agenda, Shneiderman hopes to "provoke ambitious research projects that will more frequently cope with contemporary problems such as energy sustainability, healthcare delivery, community safety an environmental protection" [352:34]. What is laid out in *The New ABCs of Research* is a sort of handbook to achieving breakthrough collaborations, which Shneiderman feels are essential for tackling these immense problems and will involve thousands of researchers over several disciplines and across sector and decades—but this should not put us off he argues, as we can plan to reach intermediatory milestones which can ensure we know we are on track for success.

Applied research is defined as having the following features: mission-driven, an outlook toward practical solutions and guidelines, and the ability to examine complex interactions between multiple variables and uses realistic (rather than idealized) scenarios (see [352 p.16] for more information). Within these features we get a glimpse of the things which drive an applied researcher—they are attracted by big problems, which normally have socio-economic aspects, they are happy when something works and happier still when the solutions can be adapted and scaled, they strive in the messy interactions which comprise wicked problems and they thrive in challenging circumstances which force them to learn more and "get their hands dirty" [352].

Basic research in contrast is defined by Shneiderman as curiosity driven, particularly in relation to developing an understanding of the world we live in, organizing knowledge and predicting behaviors. Basic research is described as being often tied to laboratory experimentation that applies reductionist models (fixing variables to deeply investigate one or more factors effect on a problem) and driven by a search for universal principles and by the reliance on simplifications and idealizations [352]. Within this a basic researcher profile emerges as someone who is driven to understand the world we live in, they require laboratories or other infrastructure to ensure repeatability of experimental evidence, they like the process of solving one problem at a time and then piecing these pieces together, then developing general theories and predictions and enjoy defining clear problem statements.

None of these approaches is superior to the other, and the ABC approach is based on blending the best of science, engineering, and design skills from both. A useful metaphor used to explain the practical applicability of the project to students by Shneiderman is: two parents, three children. When formulating a new project, he encourages groups to think about the two parents—the practical problem and the existing theory. When the project concludes the students should have three "children": the solution to the practical problem, the refinement of the theory, and guidance for future researchers [352].

By combining the applied and basic aspects of problems we are able to use both to our advantage. Generally, we lean on more traditional research methods of laboratory-based studies for basic research, which might be within HCI labs or with colleagues in other disciplines [352]. We then use in the wild methods for understanding technology use in situ [323]. The differences between in the wild research and lab-based experiments are detailed by Rogers and Marshall [323, p. 3]. In the wild studies and lab-based usability studies have produced different usability issues (e.g., Rogers [321] developing a mobile phone platform for collecting data about plants in the urban realm found very different issues when the phone was being used in the spring versus the autumn), which have led some to question if lab-based findings can be transferred successfully out of the lab and into real world settings [325]. People use technology, even prototypes, in ways we as researchers can't envisage, however as Rogers and Marshall point out this is part of the fun and the adventure of research in the world [323]. It also brings with it opportunity for basic science.

Case Study: Tacilia, Designing Interactive Technology for Blind Students
Tigmanshu Bhatnager

Tacilia started from the applied problem of *how to enable children who are blind or have partial sight to be better able to engage with Science Technology Engineering Arts and Maths (STEAM) education*. By investigating the problems faced in the classroom the need for a multiline, refreshable Braille and tactile graphic interface was identified to help children read books and explore tactile diagrams to make sense of graphs, charts, and other (normal) visual information. The project is being developed at UCL with collaborations across the Global Disability Innovation Hub, Institute of Making, UCL's Interaction Center (UCLIC), with in the wild studies conducted in India with the Indian Institute of Technology Delhi (IITD).

The Problem: Tacilia's overall aim is to address a small subset of an immense or wicked problem, that of Quality Education as defined by the UN in Sustainable Development Goal 4 (SDG4) [454]. SDG 4 ensures quality education for all children including those with visual impairments, which in turn enables upward socioeconomic mobility and is a key to escaping poverty [454:4]. It is important to note that a far greater population of people with sight loss live in lower- and middle-income countries where among children, the prevalence can be as high as 1.5 per 1,000 children [60]. We explored this situation and worked with local schools for the blind in India to observe classroom learning and teaching experiences of students and educators. What he observed was that despite the growing availability of computers and access to ICT, existing education practices for blind children are depended on printed tactile resources which includes Braille books, Tactile graphic books, Braille slates, Perkins Braille Typewriter, and other non-standard frugal tactile materials that are custom made by special educators. These mediums had significant limitations when it came to teaching and learning STEAM subjects.

Applied and Basic Research Combined: This exploration of an applied and practical problem was followed by an investigation in existing academic and market literature that showed the ways in which research across the world is trying to address the problem. Combining the practical experience and the basic knowledge, the need for development of an affordable multiline braille and tactile graphic display device was clear. This device should enable the presentation of braille and tactile graphics on the same display so that students are able to read, create and learn on a single device. Existing products have a high cost due to the complexity of actuators that are used to display tactile information on such devices. We therefore worked at a very fundamental level to invent a new reconfigurable tactile display technology which presents both Braille and Tactile Graphics as has called it Tacilia [45]. I have lab tested this display using a variety of methods based on which he has technically improved its design and performance. The display meets the Braille dimensional standards as prescribed by UKAAF and renders a sharp and clear tactile information. With its new design, new possibilities for Disability Interactions have emerged. For instance, freehand erasable tactile drawing is now possible through Tacilia, which previously was very hard for blind students [46]. Recent research work from the group has also identified a set of design heuristics to present tactile graphics and shapes on such a refreshable tactile display (under review at CHI 2022).

Tacilia is refreshable but its design largely reduces the number of moving parts and components to present tactile information, due to which it can make refreshable tactile display devices exceedingly affordable. This will help to overcome the global shortage of printed tactile resources such as paper-based Braille and tactile graphics based on thermoformed sheets or swell paper. Forthcoming research with Tacilia investigates ways to digitalize the display so that computer generated text and graphics (digital media) can be directly translated and presented in Braille and tactile diagrams. This will be facilitated through an Open-Source software with which anyone in the world can translate any static digital document (.doc, .pdf, html, .jpg, .png, .bmp, .ppt,.xlsx, etc.) into its tactile form. Educators will be able to translate books, presentations, and other educational material easily in its tactile form for their blind students while students will be able to access websites and other previously inaccessible documents in their tactile form. For visually impaired users to better interact with such a display, research is also being carried out to explore the possibility of using a voice user interface (VUI) to augment the tactile interaction.

Possibly the only way in which this work can make a real-world impact and improve the educational experience of visually impaired students is when it reaches their hands and it is being used, which will open up more avenues for further co-development. Therefore, GDI Hub is setting up the necessary platform to commercialize Tacilia. For updates about this project, please follow www.hellotacilia.com.

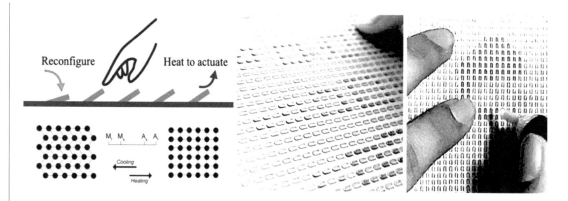

Figure 3.2: Tacilia is a passive shape-changing display made from a single sheet of Nitinol. As shown in the picture, heat can be applied using a hot-air pencil to raise the individual pins that create tactile graphics. The graphic drawn can be erased by manually pressing on the pins.

Having explored how basic and applied research can be combined in for relation of a new assistive technology we now move onto the next principle: co-created solutions.

3.1.4   CO-CREATED SOLUTIONS

This brings us to our second principle: **co-creation across a wide range of actors**. Within DIX when we say co-crated solutions, we are looking at the following users: the people who will use the technology within given contexts, and the people and systems who can enable (or prevent) this use. Building on the ABC approach we look to co-create solutions using broad teams of people who can do both basic and applied research, and translate this into guidelines or practice documents such as policy briefings for people who can facilitate the implementation of solutions. This might at first seem overwhelming, but it need not be. Let's start from co-creating with users.

HCI has a number of excellent frameworks for co-creating solutions with users. In the DIX manifesto we talk of utilizing Dan Saffer's [331] four types of interaction design practice—user-centered design, activity-centered design, systems design, and genius design. Each type of design process can be based on deep user-centered design practice. Let's look at each of these in turn for disability interactions.

Ability-based design gives us an excellent foundation of user-centered and activity-based design [433]. It builds on the approach of design-for-one [315], which developed technological solutions based on a deep understanding of a single user's needs, and applies universal design so that solutions would be more widely applicable [433]. It did this with a focus on co-design with people with disabilities to understand both the problem space and their abilities, then using technology to enhance these abilities and create new interaction possibilities [433]. User-centered design processes have also been combined with a human-rights based approach to develop new technologies, for example by Chopra et al. [90]. Chopra et al. used this combined approach to design for and with people with dementia. The human-rights-based approach acted as an ethical and legal framework alongside the co-design which enabled the authors to then realize the human rights in technology.

When engaging in co-creation of AATs it is also essential to acknowledge how much people with disabilities are already designing, hacking, and tinkering to create their own devices, strategies, and technologies that enable them to navigate inaccessible situations. Bennett and colleagues highlight how these iterative prototyping practices that take place in the everyday life of individuals with disabilities not only lead to the creation of artefacts that people feel emotionally connected to, but also contribute to professional design practices in ways that are often unrecognized [40]. The Crip Technoscience manifesto calls for four commitments to develop technology in ways that are more inclusive and critically aware of contradictions that exist within common design practices [162]. These include:

1. centering the work of disabled people as knowers AND makers, acknowledging the importance of everyday design practices, and moving beyond a more traditional view of people with disabilities as simple need-knowers to one of solution-makers;

2. committing to the idea of access as "friction" rather than pushing for inclusion as assimilation into ableist norms;

3. abandoning ideas of independence as a goal and technology as an apolitical force in favor of critical views that take into account the inevitability of interdependence and the entanglement of existing power dynamics; and

4. committing to a driving principle of disability justice that embraces the role of people with disabilities not just as technology consumers, but as transformative agents that shape technology and the world in which technology is deployed.

Co-creation and systems-level design are entirely compatible [331]. Systems design simply means designing a system—this could be a large software architecture or the design of an AT in a complex socio-technical system. In these instances, we use co-design methods to understand the full spectrum of needs necessary to make the system or technology accessible for people with disabilities.

Take, for example, the concept of Do-it-Yourself AT (DIY-AT) proposed by Hurst and colleagues in 2011—it captures the desire and rise of people's ability to design and build their own AT. Hurst and colleagues [185] found that caring was the communal element underpinning these technologies—which were developed with or for close friends and family and designed by people with no formal training in AT development. DIY-AT is in part driven by the rise of affordable, and relatively high-quality, consumer-grade digital manufacturing systems. This opens the door for co-created solutions and distributed design and manufacture at scale (see case study). In more recent research the use of digital manufacturing practices to support the education of visually impaired youth has been explored [68]. This study plots the experiences of educators in developing a practice of digitally supported learning for visually impaired youth. It demonstrates the need for a systems level understanding of the problem space, showing that 3D printing far from being a panacea can in fact create less usable artifacts for learning than other forms of tactile and audio interface. The use of this form of DIY-AT only reinforced the need for "professional transcribers" who translated ideas into objects for learners. By taking a systems-level of investigation the researchers were able to identify shortcomings of current practices and suggest new research avenues for the HCI community, specifically mentioning the need for a "collective and inter-organizations approach to digital fabrication" [68]. Overall, this demonstrates the success of the research approach and the paper in demonstrating the failure of the system.

A second example of systems level co-creation can be found in the work of Blandford's team in Digital Healthcare. Blandford [54] demonstrates these through the combination of user-centered design methods with systems level understanding to get a fuller picture of the intricacies of the tensions between disciplines, as well as then greater understanding across teams to develop products which better integrate into the needs of several user types: patient, clinician etc. For AAT we can expand our list if among the "users" we need to include not only the end user, but their social infrastructure, the purchaser, and the clinical or educational team who might help the user choose and learn to use the technology.

An example of what can happen when there is a misalignment between the characteristics of a technology and the systems within it needs to operate can be seen when we look at exoskeletons. As mentioned before, when they had first being launched on the market, exoskeletons were hailed as a technology with huge potential by much of the tech community and generally portrayed as a revolutionary aid to help people who couldn't walk anymore, to walk again. That year a person wearing an exoskeleton kicked the opening kick of the Paralympics, demonstrating at one level a radically new disability interaction—brain-controlled football! For those interested you can still watch this on YouTube. As we highlighted in Section 3.1.2, people with disabilities are often much less enthusiastic about these technologies as they can potentially contribute to reinforce ableist stereotypes. Despite controversies around the use of exoskeletons in everyday life, within the medical community there has also been considerable interests around the use of exoskeletons for gait rehabilitation (rather than as a substitute of a wheelchair) [231]. Between 2014 and 2016, through our collaborative links with the Aspire Center for Rehabilitation Engineering and Assistive Technology (CREATE) at the Royal national Orthopedic Hospital in the UK we explored how usable exoskeletons could be in the context of gait rehabilitation as provided by the National Health Service in the UK. Around this time, we trialed a less advanced exoskeletons (without brain control interaction). We found that despite the general interest in the technology, exoskeletons present huge barriers that can significantly limit their usability in clinical practice [174]. One barrier, which is rarely mentioned by many studies focusing on technological aspects, was the time it took to don and doff the suit—45 min in each instance. This is approximately the same amount of time as a standard physiotherapy appointment within the NHS at the time. Therefore, it would take at least three appointments to conduct a gait rehabilitation session using an exoskeleton, one to don the suit, one to conduct the actual gait training session, and one to doff the suit. The system of healthcare couldn't afford the cost of the service, even if they could afford the initial outlay for the device. We also found that, at least, one particular type of exoskeleton was unable to replicate human movement patterns when providing walking assistance, making it difficult to justify for rehabilitation purposes [36]. If our research would have shown that the device had been suitable for use in rehabilitation, it would have strengthened the purchase business case for the NHS. However, it did not. So, this leads to some questions: if these requirements of the users, in this case the healthcare team and system, had been known from the start how could it have influenced the design process? What differences might we have seen in the final product had the healthcare teams been integral to the design team? There are tools for us within each domain which we can draw upon to better understand the systems, such as the use of a more integrated development lifecycle for healthcare products, which has many iteration cycles between concept development to diffusion to help manage complexity as suggested by Blandford [54]. We shall come onto these in subsequent chapters

Given the great complexity within the space of disability interaction, we believe, genius design should be used sparingly. Genius design in this space is only really possibly when a designer has a deep understanding of the context and the needs [331]. We were unable to find good examples of genius design emerging from the field yet, though we are confident these will come as the sub-discipline of DIX grows and we develop more capacity globally. Within the context of disability interaction this will be more possible when we have a greater number of people with disabilities as experts in designs.

Case Study: Local Production opportunities for Assistive Technology
Ben Oldfrey

Innovation Action is a collaborative initiative led by UCL Engineering and funded by UK aid which brings together a consortium of partners working on developing innovations aiming to address global challenges. One of the key projects undertaken by the consortium focuses on the development of various mechanisms by which local production ecosystems can facilitate the co-creation of devices with AT users, local makers, and global expertise to improve access to the continued services that people with disabilities need. This is through an interconnected system of design platforms and mapping initiatives that allows for better connections throughout the design and production value chain.

Problem: Previous work analyzing the challenges of access to AT in the Global South has shown that current models by which AT are delivered to low resource settings are inadequate [179, 250]. Global supply chains, while highly efficient, do not allow the provision of devices that fully meet the needs of individuals, particularly those who have confounding disabilities, but also due to the specific environment or culture they live in. They also will never result in self-reliant local business models for the supply of AT, which would facilitate better, and sorely needed, follow-on services.

Parallel to this, during the COVID-19 pandemic it became clear that global supply chains were not capable of achieving equitable access to the supply needs of personal protective equipment (PPE) either as well as other medical supplies, including AT. They also limited sustainable design and manufacturing approaches.

Co-created new system approach: The new approach to AT production we are developing with partners globally using open ways of collaborating at scale. As part of this, the consortium is developing a series of diverse initiatives. First, we are mapping production capacities across different areas of the globe (including maker spaces, manufacturing facilities and production centers) to help designers understand what manufacturing and production capacities are available in their areas ensuring that they can develop products which can be made in their local ecosystems. Second, we are supporting the development of platforms that enable the connection between end-users who need bespoke devices with manufacturers that can create appropriate designs and make the required products. An example of this is the sharing platform called Makerko in Nepal which helps to address some of the challenges linked to fragile supply chains by leveraging distributed manufacturing and supports direct connections between users and makers to promote the development of technology that truly answers to local demands.

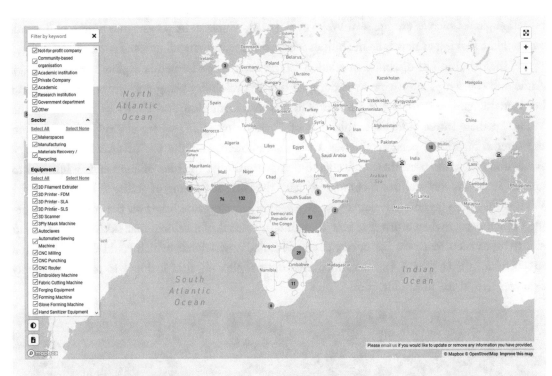

Figure 3.3: Get Connected! Want to put yourself on the map so people can find you and work with you? You can submit your details to be included on our map.

Conclusion: By promoting the creation of better local and global connections between users and innovators and by mapping available resources in local areas Innovation Action helps communities to move toward empowerment and self-reliance in when it comes to the production of AP. This can be boosted by creating peer-peer links between parallel initiatives targeting manufacturing and supply chain strengthening more in general to ensure the creation of sustainable and scalable local AT access models.

We now move to look more deeply at radically different interactions.

3.1.5   RADICALLY DIFFERENT INTERACTIONS

Radically Different Interactions. These can take place at a user level, for example advances in haptics or AI can help realize new possibilities for driving, which might open up the ability for a completely blind person to drive independently or in collaboration with the car. In a similar way, shared control is now possible for wheelchair users [441]. Radically different interactions can also take the form of new ways to do something. As an example, extended reality could be used to support the development of games which move beyond the more traditional virtual reality rehabilitation games such as examples in Weiss et al. [412], which all help to restore function. Instead, we could be looking at new human abilities which can incorporate all or a selection of our senses.

The definition of disability in relation to the augmented human is explored by Ando [12]. Ando and colleagues intertwine two concepts: the idea of ability being born from the interaction between humans and their environment Human Augmentation and ability as defined by the WHO in their International Classification of Functioning (ICF) where ability is derived from the interaction of the person's abilities, their environment, and the use of assistive technology. Ando and colleagues used these concepts to demonstrate that the idea of augmenting humans to enable "super-human" abilities is compatible with the current framing of ability as outlined by the WHO. They then go onto develop a new augmented human game based on the concept of drifting (which occurs when a driver is able to maintain control of a vehicle that skids sideways)—an ability humans currently do not possess. They designed a wheelchair which could drift and then a sport "SlideRift" (Figure 3.4). SlideRift overcomes people's physical inability to move seamlessly sideways—to "drift" in any direction.

Figure 3.4: Images of SlideRift a game which introduces a new human ability of drifting, which is enabled by the machine—a wheelchair.

Another example of radically different interaction can be seen in the production called DE-SCENT imagined and performed by the Kinetic Light, collective led by the dancer and choreographer Alice Sheppard [344]. The production retells the story of Andromeda and Venus as interracial lovers and leverages the beauty of precise and delicate wheelchair movements on a series of inclined planes to create a unique choreographic experience [ibid.]. The Kinetic Light team has also been working to enable radically different access experiences for their spectators through the creation of a mobile application called Audimance, developed by Laurel Lawson who is also a member of the collective. The application integrates traditional audio description with sonic rendering of dance movements and poetry to create a completely new experience for non-visual spectators [8].

Our experiences of the world happen through a multitude of senses. In their recent book, Valasco and Obrist [408] note multisensory experiences are a central part of our everyday lives and for the first-time technology is able to interact with these in such a way to create previously unthinkable experiences. The technologies which are being developed as part of this explosion in multisensory experiences are increasingly becoming extensions of us [408]. Given the possibilities of multisensory experiences, three laws are proposed to help shape the future mixed realities in which we will live: (1) multisensory experiences (ME) should be used for good and must not harm others; (2) receivers of ME must be treated fairly; and (3) someone and the sensor elements must be known.

Within disability, radically different interactions can be created even when one or more senses are not present for a person. Take the example of wanting to see the night's sky [160] a desire expressed by a blind person in a recent research study [160]. This is starting to be possible for people through technology such as the Argus II [455] through sensor which is surgically implanted at the back of the eye and connects to an external part of glasses with a built-in camera and small processing unit which allows light and imagery to be sent to the implant. The result is partial vision for people with retinitis pigmentosa. Combined with sensory substitution devices (SSDs) which encode information normally associated with one sense to another sense we have new opportunities for HCI design, which are all possible due to advances in technology and our understanding of disability. An example of how sensing and artificial intelligence is being used to support psychological wellbeing is given in the case study.

Glance at a Future Technology: Artificial Intelligence-Powered Physiological Computing for Better Quality of Life
Youngjun Cho, UCL

A recent report from World Intellectual Property Organization (WIPO) has introduced new emerging ATs: self-care technologies (e.g., health and emotion monitoring) and brain-computer interfaces for enhanced communication and mobility. At the center of the aforementioned ATs is artificial intelligence (AI)-powered physiological computing—a rapidly growing research area on enabling technologies that help us to listen to our bodily functions and psychophysiological needs and self-regulate. The bodily functions are measured by physiological sensors, such as wearable heart rate monitor. AI plays a pivotal role in interpreting the physiological activities into the needs. Then, captured information is fed back into us to increase the awareness of our psychophysiological states and have greater control of our body and mind, promoting positivity gradually over time [234, 353, 439].

With a closed-loop of the three components—physiological sensing, psychophysiological interpretation, and feedback—it aims to offer not only self-care intervention but also daily assistive tools to augment a person's ability. For example, EEG biofeedback, also called neurofeedback, is proven to be an effective therapeutic method for rehabilitating motor skills for people with cerebral palsy and spinal cord injury [87, 124, 235]. More recently, often with gamification, it has been explored to help regulate emotion and improve learning and communication skills for a wider user community including people with attention deficit hyperactivity disorder (ADHD), learning disability, and anxiety disorder [319]. Although more scientific evidence is required, dyslexic students can possibly benefit from visual highlighters with eye-tracking and biofeedback to enhance reading skills. Affective tutoring is another type of physiological computing application that helps tutors to understand mental demand students with learning difficulty face and to tailor teaching to the demand (Figure 3.5).

Gaining self-awareness through physiological computing can also help keep us self-driven [117]. Staying motivated is not always easy. For some disabled people, even basic everyday tasks, such as homemaking and food shopping, can be stressful and worrisome. This often demotivates and puts oneself into a negative self-perpetuating cycle. Scientifically, being aware of our physiological response and emotion is known to be helpful in improving mood and self-motivation unconsciously.

Nonetheless, it is still a long way to go for seamless integration of physiological computing technologies into our daily life given a variety of potential challenges concerning usability, accessibility, and acceptability. Having said that, future physiological computing interfaces must be co-designed with end users [e.g., 278, 295] to prevent reinforcing ableist norms, and instead ensuring people's abilities are maximized where they wish them to be. With this, I envision this type of emerging technology can make a greater positive impact on our physical and psychological wellbeing in our future.

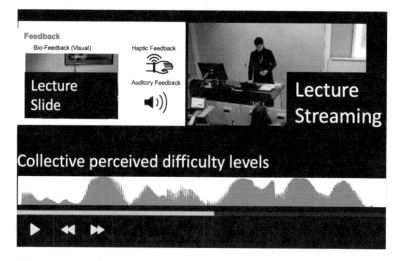

Figure 3.5: Affective tutoring with physiological computing: students' perceived levels of content difficulty are estimated, collectively gathered, and visualized for tutors to tailor their teaching to students' mental demand (Cho [87]).

Mental ill-health is underrepresented in HCI research [222]. Advances which have been made are normally developed within the digital healthcare space. These tend toward a medical model of disability and therefore design. In 2019, Ringland and colleagues [316] conducted a study to understand mental ill-health through the lens of psychosocial disability and explore the subsequent implications for assistive technology. Their related work section completes a nice history of not only the work of HCI within this space, but also the individual experience of psychosocial disability. Three highlights are pulled out here: first the scale of the problem—mental ill-health problems are immense and account for between 21–32% of health problems globally [316]. Second, the fact people experiencing mental ill-heath experience "substantial, persistent sub-threshold symptoms" [316]. These occur below the level of a formal diagnosis of a disability but nonetheless impact on a person's day-to-day ability to function [204]. Third, much of the research presented at ASSETS—the primary ACM conference for AT and accessibility research—has to date focused on physical and sensory impairments and has featured limited research in the field of psychosocial disabilities [316]. This final point is also reflected in this book, where we have done our best to ensure psychosocial disabilities are included, but we also recognize that neither author is an expert in this area, and therefore hope others will help to fill any gaps we might have missed.

It should be noted in future work that people's experience of mental ill-health is highly individual, and people experiencing mental ill-health will sometimes identify as having a disability and other times as simply having challenges they must overcome, but not seeing themselves as a person with a disability. This was also evidenced in Ringland's study of anxiety and depression [316]. When it comes to biofeedback and other therapeutic technologies that might be seen as attempting to normalize individuals, these considerations around the difference between self-identification of illness and disability in the context of psycho-social disabilities have huge implications. The strong Neurodiversity movement in the Autistic community and the recent reclaiming of the term mad by people with conditions such as schizophrenia point to a wider movement in some geographies, especially in the Global North, of resistance toward normalization of behavior and for diversity of behaviour to be the norm. This makes for interesting design spaces for radically new different interactions. For example, rather than looking to encourage people with autism to be more social, what would it look like for non-autistic people to be less social? What would it look like if technology could mediate people's experiences and help to individualize the level of social each person might wish to experience?

3.1.6   VALUE AND USEFULNESS

In HCI through user-centered design we are experts in understanding the use cases of a device in settings, we examine the activities people do and we build on their personal preferences and values to design new experiences. Just looking at web accessibility we find investigations to explore job application portal accessibility for blind people [221] to accessibility of the Internet for people with cognitive disabilities [355]. Wider than the Internet studies investigate touchscreen use by people with physical disabilities [13] and the use of Siri by blind people [3]. The focus here is on usability.

We learn as HCI researchers to be experts in breaking down usability into the following six goals: effectiveness, efficiency, learnability, memorability, safety, and utility [342]. We operationalize these goals into questions: is the system efficient to use? How long does it take a user to learn to use a new function? Rogers et al. [342] describe each of these goals. Effectiveness measures the overall ability of a product to do what it is meant to. Efficiency measures how well the technology supports productivity and task completion. Safety looks to ensure no harm or uncomfortable situations arise for a user. Utility refers to the technology having the right level of functionality, learnability understands how easy it is to start using a technology, and memorability how easy it is to continue to use it once learned. Ultimately, all together these elements enable us as designers to produce productivity enhancing technology. Usability alone is not sufficient for disability interactions. Indeed, it only forms a part of interaction design and is used in conjunction with setting user goals and developing design principles or the majority of projects [342]. But even with highly usable technology, which has followed user-informed design principles and goal setting technologies for people with disabilities are often not usable. This is because they remain unaffordable or unobtainable for users.

From an innovation point of view, we will have proven a wonderful user-product fit. Yet, we would have failed to show the ability for a product-market fit. A lack of market-fit is a contributory factor to a number of useful inventions not yet making it to market. For example, in the World international Property Organization's recent review of assistive technology related patents they found WIPO only 17% of patents are commercialized. This alongside a systematic review of innovation in assistive technology has led to the term: technology-readiness level- (TRL) 5 challenge, which indicates when initially successful ideas get stuck at the proof-of-concept stage. In Figure 3.6, we show the valley of death alongside the TRL levels can and should extend the area of influence of HCI research. A lack of market fit might seem beyond the scope of a HCI designers, and funding agencies often don't fund beyond the level of TRL4 (which is just before going to market). We would argue that this is one of the challenges facing the sector—a disjointed funding landscape. However, we can help overcome this and other challenges, and in the process enhance our designs by using one of the following strategies.

A proven a collaborative model for AT development, is the GRID (Grants-Research-Industry-Dissemination) model [373]. Developed IIT Madras this model has resulted in two new technologies reaching the marketplace: **Arise** Standing Wheelchair and the **NeoFly-NeoBolt** for seamless indoor-outdoor mobility. These devices build on the use cases which look not only at the individual but also of society, designing for the local context and with local manufacturers and distributors from the start of the process, to tighten design requirements and ultimately ensure the research would be useful to individuals.

A second method to support more impactful delivery of innovation is for HCI researchers and designers to work with people who help set budgets, and with people who help influence these budgets. An example here is in the product narratives developed as part of the AT2030 program. These were led by the Clinton Health Access Initiative to help support not only AT2030 but also the new Global Partnership on Assistive Technology—ATscale. Within the elaboration of these product narratives, HCI researchers GDI Hub contributed technical expertise for CHAI to ensure they were fully acquainted with the latest advances in technology and were connected to innovators in the AT field. This collaboration, which stretched across the AT2030 partners resulted in five-landscaping documents which clearly set out the supply and demand challenges for product sectors such as mobile phones as assistive technologies [19].

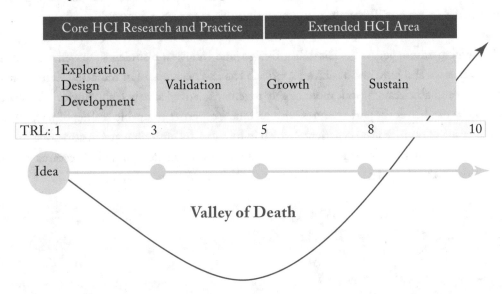

Figure 3.6: Valley of death diagram showing the innovation journey from idea to sustainability across the technology readiness levels 1–10.

Another example of landscaping documents is the GSMA disability digital divide report which was the result of over 80 interviews and 2,000 survey responses form people with disabilities in Bangladesh and Kenya. The report helped galvanize mobile phone operator responses to making their services and operations accessible through a continued commitment to evidencing and monitoring the disability mobile gap (see subsequent 2020 report), a dedicated technology accelerator for mobile—GSMA Assistive Tech Program [153]. Knowledge from these initiatives culminated in the launch of "The Principles" for the Digital Inclusion of Persons with Disability which has now has a range of mobile network operators as signatories including Vodacom, Orange, Telfonica, and Safaricom [154]. The initial 2019 research also provided a rich data set of the usability of current systems and the usefulness and value of having a mobile phone for people in low-resource environments.

A third method is to open and share our user-centered design practices with other disciplines, especially into and supporting entrepreneurs. Currently, there are a number of technology accelerators that are focused on helping AT and accessible digital technology to market. Accelerators are part of the innovation ecosystem. They normally take a cohort approach to helping new technology and ideas to market. A cohort—anything from a handful to tens of ventures—is brought together and supported through a program where they learn to sell their idea, develop a business plan, connect to partners, and test models of scale. In developing their business model, a venture is looking to measure usefulness and value so that they can then derive a pay structure for people to purchase their product or service. There are many opportunities for partnership with accelerators such as Remarkable, InnovateNow, and Social Alpha, and ventures within these. We have found it particularly useful to ensure our M.Sc. Disability, Design, and Innovation students are well connected to local accelerators and have heard such an approach has also been useful in India and Kenya—where universities and accelerators work more closely together to advance new technologies. Universities, in particular, can better support ventures with technical expertise to enable scaling of technologies, and validation of positive user-experience which in turn can aid entrepreneurs in attracting funding.

We now present a case study of value and usefulness which combines HCI research methods and assistive technology development: the case of the innovATe wheelchair.

Case Study: Motivation InnovATe Wheelchairs, Reimagining Wheelchair Bespoke Wheelchair Manufacturing Through Technology

Jake Honeywill and Nancy Mbugua

Motivation InnovATe [272] is a trial model for locally producing made-to-measure wheelchairs that are fully customizable to the needs and preference of each user. The process starts with a wheelchair assessment; a trained clinician works with the user to establish their requirements and priorities, and to obtain accurate body measurements. This data will directly inform the design of the wheelchair; it is fed into a parametric Computer Aided Design (CAD) model which automatically generates a bespoke wheelchair design that provides the optimum fit for the user. The wheelchair is then fabricated using a combination of unique3D printed parts and metal tubing cut to length enabling localized production of consistent high-quality. The InnovATe model has been developed by Motivation UK and tested with local users and clinicians in Kenya as part of the AT2030 program.

The Problem: In Kenya there are more than 500,000 individuals with physical disabilities, many of whom need access to appropriate wheelchairs. Current wheelchair provision models rely on donor-funded projects, donation of imported chairs by philanthropic organizations and charities, or small-scale local production. These models are unsustainable, with time-limited funding, costly importation that is susceptible to disruption, and wheelchairs that are often inappropriate for their intended user—the wrong size, with product features which do not match their environment or lifestyle. At the same time, local manufacturing struggles to produce wheelchairs of consistent quality and quantity. The gaps in these production models, alongside gaps in wheelchair services, result in wheelchair users lacking access to the AT they have a right to, which impacts on their independence, health, and inclusion in society.

Value and Usefulness, Co-Created Solutions: The Motivation InnovATe model leverages technology to address manufacturing issues, and promotes a de-centralized approach to wheelchair development that shifts the ownership of the wheelchair design and production process directly into the hands of the user and the local clinical and technical team. Throughout our trial we observed how the deep collaboration required between all parties involved at every step, from assessment and design to production and fitting enabled not just users, but also clinicians and technicians to feel empowered. In particular, users felt, often for the first time, in charge of the process that leads to the production of wheelchairs that match not only their physical needs, but also their personal identities [34].

Figure 3.7: Participant involved in the motivation innovate trial in Kenya is testing her bespoke wheelchair (picture by Motivation).

Open and Scalable: The hybrid manufacturing process of the Motivation InnovATe wheelchairs that combines digital technologies such as CAD and 3D printing with traditional assembly, allows for great flexibility, creating a model that can scale across context with different requirements and resources. Materials and components used to assemble the wheelchairs can be changed according to what is available in the country. Similarly, the design of the wheelchairs can be adapted according to the different characteristics of the environment. This flexible approach has great application potential for the development of other assistive devices such as crutches, walking frames, and postural devices components enabling the creation of a library of customizable assistive devices that could be manufactured leveraging the same materials and equipment supporting scalability across different products.

Choice, Power, and Value of AT

One underpinning issue with advancing the adoption of assistive technology lies in how healthcare is funded more broadly. This is more explicitly explored in Chapter 6. The range of products and services available to people within healthcare services are available at this discretion of the healthcare provision system. The main issue is how health is financed. Healthcare is expensive—for example it will account for 20% of Gross Domestic Product (GDP) of the U.S. by 2024 [252]. Healthcare is normally financed through two systems—general tax base or insurance-based systems. They can also be financed or supported in their finance by donations or grants, something which is more prevalent in LMICs.

How a country chooses to finance a health system and the importance of AT within this, alongside the guiding philosophy or principles, all influence the experience of the person with disabilities. Insurance-based systems such as those which prevail in the United States.

There are two countries which are interesting to explore in their attempts to make AT provision equitable. The first is Australia and the second is Norway. The first picked due to the recent review of the choice-based system led by Emily Steel [e.g., 366,367, 368], the second as it is often used as an exemplar by the WHO.

The Australian National Disability Insurance Scheme (NDIS) recently adopted a policy for assistive technology which aimed to balance "participant choice and control" [456:18]. While doing this the strategy looked to balance maximizing individual choice [456:18] and outcomes with financial benefits for the scheme [456:17]. A recent review of this policy was undertaken by Steel in 2019 [366]. She found there were inherent tensions between these two aims. On the one hand, maximizing return of the scheme, meant implementing a form of collective choice. This, Steel observes, is not "counter to human rights principles" as it aligns with self-determination theories for example which can be considered a collective process [ibid.]. However Steel questions how meaningfully disabled people were a part of the process of collectively determining the choice of products available for them to use [ibid.]. Steel further highlights the problem of choice within this economically restrained policy, which has a strong focus on products and rational choice, over and above the provision services and social bonds within constitute a user's life and choices [ibid.]. The fact finances are devolved to local organizations (as is the case in Australia) can further exasperate inequalities within healthcare systems [ibid.].

Choice within health is closely aligned to where power rests. There are competing arms of neo-liberalism within this paradigm. The first being the right to individual power and choice, the second that this will bring about economic growth. However, as is demonstrated both in Steel's review of the Australian AT strategy and by other authors such as Clarke [93], choice is complex and ambiguous. Choice is an emerging key idea within reform of public services within the UK and globally [93]. Choice is ambiguous—it can have different levels of specificity [93]. For example, choice within a sub-set of assistive products or choice of which health service center you would like to use [93]. Choice can also be opaque, masking, or being perceived to mask agendas such as privatization [93]. Choice can also be antagonistic as it can create inequality, change power paradigms, and introduce the idea of private into public services [93]. The disability movement has been at the vanguard of challenging the idea that public service individuals know best and have championed the idea of the disabled person "being the experts of their own condition." However, what we are seeing in current choice-based policy is an implementation of choice Individuals where those with greater social capital and who are better able to express and argue for their needs will, within a free-choice system, prevail with better outcomes than people less able to advocate [366]. When we return to evidence from the NDIS of Australia, we are presented with evidence of how AT users value the role of healthcare practitioners in enabling choice of AT [356]. However, due to excessive delays in gaining access to AT, people felt their control was diluted. Not having access to the AT needed meant they were unable to control other important aspects of their lives [356]. The question therefore remains—how best to enable this expertise of disabled people to be combined with external expertise (when wanted and needed) within a public system?

An answer to the above question might come from AT provision within Norway and Sweden derives explicitly from a human rights approach. This changes the power and choice dynamics. The Norwegian Assistive Technology Service Delivery system started as a pilot in 1977 and was driven by a close collaboration across: Ministry of Health and Social Services (MoHSS), Disabled People's Organizations (DPOs), professional organizations, and the applied research agency SINTEF [238, 375, 376]. SINTEF led the process and housed the secretariate of the Council for Assistive Technology. Importantly, the assistive products within the AT service are a library, they are not owned by any one individual and instead are leaned to individuals as needed, then returned when not needed [375, 376]. The results of a well-resourced and human-rights-based approach system which is seen in Norway and paralleled in Sweden are that people can have choice of products which suit their lifestyles, e.g., a wheelchair for skiing, one for commuting and one for use in the home. The demand for products drives the need for procurement and private companies compete to get their products into the catalogue used within each of the Assistive Technology Centers.

3.1.7   OPEN AND SCALABLE

As we have seen, accessible solutions and ATs are yet to fully reach their potential due to a lack of market-fit validation, and restricted routes to market. One way to help solve this is promote the use of open and scalable solutions.

A recent review of the innovation landscape for AT as part of the background papers for the WHO World Report on AT found only 91 studies which combined innovation and assistive technology [181]. Reviewing these papers alongside 72 case studies the authors found there was a large focus on product innovation with gaps for innovation present in the systems which support the provision and supply of AT [181]. Open innovation strategies combined with systems strengthening were proposed for the future of more successful innovation strategies for AT [181].

HCI researchers have explored how design sharing platforms such as Thingiverse can also be used for accessibility. Bueler et al. [70] surveyed all AT available on this site, as well as the designers of AT solutions, examining their motivations for AT design and sharing practices. This DIY-AT approach which we focused on in co-creation principle demonstrates the ability to use technology to create new interactions. However, as we saw this type of sharing and co-creation has limitations when scaling. This is not a criticism of the approach, developing technologies for individuals is both useful and rewarding. Moreover, its caring agenda is only implementable through empathetic design, generating outputs which are usable, useful creations for people who needed them. However, this type of design would be even more impactful if it was built within communities, which had ready access to the assistive technologies and accessible solutions. How then can we begin to use sharing platforms for more scaled approaches to design?

We draw on two examples where digital AAT infrastructure can be designed to be more open and scalable: Information Interaction and the Circular Interactions before concluding with a case study of an open and scalable disability interaction example of from IIT-Bangaolire of their Open Source Learning Management System (LMS), Subodha.

Information Interaction: Recent examples of this infrastructure include the recent InnovationAction project [133] which is bringing together data from a range of projects to develop a more integrated understanding of the possibilities for local production in low and middle income. A second example is the Open Know Where Project [244], which uses a common data standard to allow different mapping initiatives to cooperate more easily, with a common data standard. However, as these datasets are generated, there are questions about how to make them most useful and usable. Ultimately, having the data is just the first part of the problem; next we must work collaboratively to make it useful.

This is an area where HCI can help greatly. We can build systems which enhance the possibilities of interactions between information (data) and people to create actionable insights on insights from other areas to help develop more interaction with the information being collected [53, 100, 306]. Design can also help contribute to the information conversation which takes place between people and the platforms they engage in [245].

Circular Interactions: Recently, a circular AT provision model has been developed which highlights the links between local production of AT and systems level thinking. As seen before, a systems approach is not new, and neither is the idea of localized, distributed manufacture. Systems strengthening has been proposed by a range of authors, e.g., MacLachlan [240], Blandford [52], and Holloway [181]; and a history of craftwork predates the industrial revolutions. What is new is the demand—the increasing need for adaptable, affordable, high-quality AT, and the ability to develop new levels of scale for supplying this demand.

Building on the work of Thingverse and other design sharing sites there are opportunities to focus in on repair culture, and also develop new methods for clinical trials which may include distributed manufacture processes. Finally, though our socio-technical investigations we can look at schemes which better support re-use and loan schemes.

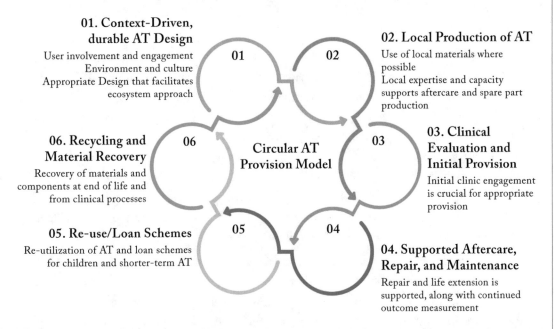

Figure 3.8: Diagram showing the Circular AT Provision Model articulated across six principles: Context-Driven Durable AT Design; Local Production of AT; Clinical Evaluation and Initial Provision; Supported Aftercare, Repair and Maintenance; Re-Use/Loan Schemes; and Recycling and Material Recovery.

Case Study: Creating Accessible STEM Content and Making It Available at Scale Through Subodha

Supriya Dey, Vision Empower, Bangalore, India; Amit Prakash, Center for Accessibility in the Global South (CAGS), IIIT Bangalore, Bangalore, India

The design of an Open Source Learning Management System (LMS), Subodha, accessible for students and teachers with visual impairment. Vision Empower (VE) specifically designed a content creation process to make the largely visual curricular content, especially that of Science, Math, and Computational Thinking, accessible for these students and teachers. Subodha was created through a collaborative research effort between VE and IIIT Bangalore, where the not-for-profit enterprise is incubated.

The Problem: The challenges of education for visually impaired students within India include large numbers of rural and underserved children huddled in special schools for the blind, inconsistency in the pedagogical approach due to diversity of languages and lack of awareness about the possibilities of affordable and inclusive education [384]. Apart from lack of appropriate technology to learn Mathematics, Science, and Programming in higher grades, there is a dearth of trained teachers in India who can train students with visual impairment, especially on STEM subjects and on the usage of digital platforms [108].

Co-Created Solutions Across a Wide Range of Actors: The Vision Empower Subodha LMS was specifically co-created using a participatory design method by the VE-IIITB team along with visually impaired users, who were key contributors in the design process. They were either expert users of technology, or teachers, students, and their experienced mentors. Content for Subodha is being created in collaboration with multiple VE partner organizations in various regions of the country engaged in the support of educational needs of students with visual impairment [297]. The accessible content for both teachers and students includes Teacher Instructor Kits and accessible reference material for teachers and students, designed following the VE Content Creation process, which was created to address the needs of accessible STEM content for students with visual impairment.

Open and Scalable: The VE Subodha LMS was initiated through an academic collaboration with IIIT Bangalore. It was designed based on the open architecture of the OpenEdX platform. The primary motivation of the LMS was to leverage the accessibility features of a proven platform and enhance the design to disseminate easily accessible STEM content for use by persons with visual impairment, make it available on demand by the community and ensure that the enhancements were made openly available to developers for the future. The LMS is available in English and five Indian languages for use in states (provinces) where VE is currently engaged. So far, teachers in 83 schools across these 5 states in India have been trained on the Subodha LMS (http://visionempowertrust.in/news-events/). In addition to accessible Science, Math, Special Skills, and Computational Thinking courses, Subodha also offers accessible Digital Literacy training content for both students and adults. In collaboration with other NGO partners, VE is training 1000 teachers who are visually impaired on Foundations of Digital Literacy using the Subodha LMS. The VE conviction is that the platform will reach and help every student with visual impairment in the country, their teachers and caregivers who are often themselves visually impaired, through this consolidated repository of accessible educational content, freely available on demand. State governments of Karnataka, Tripura, and Tamil Nadu have approved the use of the LMS for all special schools for the blind in their respective states.

3.2   A FRAMEWORK: DIMENSIONS OF DIX

We have seen that the principles of DIX exist at a high level, and some seem like core competencies of HCI research such as co-creation, while others might appear beyond the scope of HCI like disability inclusion as a wicked problem. Therefore, one could legitimately ask how can we operationalize it, and what specifically differentiates disability interactions from other HCI theories (e.g., Ability-based design) or frameworks (e.g., Computing for Wellbeing)? Good questions.

DIX is in many ways a framework of frameworks and so we present it though the four- dimensions of DIX, which are shown in Figure 3.9.

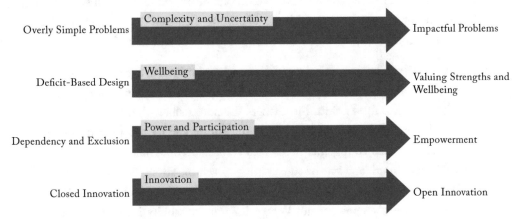

Figure 3.9: The dimensions of DIX.

The DIX dimensions are measurable on a finer scale than the principles and allow us to build the framework for operationalizing the DIX agenda. The four dimensions are as follows.

- **Complexity and Uncertainty:** Complexity refers to the number of interactions and scale of these; uncertainty to the number of known unknowns within a project. We move from overly simple problem definition (completed in isolation) to tackling impactful problems. These impactful problems will have a very definite social responsibility framing and involve a high number of disciplines and researchers solving the problem. Highly uncertain projects could involve a fundamental new material or interaction type where certain characteristics are completely unknown or could result due to institutional or organizational changes, e.g., a change of CEO or of funding arrangement mid-way through a project. COVID-19 has made helped many appreciate the nature of uncertainty—it brings both opportunity and challenge.

- **Wellbeing:** This dimension is heavily influenced by Calvo and Peters' Positive Computing approach. Technologies which are designed for deeper meaning, happiness, and human flourishing are included in this dimension. We seek technologies which are built on user and community values, and which include enhancing ability but also improve three elements of psychological wellbeing: (1) affective quality, (2) engagement/actualization, and (3) connectedness of experience. However, in pursuing this goal we must be careful to not seek to develop technologies which are simply trying to normalize or reform the behaviors of people with disability from an ableist view of being well. For this to occur it is important to take notice of the rising influence of what Williams calls the "metaeugenic" vision of a future without disability—where an "undercurrent of cultural norms, ideals, values, and demands" "warp and twist deviant bodies into conformity via a desperate drive for survival and future" [429].

- **Power and Participation:** This dimension measures how much agency is being given to both individuals with disability and local communities in the research program or project. There are two focal points. First, where the power sits within the research design, this focal point aligns well with wellbeing dimension and we see a future where both dimensions are defined together in research studies. Second, there is a particular focus on the Global South and low resource settings given the strong link between disability and poverty with 80% of persons with disability living in the global south. We move from exclusion to empowerment. When designing disability interactions along this scale agency is a useful measurement. Full agency will be achieved when we have diverse teams tackling a problem with researchers having lived experience of disability and the context of technology use. For this to be achieved ableist approaches must diminish.

- **Innovation:** Innovation is defined as attempting something new, and open innovation as a process that sees information or knowledge from internal and external sources being used to advance innovation (466). Therefore, as we move along this DIX dimension we are looking to work in partnerships and acknowledge the need for a variety of actors to bring a new technology or idea to market and then to scale.

We will now take a closer look at each DIX dimension, illustrating each with a case study before exploring the theoretical basis, methods, and tools which can be used to measure each DIX dimension.

Each dimension is informed by the theories from HCI and beyond, where these theories are not yet fully formed, we draw upon other relevant emerging literature. This collection of theories and literature helps to inform design and research strategies, methods and tools. Together, these elements complete the DIX framework—summarized in Table 3.1.

We will now take a close look at each of the dimensions within the framework before concluding the first part of this book with a case study.

Table 3.1: DIX framework

Dimensions	Literature and Theory	Strategies, Methods and Tools
Complexity	Systems thinking and agile methods Managing the unknown: A new approach to managing high uncertainty and risk in projects [467] Prefigurative politics	Speculative Design: Design fiction, future scouting toolkit Longer-term studies and interdisciplinary teams: Agile project management, team building Contextually appropriate theoretical frameworks Action research
Wellbeing	Ability-based design [433] Positive computing [80] Positive technologies [469] Experience design [470 Positive design [471] Humanistic HCI Multisensory experiences Metaeugenics [429]	Wellbeing design cards (468) Motivation, engagement, and thriving in user experience (METUX) model Value-based design xSense design cards for multisensory experiences
Power and Participation	Critical theory In the wild Ableism Capability approach (sen) Interdependence theory Competency and assistive technology Metaeugenics [429]	In the wild Handover approach to research Participatory design Human-rights-based design disability documentaries
Innovation	Open innovation Roger's diffusion theory	Mobile-based solutions Sustainability: Digital and distributed design and manufacture The business model innovation grid

3.2.1   COMPLEXITY

There are multiple people speaking about this need for different scales of investigation. In designing for emerging technologies, Follet describes how the next generation of technologies will disrupt rather than accelerate innovation and that for designers to truly be able to harness the emerging technologies we will need to develop eight core skills or tenets, among these are the ability to operate at different scales, work in interdisciplinary teams which provoke and facilitate change [128]. Shneiderman approaches the matter slightly differently as he describes the need to work on both applied and basic research simultaneously [352]. Regardless of the nuances of each approach, both are speaking to the role of systems thinking and how we develop our core skills at different levels. If we are to fully commit to this new way of delivering HCI for disability inclusion, then we will also need to ensure capacity is built globally and not just in the Global North. We look further at this paradigm shift in the next chapter.

Designing and researching technology for people with disabilities is complex as the nature of disability is complex. Scholars have drawn from the Disability Studies literature to develop theories which can help us advance DIX. One such theory is Interdependence theory, which acknowledges the complexities of collaborative access to technology. It starts from the point that we all depend on technology and others to live our lives, however, when a person is not disabled these dependencies are normalized; this is not the case for people with disabilities [38]. There is often a lack of resilience within the mediated interactions technology plays in the lives of people with disability. An example given in Bennett et al.'s paper comes from the field of Science and Technology Studies and involves the use of a wheelchair life being out of order on a train and therefore preventing a wheelchair user from boarding the train [271]; a common issue in the United Kingdom is finding oneself stuck on a train as ramps are manually deployed by people who can forget to come and deploy them. Building resilience alongside equality of experience—not just access to an experience adds complexity to designs.

In their paper titled "Accessibility Infrastructure in the Global South," Pal and colleagues [289] make the case that policy alone will not solve the problems of digital accessibility, calling out the issues of stigma and a lack of an inclusive network. They argue we must go beyond the individual ability expressed in ability-based design and look at how the accessibility infrastructure enables, or indeed disables people from being able to participate in society. Pal et al. build their accessibility infrastructure framework on the experience of visually impaired users of mobile phones, however, postulate the theory has much broader applicability to assistive technology in general.

In the Global South, Sambasivan's concept of human infrastructures has also emerged as crucially important [333]. These human infrastructures can be low-cost and robust, built on a substrate of trust. They can operate over multiple communities of practice which reconfigure and sometimes contest one another. By understanding these complex dynamics, we have an opportunity to design technologies which take advantage of human infrastructure and its social nature to design technologies and interfaces which better express determinant factors of wellbeing. For example, Pal et al. have explored the use of ride-sharing [200] and mobile phone use [292] by visually impaired people in low-resource environments, where human infrastructure is more prevalent in technology mediation. Through their exploration of technology use, they propose the following set of features as essential one to be measured throughout different interactions: independence, safety, productivity, economic participation, income, social circle, and mobility.

AT, as described by Pal, refers mainly to digital accessibility. However, there is also a role for accessibility infrastructure when looking more broadly at AT as described by the World Health Organization (WHO). The WHO define assistive products in the same way HCI professionals describe technologies. For an assistive product to become a technology for the WHO it must be paired with services which allow a person to receive and if necessary be trained in how to use the product.

Traditionally assistive products were provided to people through clinical or educational settings with specialists assessing the user, selecting the product, and then providing training for use. This service, combined with the products and the policy and provision systems are together termed "technology." There are guidelines on how to provide for example wheelchairs to people. These guidelines were set via consensus to prevent poor quality products being given to people (e.g., devices which were dangerous, would break easily or were given with little or no training rendering them all but useless). The 5P's defined by the WHO's Global Cooperation on Assistive Technology: Policy, Provision, Personnel (i.e., trained clinical experts), People (users), and Products almost perfectly describe a wicked problem as seen in the previous chapter. However, elements of the problem can be deconstructed and made solvable, all the while ensuring we are able to honor the overall complexity. We now move to explore the second dimension—wellbeing.

3.2.2   WELLBEING

In the wellbeing dimension, we seek to move beyond designing to enhance and optimize functional abilities and toward a more rounded concept of wellbeing. We build on the solid foundations of ability-based design principles and participatory and co-design design methods; adding the foundational work of Positive Computing and its evolution to Psychological Wellbeing. In their original work, Calvho and Peters explore the entry point of teams to Positive Computing, which they posit could be with one factor or **Circumstantial Conditions** and **Determinants Factors** of psychological wellbeing. Some circumstantial elements fall outside the scope of Psychological Wellbeing—personality type, multiple intelligence levels, and socioeconomic status, while others such as learning, physical environment, and social relationships are often mediated through technology and offer huge opportunity for design work by working to design meditations which support the **determinant factors of wellbeing**, namely: positive emotions, motivation, and engagement, self-awareness, mindfulness, resilience, gratitude, empathy, compassion, and altruism. Why are these important for DIX?

In a recent study of open space use by people with visual impairments the PLACES (Plan, Access, Contribute, Engage, Share) framework was proposed [28]. Central to the framework was the idea of contribution of the person with visual impairment to all aspects of a trip to an open space. The concept of contribution combined with Psychological Wellbeing opens up an interesting design space. To be able make a trip to an open space fully inclusive one needs for example to be self-aware and to have empathy. Moreover, to allow individuals to share the experience of an open space, the space itself will need to be designed to allow interactions which go beyond simply following a route from A to B and allow learning and exploration of the individual—all of these aspects: learning, environment, empathy, and self-awareness can be designed with the help of Psychological Wellbeing.

Interestingly, the concept of Psychological Wellbeing, which has now matured into the recent Motivation, Engagement, and Thriving in User Experience (METUX) model, does not mention independence. Frequently, independence has been deemed the goal of technology use by people with disabilities. However, as was explored by Soro et al., independence more broadly in HCI can be used inaccurately and almost lazily to represent a wide range of topics such as: agency, dignity, autonomy, freedom of choice, and participation.

3.2.3   POWER AND PARTICIPATION

There is a lack of people with disabilities as active members of the HCI research community, this means that the diverse perspectives which people with disabilities would bring are lacking from teams. This contributes to an ableist approach within HCI research which is pervasive, and in need of change. Furthermore, there is an even more severe lack of trained HCI researchers and designers in the Global South, this can lead to approaches where researchers from the Global North parachute in, conduct research, and then leave.

When conducting a relatively recent study in Kibera, Kenya we were asked: "What makes you different from all the others?" The "others" being referred to here are the myriad of researchers who cross-cross the lives of people living in Kibera, but without change being observed as a result by Kibera residents. We hoped to be different and leave a more lasting legacy by the lens of human infrastructuring [333] and the idea of a hand-over approach to technology creation [322]. By this we mean to hand over control of the research agenda to the people for whom the research is being conducted and the local teams who will be able to continue building a research agenda locally within this space. We combined these with a focus on developing the capacity of the people with whom we are working, some were Kibera residents, so that the people with disabilities themselves in low-resource settings were integral part of the team and developed skills they didn't otherwise have access to. We continue to work with the local teams through our innovation stream of work in AT2030. As part of this program we have supported a local innovator, Lincoln Wamae, who is building wheelchairs from scrap materials which are robust to the local, hostile built environment. Lincoln's wheelchairs have since been shown on the BBC and other news outlets as he built his business and profile. Next year will see a broadening of this research to cover virtual live lab networks which will connect local residents and groups with global expertise that can support the development of contextually appropriate innovations. Interestingly, this would have happened this year, but due to COVID-19 and the resulting constriction of the UK economy the UK Government chose to reduce the overseas development aid budget from 0.7% to 0.5% of Gross Domestic Product. The decision has been condemned by many, and said to reinforce colonialist constructs, while undermining trust between the UK and low- and middle-income countries. It certainly hasn't helped our efforts to build capacity.

Returning to the lack of disability diversity within HCI and the reflections of Hoffman et al. on the issues facing researchers with disabilities within our community, we see the following issues: ableism in research, oversimplification of disability, and human relationships around disability. Ableism is something which affects disabled and non-disabled people alike and must be acknowledged if we are to move beyond it [177]. The authors argue the need for accessibility researchers to hold the dualist perspective: to support disabled people's need to co-exist within the current ableist society, while also enabling a complete rejection of said society and creation of a new society, which we suggest would be more accepting of diversity, pluralist and fairer.

Crucial to this subversion of power is the idea to shift perceptions toward the desirability, or undesirability of ATs. Within this context, we argue for the creation of design experiences which allow people with disabilities to both desire their technology, and to ensure technology used by them enables expression of self. Instead of promoting the usually popular stereotypes of persons with disabilities as either heroes or people in need of saving, we should allow for choice and expression which can on one day be to simply blend in and another to stand out. What we are aiming for here is beyond inclusion to expression, but especially empowerment of choosing one's own self-image.

We have seen glimpses of this in the design and choice of prosthetic devices, with children being able (and we should ask, why only children?) to choose a superhero limb through open bionics partnership with Disney. Another important aspect within this dimension is that of competency. Many ATs take a great deal of skill to master, something which is often overlooked by non-disabled users; people do not see let alone value the competencies an AT user has developed in order to become a proficient user.

Figure 3.10: Open bionics collaboration with Disney to produce character prosthetic arms for children.

Promoting greater participation also requires us to adopt a critical outlook as described by Rogers [320]. When applying critical theory to HCI we take on the role of skeptic and expert within a cultural topic; for disability this means being an expert in the field of disability studies and applying that expertise critically to the nature of HCI design practice or to a specific process or product. Critical theory is complex to put in practice difficult due to the need for this level of subject and design expertise [320]. People need to have great knowledge of the subject or can run the risk of oversimplifying the problem space due to a lack of expertise which leads then to cherry pick concepts rather than being able to unpick and explain the multiple levels and theories which are at play within the space care therefore must be taken when applying critical theory [320]. In 2021 at the Paralympic Games, one such shift will take place at a global level, as a campaign launches to transform people's perceptions around designing for disability. The campaign will seek to shift the conversation toward harnessing the power of the 15%. The power of the 15% refers to the 15% of the global population who live with disabilities. The #wethe15 campaign will last for 10 years and it will be interesting to see how technology such as social media is used to connect conversations and amplify messages of inclusion during this time. What is crucial in such campaigns, as well as in scientific enquiry is the need for diversity and inclusion to shine through; for normalization of diversity and inclusion to take place rather than the normalization of individuals with disability.

Despite advances in participatory methods, there are often cases where people with disabilities are inadvertently victimized as part of research. Williams has been conducting research into the types of studies conducted on behalf of autistic people. In 2019, he published a survey with Gilbert [426] on wearable technologies which showed that there was a prevalence for using such technology to encourage social normative behaviors of autistic children and adults. Commenting on this study and quoting verbatim from exemplar studies William explores the role of what he defines as *Metaeugenics*—something he sees an endemic to the research aims of AT for people with autism. By this he means a number of things [429]. First, that researchers persist in developing technologies which look to repetitively reinforce behaviors and fail to explore the instances when the child or adult clearly demonstrate their displeasure of being controlled as simply another failure to achieve a normal behavior. Second, conducting experiments in small spaces which are confined and within which the end goals of the technology development are seen as superior to the adverse effects on the child taking part in the experiment. Here an example of robot assisted therapy is given where a child clearly moves away from the robot only to be followed by it. While this is reported as a negative reaction by the initial authors, Williams questions why the robot should be able to demonstrate poor social skills—chasing the child, when. Supposedly designed to help the child learn social skills. Finally, a description is given of a therapist-based intervention compared to a technology mediated intervention. The technology is less bad, it produces less resistance and distress from the autistic person; but Williams asks, why was the therapy distressing in the first place? Williams urges us to be attentive in our research design [429] and for the necessity of community-led research if we are to have an ethical progress in AT design and development [426].

Finally, another way to shift the power balance in HCI and DIX research is to move from researchers-controlled lab-based studies to in the wild studies controlled by participants. In fact, these studies show how people come to understand and appropriate technologies in their own terms and for their own situated purposes. In these contexts, the focus of control shifts from the experimenter to the participant of a study and from the isolation of variables we move toward the need to understand the interdependencies at play. Rogers advocates that to make sense of things in the wild, we first need theories from outside HCI which have been developed to understand and explain behavior in the real world. These theories can then be recontextualized for HCI studies, and the subsequent findings of these studies then used to create new "wild" theories.

Ultimately, we are looking to move beyond a design to address problems which create social exclusion to one which embraces the possibilities for inclusion, empowerment, and equal participation of all people, regardless of abilities and competencies. This might seem like a subtle shift, but in the same way Ability-based design shifted the perspective from a deficit mindset to one of abundance or surplus. When we begin to imagine interactions which will incorporate people with a wide spectrum of sensory abilities for example, we are forces to explore multi-sensory design methods, and think of how best to substitute information across and between senses for an equivalence of experience for all people.

3.2.4   INNOVATION

The final dimension is one of innovation. In the DIX manifesto we look toward the power of ICT and distributed design and manufacture to power more open and scalable technology [392]. At the time the FabCity movement was referenced, which looked to design 50% of all technology within a city to create more sustainable manufacturing systems. Since that time COVID-19 has come and disrupted our lives completely. It has demonstrated the fragility of our global supply chains [258] but also the ability for technology and human ingenuity to develop novel, more local products, and services. COVID-19 has not affected everyone equally; minority groups the world over, and poorer nations have suffered the effects of the virus more severely than their better-off neighbors. People with disabilities are no exception. People with disabilities have seen healthcare [359] and education provision disrupted. However, it has also exposed the social nature of disability to the global population in an unexpected way—people have more experimental knowledge of what it is like to have environmental factors limit their freedom of movement and restrict their ability to "feel informed," they have also reported feeling "different," all things people with disabilities encounter daily [119]. Furthermore, mainstream, accessible technologies such as Zoom and Microsoft Teams have transformed the workplace. In 2018, people with disabilities who encountered challenges in accessing their workplaces and would have benefitted from flexible and remote work arrangements, found it difficult to make the case, now these arrangements are the norm for the majority of office workers. These technologies scaled, albeit sometimes with glitches in a manner which has accelerated both their acceptance and use.

As Blandford points out in her review of the challenges and opportunities in HCI for health and wellbeing, there are paradoxes in healthcare for the HCI community: "on the one hand, there is substantial investment in innovative health technologies, particularly around "big data" analytics and personal health technologies; on the other hand, most interactive health technologies that are currently deployed at scale are difficult to use and few innovative technologies have achieved significant market penetration." When it comes to Disability Interactions we can see a similar dynamic at play: on the one hand, we have an increasing number of inventions in AT in areas such as smart homes, robotics, and AI [431]; and at the same time, we have 90% of people unable to gain access to the most basic of technologies to assist them in their lives.

Since publishing the *Manifesto*, the problems surrounding the diffusion of AT have been reviewed systematically in a scoping review. Here, a lack of open innovation and larger mission setting were identified as barriers to products being able to overcome the valley of death. The valley of death, where innovations fail to scale due to a lack of investment and traction at key points, is known to be longer and deeper for AT—meaning many more innovations fail on their route to market. It is more complicated for assistive products to reach the market and for entrepreneurs in the space to create sustainable businesses as investors often believe disabled people will not be able to pay for the technology (recent finding of the AT2030 Impact Fund), the products are classed as medical devices and must pass regulator testing and approvals (which can also be the case for accessible technology, something inventors can be unaware of) and devices which are produced for batch or small levels of distribution may not scale well from more mass manufacturing.

The conversation about scale has been detailed in Chapter 2. Here, we simply reflect on the growing number of initiatives which are looking to support AT, disabled entrepreneurs, and inclusive and accessible solutions. As stated previously, dedicated accelerators for AT now exist in London, Australia, India, and Kenya [181]. Within the AT innovation landscape AT accelerators are a relatively new initiate, which combine traditional start-up entrepreneurship model and values with short development cycles, rapid viability discovery, business-driven experimentation, iterative product releases, and validated learning [181]. They blend social impact and commercial business models with most sharing at least some of the following characteristics [181]:

- an application process that is open to all, yet highly competitive;

- provision of pre-seed investments;

- a focus on small teams not individual founders;

- time-limited support, usually between 3–6 months, comprising programmed events, and intensive mentoring; and

- cohorts or "classes" of start-ups rather than individual companies.

All of these are great examples of open innovation where start-ups are connected to manufacturers, venture support as well as academic expertise. There is even a dedicated AT impact fund now for this purpose, which gives bespoke venture and technical support to ventures through a "Scale Studio" [134]. When we look back in 10 years will AT be as successful as FinTech for example? It is possible. However, it will need significant levels of investment and technical expertise to help the sector grow. The combination of open innovation approaches—where no one entity believes they alone can design, manufacture, market, and scale an invention—combined with central policy missions such as age friendly or carbon neutral cities which are each infused with a disability inclusion lens, will allow for a thriving investment space. However, this will only be possible when systems thinking is infused from the start of design projects to ensure that these interventions do not act in isolation but act as a coordinated portfolio of initiatives sustaining the design, development, distribution, reach, and use of AT from start to finish.

Before concluding this chapter with our case study, it is worth pausing and adding a word of caution on the roles of innovation with disability interactions. We have demonstrated the need is growing alongside demand for inclusively design products and services, and AT. This is good news for routes to market, for entrepreneurs and investors alike. However, the drivers for innovation are often profit driven—the technology will level the playing field for an individual to become a productive member of society as defined through a capitalist lens as someone who can generate monetary wealth. However, as noted by Williams, people with disabilities may be unable to, or simply not have the desire to, overcome the many systematic barriers in their way to enter into the workforce; they are none the less valid and worthy humans [429]. It is important therefore to remember within the ecosystem of AAT innovation we should ensure technology supports all people and should see solutions to systematic barriers. These will only be possible through a non-ableist co0designed agenda to the ecosystem.

3.3   CASE STUDY: DIX WITHIN THE AT2030 PROGRAM IN KENYA

We now take a look at how a DIX approach has played out in accessibility research and assistive technology research within the AT2030 program [135]. Throughout this program we strive to incorporate all the elements of a new approach to DIX research. This is not to say of course that the program itself is perfect, as it is of course not the case, but its large portfolio of activities contains all the ingredients to test the DIX manifesto and develop new solutions and theories, in keeping with the ABC approach to research of Shneiderman which forms one of our core DIX Principles.

AT2030 is a £19.8m program of research funded by the UK's Foreign, Commonwealth and Development Office (FCDO). It was launched at the Global Disability Summit in London in 2018. The GDS was a significant event where world leaders convened to make pledges for disability inclusion. The UK Government co-hosted the event with the Government of Kenya, and our AT2030 program had been co-designed over 4 months leading up to the Summit. The program is global—it operates in 35 countries and contains over 50 partnerships, with a focus on East Africa and Kenya in particular (see Figure 3.11). The number and type of partners changes as the program evolves. As part of the AT2030 program GDI Hub has, in Kenya, partnered with the GSMA, CHAI, the Government of Kenya, and local Kenyan-based charities including Kilimanjaro blind Trust and Motivation Wheelchairs. For example, the Clinton Health Access Initiative supports the Government of Kenya in developing policy, while GDI Hub helps scope the innovation landscape. Other partners such as AMREF Enterprises deliver the GDI Hub-powered Innovate Now accelerator, which works with local partner Kilimanjaro Blind Trust Association to deliver the Live Labs network. The growth of AT2030 happened from additional funding from FCDO as well as nearly £10m in matched funding from partners big and small linking into and amplifying the reach and impact of the program. Cross-sectorial partnerships have been key to this approach.

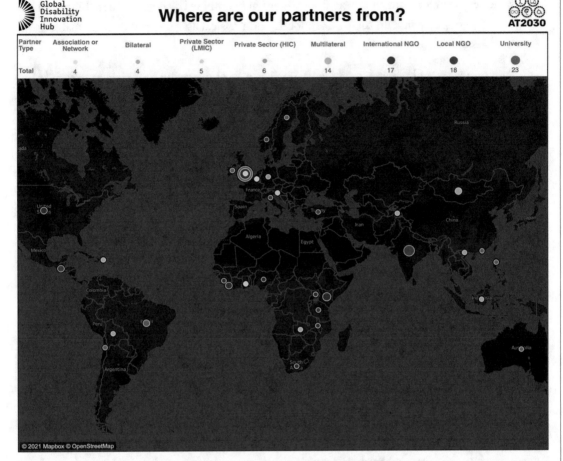

Partner Type	Association or Network	Bilateral	Private Sector (LMIC)	Private Sector (HIC)	Multilateral	International NGO	Local NGO	University
Total	4	4	5	6	14	17	18	23

Figure 3.11: Map showing the location of all the partners of the AT2030 program.

A number of projects which form the large portfolio of the AT2030 program have been conducted in Kenya, some of these are fully contained within the country, whereas some others are part of a wider multi-country or global study. These projects include:

1. landscaping studies for mobile phone access and access to digital and physical assistive products;

2. working with the Government of Kenya to develop a wheelchair provision plan, a mapping of AT provision and innovation spaces across Kenya and a country capacity assessment to understand where systems need strengthening;

3. local research within an informal settlement in Nairobi with people with mobility and vision impairments on the role of mobile and physical assistive products in enabling access;

4. a campaign and research study with *Shujazz*, a local magazine that reaches over 50% of Kenyan youth to understand attitudes toward people with disabilities and look to use behavior change methods to help shift attitudes toward greater inclusion and positivity;

5. an innovation accelerator for start-ups that has seen 16 ventures supported through a bespoke designed inclusive entrepreneur toolkit; and

6. three pre-clinical trials of technology (a hearing screening tool and aid, an in-part 3D printed wheelchair and a new prosthetic service that leverages thermoplastic materials. In the case of the hearing aid, the mobile-based screening tool, and hearing aid the innovation being trialed are not just at technological level, but they include a new financing model to test affordability of solution at a local level.

A mapping of these projects of the AT2030 program against the dimensions and principles of DIX is given in Table 3.2. All projects encompass each of the DIX principles, however, some are more strongly associated with some principles than others, and within the table this is demonstrated.

The wicked nature of disability inclusion is acknowledged within the country capacity assessment work and the product narratives which act as sort of landscaping studies for why markets are broken globally and what actions can be taken to help shaping them into more functioning markets. An opportunity for better wheelchair provision services came out of this work which has been developed with local stakeholders including Motivation Wheelchairs. This raised awareness within governments and with the work completed to understand the role of new technological approaches to product design and service delivery as well as the innovation accelerator helped to develop the AT innovation map of Nairobi which is housed on the www.innovationAction.org site.

This mapping was completed alongside work to understand the markets for assistive products and also the disability mobile gap [151]. The former completed in partnership with the Clinton Health Access Initiative (CHAI) (see wheelchair [20], prostheses [21], eyeglasses [22], digital [19], and hearing aids [23], the latter with GSMA). The research which informed the reports has also been analyzed more deeply and detailed individual studies have been published in a wide range of venues [30]. These more detailed insights have led to new grant proposals for basic research.

We also conducted a number of user studies around the use of different types of ATs. Initially, these were in two main areas: Kibera, an informal settlement where we investigated the role of mobile in enabling opportunity and access for people with mobility and visual impairments; and the second in clinical settings where we tested and assessed new products and services for wheelchair users and prosthetic users.

Table 3.2: Example of AT2030 research across the DIX principles and across the DIX dimensions. All projects strive to encompass each of the DIX principles. However, some are more strongly associated with some principles than others, and within the table this is demonstrated

	ABC: Basic and Applied	Radically Different Interactions	Co-Created Solutions	Value and Usefulness	Open and Scalable
Complexity	AT2030 Program			Product narratives Mobile disability gap report	
Wellbeing	Motivation Wheelchair study				
	Amparo Prosthetic Study				
		HearX hearing aid trial			
			Wazi vision eyeglasses investment		
Participation		Kibera User Studies			
			Shujaaz attitude change		
		Kibera User Studies			AT and Innovation Mapping
Innovation		Innovate Now technology accelerator			
				AT Impact Fund	

The studies in Kibera are further unpacked in terms of their research findings in Chapter 4. Here, we briefly touch on two things, the capacity building work, and the links between basic and applied research. As mentioned above, in capacity building we adopted a handover approach to research with the local community, hiring and training local Kiberan residents to be part of the research teams, including authoring teams. This partnership, facilitated through the Kilimanjaro Blind Trust (KBT), has continued and led to further collaboration on different projects. For example, KBT has developed a pipeline of research testing for innovators within the innovate now (www. innovatenow.org) technology accelerator.

This close partnership on applied research—testing new products and understanding user needs in the wild—alongside another partnership in India with IIT Delhi, has exposed the chronic need for children with disabilities in low-and middle-income countries (LMICs) to have better access to tools which enable STEM education. This has led to new basic research into shape memory alloys for a new tactile array which allows children who are visually impaired to draw, and to explore graphs and charts as well as shapes and geometries [45].

Finally, we reach the work to change attitudes toward people with disabilities and assistive technology users more broadly. Through the partnership with Shujaaz we co-designed story lines for a local magazine using focus groups of local youth across Kenya. Thanks to multimodal engagement with young people with and without disabilities, we gathered baseline evidence and then ran a campaign showing people with disabilities simply integrated into story lines, without a focus on their impairment or AT. Al the reports for the multidisciplinary work carried out by different institutions can be found on the AT2030 website (www.at2030.org).

3.4   CONCLUSION

In this chapter we have unpacked the six principles of DIX, developed the framework for DIX along a number of dimensions and used the AT2030 program to demonstrate how these can be used within HCI research. We now explore the different domains where DIX can be applied, starting with the Global South.

CHAPTER 4

Exploring Geographies: DIX in the Global South

4.1 GEOGRAPHICAL IMBALANCES OF DISABILITY AND AT RESEARCH

If you are a graduate student living largely on instant noodles and joining pretty much any society event on campus on condition of free food provision (especially pizza!), you might at first disagree with us, but research, or more precisely what is counted or legitimized as academic research in technology and many other scientific fields, is shaped by a system of hegemony of power which is largely built on a dynamic of colonial power and privilege [165]. Academic research often requires large investments from public or private bodies which are more likely to be available in richer countries of the Global North. The 2021 UNESCO Science Report highlights how, despite a 19.2% global growth index in research spending between 2014 and 2018, there are significant differences between the Global North and Global South on how much of the annual GDP is invested in scientific research [397]. For example, the EU and the Unnited States, respectively, spend approximately 2.02% and 2.84% of their total GDP on research. On the other hand, Latin America, Sub-Saharan Africa, and South Asia only allocate, respectively, 0.66%, 0.51%, and 0.60% of GDP on research every year [ibid.].

Higher amounts of investments often mean greater number of researchers and higher volumes of publications and patents. As shown in Figure 4.1, the data from the UNESCO 2021 Science Report show that G20 countries employ 88.8% of researchers worldwide, produce 90.6% of the global share of publications, and own 96.4% of the global share of IP5 patents[2] [397]. Similarly, in 2018 BioMed Central carried out an internal survey across four journals published by the group (*BMC International Health and Human Rights*, *BMC Medical Education*, *BMC Medical Ethics*, and *BMC Public Health*) and found out that 71% of authors listed across all the papers in the various journals were from high-income countries [57]. Furthermore, a recent study by Dimitris, Gittings, and King [111] looking at the geographical distributions of authors publishing research in Global Health reported that, although 86% of published papers had at least one author from a Low-and-

---

[2] IP5 is a consortium made of the five largest intellectual property offices in the world, namely the U.S. Patent and Trademark Office, the European Patent Office, the Japan Patent Office, the Korean Intellectual Property Office, and the National Intellectual Property Administration in China.

Middle-Income Country (LMIC), among the studies actually carried out in low-income countries the percentage of publications with a LMIC affiliated author was only 58.7%.

The reasons for this disparity of published research are both complex and numerous including lack of funding, inadequate human resources, language barriers, procedural difficulties and unbalanced power dynamics in the academic research and publishing world that contribute to perpetuate inequalities [457]. Although the aim of this book is not to identify or discuss the mechanisms that reinforce the colonialist approach that promote research inequalities (nor the most qualified or appropriate researchers to do so given we are white researchers living in high income countries), it is important for the reader to acknowledge this and become aware of the significant implications that it has in relation to disability and AT research.

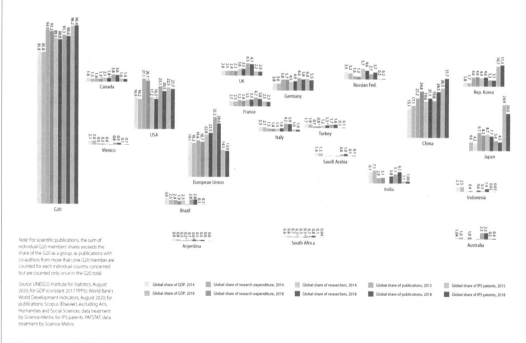

Figure 4.1: Global publications taken from the UNESCO 2021 science report.

Of the 1 billion people with disability in the world, it is estimated that approximately 80% live in the Global South often in conditions of poverty and with very limited access to essential services [179]. Yet, when Morgado-Ramirez et al. [265] searched the ACM library using a series of relevant keywords (including low-resource setting, Global South, low-income country, Emergent country, rural, and HCI4D), only 46 relevant references were identified. Of these 27 were discarded from further analysis as they did not report primary research or failed to actively include people with disabilities in the research. Furthermore, Ghai et al. [137] found that none of the over 2000 papers on disability and AT research published in the proceedings of the CHI conferences in the three years between 2016 and 2019 makes any mention of the emerging field of Disability Studies in the Global South. This means that our interpretation of the disability experience very largely disregards the reality of the majority of people with disability in the world.

Moreover, much of the international development agenda on which both the fields of Information and Communication Technology for Development (commonly referred using the acronyms ICT4D or ICTD) and HCI for Development (HCI4D), have come under significant criticism from postcolonial scholars [130, 241, 434]. Madianou [241] highlights how many of the practices associated with the use of digital technology and the management of data in many humanitarian settings reiterate the unbalanced power dynamics that reinforce colonial relationships. These practices, labeled as technocolonialism, are defined as extractive in their nature and formed around models in which vulnerable individuals produce value through their participation in humanitarian research which is leveraged for the benefit of funding stakeholders which include private companies [241]. Furthermore, both Erevelles [125] and Puar [309] warn us of how many exploitative and oppressive practices associated to technoscience research in the Global South can become even more prominent when it comes to research involving, or more often targeting, people with disabilities dure to intersectionality issues combined with limited perceived agency.

Finally, as noted by Getch [145], colonialism and decolonization are not fashionable metaphors, but historical and material processes that need to be analyzed in their violent narrative to understand their effect on shaping reality. Gretch [145] argues that colonialism and imperialism are one of the few shared experiences among the heterogenous and diverse regions which are clustered under the term "Global South." First of all, state violence, resource exploitation by colonial powers, and cultural eradication practiced with the purpose of exercising control lead to massive increase in the number of people with disabilities in much of the colonized territories as a result of imported disease, famine, and brutality [145]. Second, colonialist powers significantly contributed to the reframing of disabled bodies as something to be feared, repelled, or, at best, pitied laying down the structure of disempowering charity models of white saviorness that remain prominent to this day [145]. These historical aspects have significantly contributed to the materiality and the conceptualization of disability in the Global South and the International Development agenda within and beyond HCI, and it is important to remain critically aware of their potential influence not only on the reality of the context of our research, but also on our positionality as scholars and researchers.

Throughout the rest of this chapter, we will examine some of the relevant work on disability and AT in the Global South by researchers both within and outside HCI to highlight where different disciplines can better support each other to capture the complexity of DIX in the Global South. Through this we strive to identify ways in which we can maximize the impact of the excellent work of AT and accessibility researchers in a way that is appropriate to the needs and values of individuals with disabilities living in the Global South.

4.2   UNPACKING CONTEXT IN THE GLOBAL SOUTH THROUGH HCI RESEARCH ON MOBILE TECHNOLOGY

HCI researchers and practitioners have acknowledged for years that the context in which a person lives has an extremely important effect on the technology that they have access to, how they use it and what they use it for [312]. Räsänen and Nyce [312] reminds us that, when we think about context in HCI, we often focus on the immediate context of an action that involves the use of a technological artefact. This is undoubtedly important. For example, a visually impaired person using a GPS navigation app on a mobile phone in Bangalore is likely to have a different experience compared to another visually impaired individual using the exact same application in Seoul. In the study by Pal, Viswanathan, and Song [293], the authors showed how the different characteristics of the two cities, including the availability of services and the transport and road infrastructures, significantly affected the challenges encountered by users during independent navigation [293]. Participants from Seoul struggled with orientating themselves in the indoor environments of public transport stations, where wayfinding could be extremely problematic due to poor reception underground, leading them to rely on the assistance of station staff [293]. On the other hand, in Bangalore challenges were more likely to emerge during outdoor navigation where the application could provide incorrect or incomplete instructions due to map inaccuracy (missing street names, failed detection of non-permanent structures, etc.) [ibid.]. The physical and technical infrastructural context in which technology operates are of course extremely important. However, by adopting a broader interpretation of context which encompasses the cultural and historical factors that shape individual and societal beliefs and behaviors, leveraging theory and methods from anthropology and other social sciences, we can better capture some of the fundamental differences that affect the way people with disabilities in the Global South relate to not just technology, but to disability itself [312].

Most of the HCI work involving people with disability in the Global South has been largely focused on mobile phones. This is primarily linked to the high penetration rate of mobile devices compared to other, more costly and infrastructurally heavy technologies such as personal computers and laptops, the latter devices are generally more expensive, requiring more significant access to electricity due to larger batteries and higher computational power and consuming much greater amount of data [194]. Thanks to their versatility mobile phones can effectively pack multiple AT in a single device, leading to a huge empowerment potential for people with disabilities [59]. However, to ensure that mobile-based innovations are able to reach and positively impact the lives of people with disabilities in the Global South, it's essential to understand the infrastructural challenges that affect if and how people with disabilities are able to access and use mobile technology [30].

An example of this is the Enable Vaani voice-based social platform designed by authors in Dubey et al. [113] that has been used by over 25,000 people in India and has recorded over 300,000 messages since its launch in 2016. The Enable Vaani platform can be used to access and share stories, information, and opportunities that are relevant to people with disabilities living in India [113]. Traditional social media platforms such as Facebook, Twitter, or Instagram require the use of internet-connected devices such as smartphones, tablets, or computers. Moreover, to access these social networks, the person must be in an area where the Internet signal is sufficiently strong and be able to cover the cost of data for navigation. As mentioned before, most people with disabilities who live in the Global South are poor and have very limited access to services, including technological devices and internet connection [149]. To enable people with disabilities to access the platform using more widely available basic phones and to avoid the significant costs associated with internet data, Enable Vaani users can make a free "missed" phone call to a dedicated number. The user then receives a call back by the system, and they can navigate through the platform thanks to an Interactive Voice Response system and choose if they want to listen to existing content or create new content [113]. A similar voice-based social forum with the name of Sangeet Swara was created by Vashistha et al. [405], who also leveraged community moderators to categorize and evaluate posts made by users in order to bypass the need for dedicated moderators which often limits the scalability of voice forums. Both of these examples show a deep understanding of the social infrastructure and therefore complexity of the problem space. This was achieved through a co-design approach with users leading to technological outcomes that were socially acceptable (even desirable) to use.

Although we were unable to find out if Sangeet Swara was still operational, we were happy to find out that, thanks to the work of the NGO Enable India, the Enable Vaani is still active and can count on over 38,000 users across 20 Indian states (you can check out the appropriate page on the Enable India's website if you would like to read more about it). The success of Enable Vaani is a testament not only to the great work of Enable India, which ensured the sustainability of the project, but also of how mobile technology is able to boost users' ability to connect with each other, share opportunities, and access valuable support. In previous chapters we discussed how the social context can have a huge effect on the decisions that people with disabilities take around the use of AT. However, this relationship is not unidirectional. The cases of Enable Vaani and Sangeet Swara show how mobile phones and mobile-based technologies can represent a key gateway to increased social opportunities for people with disabilities, and through this better disability interactions through access to healthcare, education, and employment opportunities [192].

Together with colleagues in the UK and Kenya, in 2019 we conducted two studies to better understand the dual relationship between mobile technology and the social context of people with disabilities in the Global South [35]. For both studies we chose the informal settlement of Kibera, on the outskirts of Nairobi as a setting for our research. Kibera is famous for being the largest slum in Africa, and one of the largest in the world, covering an area of approximately 2.5 km² and with an estimated population ranging between 200,000 and 1,000,000 (the variation in numbers gives you an idea of how hard it is to collect reliable population data in areas where there is no government infrastructure) [275]. The reasons for our choice of context were multiple. Some of these were based on the uniqueness of informal settlements as communities that combine the scarcity of services, overpopulation, and low standards of living common to many deprived areas with social dynamics that are less constrained by the rigid canons of traditional rural communities [395]. However, the main reason for our choice of setting was of a more practical nature. As part of our work on the large UK FCDO-funded project called AT2030 (https://at2030.org/), we had been able to create strong collaborations with the University of Nairobi and a number of DPOs and NGOs working in Kenya, especially the Kilimanjaro Blind Trust Africa and Motivation Africa, all these institutions had amazing community staff working in Kibera that were willing to actively engage with us and become key members of the research team. These partnerships and strong collaborations are essential for conducting ethical and good quality research in any area or setting, and especially when working with people with disabilities living in the Global South. Local organizations and researchers don't simply facilitate access to participants or provide translations from local languages into English, but they have essential practical knowledge which is needed to select and adapt research methods that are appropriate to the context and ensure that the interpretation of data is not re-framed to suit western narratives [190, 374]. Even more importantly, these organizations have gained the respect of the community you want to engage with, and are essential to generate the kind of buy-in from participants which is necessary for sustainable and impactful research [265].

The aim of these two studies, looking at how Kibera residents who had visual or mobility impairments accessed and used mobile phones in their daily lives, was to understand not only how the social settings impact mobile use, but also the effect of mobile use on participants' social interactions [31,35]. What we found was that participants leveraged their social networks to break the mobile phone access barrier. For example, a person with visual impairment might ask a sighted friend to read a text message on a phone without a screen reader, or a wheelchair user who did not own a mobile phone would borrow the handset from their husband to make a call [31, 35]. Depending on the degree of agency that participants felt they had in these interactions with mobile phones we classified them as *direct*, *supported*, *dependent*, or *restricted*, expanding on the framework of human infrastructure of ICTD previously defined by Sambasivan and Smyth [333] (see Figure 4.2). When engaging in *direct* interactions participants were fully in control and able to complete a particular task independently. Supported interactions were characterized by the assistance of friends and family, whereas dependent interactions required the direct action of someone outside the individual's social circle to complete the operation on behalf of the person The Social Network [35]. Finally, restricted interactions remained inaccessible to participants, regardless of their ability to draw on their own social capital due to limitation of the mobile phone, lack of accessibility feature, low digital skills, or individual beliefs about technology such as the fact that address books on mobile handsets were simply "it is not for persons living with visual impairment" [35].

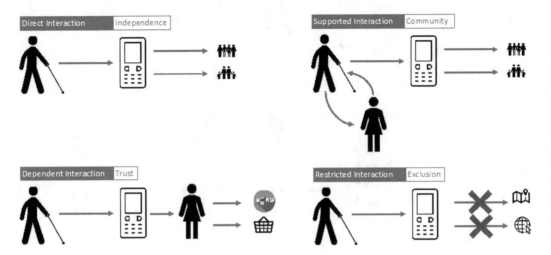

Figure 4.2: Mobile phone interaction types when used by visually impaired people living in an informal settlement.

At the same time, participants reported that being able to access and use mobile phones enable them to connect with their communities and bridge the gap that was often created by the inaccessibility of the environment (Figure 4.3) [31]. Participants who used wheelchairs for mobility were often unable to navigate the harsh physical environment of Kibera on their own as narrow roads, rough terrain, and the presence of mud following torrential rain made it impossible to use manual wheelchairs in many areas. Thanks to their mobile phone they were able to connect with friends and family, ask for assistance when required, but also manage their own work or find out about employment opportunities [31]. In a way, as much as the social network could help to navigate the accessibility challenges of the mobile phone, the phone allowed people to further unlock their social support system [31].

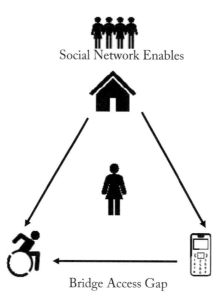

Social Network Enables

Bridge Access Gap

Figure 4.3: Ecosystem of accessibility enabled through social networks for wheelchair users living in an informal settlement. The person with disabilities is represented by the human icon in the middle of a triangle featuring at the top corner a house, which represents the environment. At the bottom of the triangle two icons representing, respectively, the wheelchair and the mobile phone connect with each other as they together help to bridge the access gap. The triangle is surrounded by a circle indicating the social network of the person which support access to both assistive technologies and to the environment.

Finally, the mixed methods research carried out by Pal et al. [289] across six cities—including Blantyre, Freetown, Kigali, Mumbai, San Jose, and Seoul—represents a poignant example of the need to look at concepts such as infrastructure and context much more broadly in relation to AT and accessibility research in the Global South. Through a combination of surveys and interviews with relevant stakeholders the authors look at the gap between the promise of accessibility, enshrined in the United Nations Convention for the Rights of Persons with Disabilities (UNCRPD), and the reality of how many people with disabilities are able to access and use AT and other relevant technologies [289]. Results showed that stigma and ableism still play a major role in determining their level of access to mobile technology and the impact that it had on their lives [289]. Many people with disabilities were economically dependent on family members, hence they lacked the power to make the financial decision to invest in mobile technologies and other ATs, having to rely on others to make these decisions for them. Marketing materials for mobile phones are generally only targeted at individuals without disabilities, and this has the effect of failing to highlight the positive impact that mobile technology can have not only on the person with disabilities, but also on their social sphere [289]. For example, a person with disability might struggle to physically reach the workplace because of environmental barriers that increase the chances of delays, sick days, and reduced productivity once in work. However, access to a mobile phone might enable the person to use ridesharing services that allow them to get to work on-time and without wasting unnecessary energies [200]. As shown during the pandemic, ICT can also enable people with disabilities to carry out their work from home where possible, which provides benefits not only for the worker with disability, but for the employer as well [290]. Finally, Pal et al. [289] also found that people with disabilities who were able to access smartphones managed to expand their accessibility human infrastructure by tapping into existing online communities and creating new ones to share information, ask for help, and support each other.

4.3 UNDERSTANDING THE NOTION OF CONTEXT IN DISABILITY AND AT ACCESS RESEARCH IN THE GLOBAL SOUTH

4.3.1 INTERPRETATIONS AND EXPERIENCES OF DISABILITY IN THE GLOBAL SOUTH

Researchers working on disability and AT in the Global South beyond the boundaries of HCI have also invested great effort in highlighting the importance of understanding contextual differences between much of the Global North vs. the Global South [296]. One of the strongest arguments made by scholars in Disability Studies in the Global South is that, although at a granular level, some of the interactions between persons with disabilities and technologies might appear the same, the experience of disability is completely different in most Global South countries compared to the Global North. Over two decades ago one of the Zimbabwean participants from Stone 1999 argued "While people in the rich world are talking about Independent Living and improved services, we are talking about survival" [371]. Since 1999, particularly thanks to a growing global movement of disability justice and the formulation of the UNCRPD in 2006 (which in 2021 has been ratified by 184 parties), the situation of many people with disabilities around the world has dramatically improved. However, the gap between the Global North and the Global South has arguably remained as wide as ever [253].

When considering how context shapes the experience of disability in the Global South, one of the most prominent factors that have been studied by researchers is stigma [65]. Disability stigma is by no means a phenomenon that is exclusively present in the Global South. Nonetheless, stigma is deeply rooted in the cultural interpretation of disability which is highly contextual. Furthermore, disability stigma is both more widespread and has more severe consequences in the Global South due to the lack of institutional protection and empowerment opportunities for people with disabilities [65]. In many regions of the Global South the beliefs that disability might occur as a result of a curse or as a form of moral retribution for wrongdoing of the individual or their family is still highly prevalent [249, 338]. The prevalence of these "moral" disability models often lead to high levels of stigma, discrimination and abuse toward people with disabilities [281]. Once again, it is important to remember that these moral models of disabilities are generally more present in the Global South, but can also be found in the Global North, particularly in connections to fundamental religious communities or nationalist state-driven narratives [211, 227, 229].

The protection of the rights of people with disabilities, including their rights to access AT is, in most countries in the Global North, largely the responsibility of the state. Most countries have implemented specific laws and protocols detailing frameworks and procedures stating not only what are the rights of people with disabilities, but also what parties are responsible to ensure access to these rights [146]. In fact, much of the discourse surrounding disability rights and access to AT at a global level have been shaped by the broader concept of human rights. However, several scholars and activists have argued that this human rights lens runs the risk to further exacerbate inequality [91, 203, 256]. Meekosha and Soldatic [256] argue that the rise of human rights has formalized and institutionalized what were previously grassroot practices of community building, social inclusion, and empowerment; moving power to promote inclusion away from communities and toward the state, which can be extremely problematic if the state is a complicit actor of oppression toward people with disabilities. Furthermore, even when governments have the goodwill to advance the disability rights agenda, they often struggle to translate global treaties such as the UNCRPD into national laws and actionable policies [256].

The human rights lenses also shape the conceptualization of disability as a form of social oppression which has several potentially problematic implications. First, as highlighted in Section 4.1, colonialism and imperialistic practices carried out by many countries in the Global North have huge historical responsibility for both the higher incidence of disability in the Global South and its negative conceptualization [256]. For many people with disabilities in the Global South impairment itself occurs as a result of wars, violence, and abuse which are linked to practices of imperialism and colonization rather than through natural processes [256]. Moreover, in a colonial society where mutilation was often inflicted as a punishment for resistance, the moral model of disability became automatically incentivized and leveraged to promote oppression by the dominating power [145]. The risk of reframing disability purely as a contemporary social construct risks shifting the responsibility of disability oppression solely toward national governments and local communities instead of acknowledging the responsibility of colonialism and international oppression [345]. In turn, this can hinder the formation of alliances focused on redistributive justice [345].

Second, Human rights and other models of disability that depict disability solely as a social phenomena can deny some of the key individual aspects of disability that shape personal experiences [340]. Critics of these models of disabilities highlight how while the shift from a purely individual to a purely social model of disabilities can, on the one hand be empowering, it can also lead to overlook key personal aspects of disability, such as impairment, which is described as "natural and unavoidable" [202, 256]. Shakespeare [340] points out how separating impairment from disability in everyday life is both impossible and counterproductive. Furthermore, he highlights how narrative of disability as social oppressions can contribute to disempowering visions of people with disabilities who are consistently portrayed as victims [ibid.]. Finally, the reframing of disability away from the concept of impairment, might lead to a perceived "Westernization" of the interpretation of disability and promote mechanisms for inclusion that fit well within neo-liberal societies in the Global North but disregards the strong grassroot community tradition of much of the Global South [256].

4.4   GLOBAL SOUTH AND AT ACCESS

When it comes to AT in the Global South, researchers working outside of HCI have mainly focused on unpacking the systemic issues which prevent people with disabilities form being able to access ATs that matches their needs, rather than focusing on developing new technologies or tackling specific mismatches between individuals with disabilities and particular types of AT [115]. However, we believe that there are strong overlaps between the interests of HCI researchers and other disciplines focusing on issues of AT access in the Global South.

As mentioned in Chapters 2 and 3, AT is part of a complex system of actors from people with disabilities, to service providers and officials working in nationals and international organizations, all of which operate at different levels to create the chain of policies, devices and practices that enable AT access and provision. As a way to untangle this complex web of relationships, MacLachlan et al. [239] developed a Systems-Market for Assistive and Related Technologies (SMART) Thinking Matrix, shown in Figure 4.4, which shows the relationship between the levels of the systems of AT provision and the level of efficiency of a "market" which encompasses everything from product to provision and service delivery systems.

The three system levels (Micro, Meso, and Macro) which appear on the vertical dimension of the matrix help to understand where the different challenges that affect access to AT might be located, and who are the actors that would most likely benefit from interventions to tackle specific barriers [239]. For example, in the previous section we highlighted how, beyond lacking the historical perspective to fully understand the experience of disability in the Global South and running the risk of overlooking important personal aspect of disability which are linked to impairment, most of the national policies and international treaties that outline the rights of people with disabilities, including the rights to access ATs such as for example the UNCRPD, are aspirational more than practical. These can lead them to ail to couple broad and significant aspirations with detailed implementation plans that include appropriate allocation of budgets and resources to ensure that rights

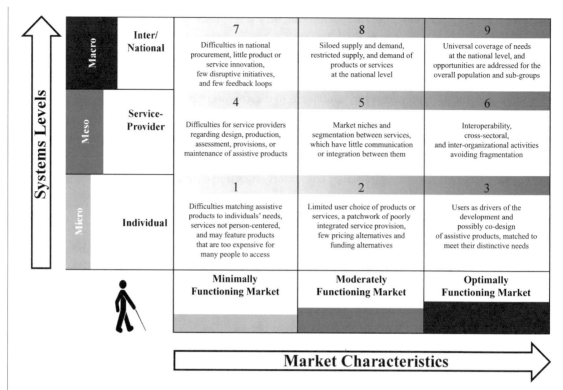

Figure 4.4: SMART thinking matrix for assistive technology. Source: [239].

are turned into reality [238]. This is quite clearly a macro-level issue that should be addressed by providing support to government departments in charge of writing these policies, ensuring that governments prioritize AT provision and allocate appropriate resources to it, and develop mechanisms for evaluations so that countries can show their progress toward the goal of AT access (and be held accountable by their citizen when there is a lack progress). One way which HCI researchers can help here is in data representation—and enabling better data sets. Moving down a level, if we identify, in a particular country or region, that one of the roadblocks to AT provision is linked to the fact that healthcare personnel (or other relevant professional figures) lack the competencies to adequately assess people with disabilities and provide support and recommendation for AT, this can be categorized as a meso-level system failure. Measures to address this gap should include the provision of training to local professionals, establishing pathways to referrals where necessary and the creation of better connections between users, providers, and developers of AT to ensure maximum communication [358]. Here HCI research, and technology research more, in general, can help develop new screening tools, or remote education platforms or help develop interventions for community health practitioners. Finally at the micro level we look at interactions at the level of the user, potentially including carers and social relations if appropriate. These aspects might include research focusing on developing training to use an assistive product or exploring how a particular assistive product might affect social relations in a way that makes it more, or less, acceptable and suited to one's needs. In reality, the division between different levels of the system is rarely as clear-cut as in the examples we provided above. However, the SMART matrix can help researchers and practitioners reflect on the complex nature of AT provision systems and identify what interventions might be needed at different levels [239].

The horizontal dimension of the matrix can be used to determine the current level of market functioning, from minimally functioning (where significant difficulties are shortcomings are present within a certain level of the system, effectively preventing the majority of people with disabilities from accessing necessary ATs) to optimally functioning (when all user in a country have universal access to user-centered services that ensure appropriate provision of AT that match their needs and priorities). For example, at the macro level, in the case of national policies we have outlined above how, a minimally functioning market could be represented by a country that, despite having potentially ratified the UNCRPD, has no established policy concerning AT. This probably means that the government has not established supply chains and procurement pathways for products ranging from wheelchairs to Alternative and Augmentative Communication devices (AACs). Some form of provision might exist, but it's largely dependent on charitable donations form NGOs or international actors that are unable to guarantee consistent supply of quality products appropriate to the setting. At the meso level this might translate in a company limited ability to develop AP that reach the market, or a hospital having low capacity to appropriately assess individuals AT needs and provide suitable products. Finally, this is likely to trickle down to a micro level where individuals with disabilities and their families have limited capabilities to access the AT that they need due to financial constraints, accessibility issues, lack of awareness, or other potential reasons. Alternatively, in moderately functioning market there might be established supply chains for certain types of devices rather than others or provision pathways of ATs that function well for persons who are in charge of the healthcare system, but not for children in need of AT for education or adults who require access to particular technologies in the context of employment [432].

It is important to remember that the SMART matrix aims to be globally applicable and does not aim to be used exclusively in the Global South [239]. However, its modular and multi-dimensional structure allows researchers to capture how context across different countries affects access and provision of AT. It has been used recently to map AT innovation activities [181] and in a recent study by Ebuenyi et al. [120] in Malawi the SMART matrix thinking helped highlight how, despite the presence of numerous national policies which are relevant to disability inclusions, none of them included clear guidelines about AT provision. Through a multistep and multi-stakeholder process and using a variety or relevant tools that range from the SMART matrix to the Country Capacity Assessment tool, designed by the WHO to evaluate the ability of a country to finance, regulate, procure, and provide AT, the authors have launched a project that aims to create a framework to support the development of effective national AT policies which will initially be implemented in Malawi [120]. Malawi, as several other countries in the Global South, didn't have a specific policy that focuses on AT, which can lead to poor coordination among national and international stakeholders working in the space, both within and outside government [120]. The project leverages a collaborative action research approach where relevant stakeholders from government, NGOs and DPOs in Malawi work together to establish priorities and assess availability of evidence and national resources to develop realistic and contextually appropriate policies to spearhead the AT agenda.

This type of work shows how the problem of AT access in the Global South is characterized by systemic barriers that require understanding of the broader provision system at both local and country level to ensure that existing, and newly developed, technologies can reach the hands of the millions of people with disabilities who need them.

4.5   THE ROLE OF DIX IN INCREASING ACCESS AND IMPACT OF AT IN THE GLOBAL SOUTH

Throughout this chapter we saw how researchers in different fields have recently started to turn their attention to understand how the way in which people with disabilities who live in the Global South are able, or more often unable, to access AT, and other types of technology, in their everyday lives. We believe that the five principles of DIX can really help to capture the importance of contextual factors from individual to system levels and push researchers to consider multidimensional factors when developing new technologies, or promoting the diffusion of existing ones, in a way that is mindful of the differences between Global North and Global South.

4.5.1   ACKNOWLEDGE THE WICKED PROBLEM

This is arguably the most important consideration that we should keep in mind when engaging in DIX research in the Global South, especially if you are a researcher from the Global North or if you are conducting research in a country in which you are not necessarily familiar with the context. Keep in mind that acknowledging the complexity of issues that affect AT access or disability inclusion in the Global South does not mean you need to tackle all the different levels of the problem at once. But, you need to be mindful of the existence of different barriers and strive to understand how contextual elements ranging from cultural beliefs, availability or technology, infrastructural requirements, and policy frameworks affect the experiences of people with disabilities and how they access AT. One example of how we tried to do this is through our work in stigma reduction in Kenya as part of the AT2030 program. Previous research had identified stigma as a significant barrier to AT access for people with disabilities in Kenya [179]. The aim of our project was to develop effective strategies to reduce negative beliefs surrounding disability that were held by young

Kenyans without disabilities, increasing awareness, and reducing stigmatizing stereotypes. In this project we partnered with a network of social ventures based in Nairobi, but operating across all East Africa, that focuses on engaging and empowering young people on meaningful topics ranging from sexual health, governance, and economic empowerment. As part of this project we conducted two studies that aimed to understand how Kenyan youth view people with disabilities in their communities and beyond, what interactions they routinely have with them and how AT relates to their own vision of disability [32].

These studies helped us to paint a picture that highlights how young people often have contrasting beliefs about disability and AT. While beliefs about disability occurring as a result of a curse or punishment were still present and people with disabilities were often seen as powerless and incapable, many young people felt strongly about the role of society in the construction of disability [32]. AT was seen as an indicator of disability, but also as a tool that could enhance function and show that the individual had access to personal resources that could help navigate the challenges linked to disability. Understanding the complexity of beliefs causing disability and AT stigma enables us to make some concrete suggestions for tackling disability stigma. The first one, which is relevant to both professionals designing inclusion campaigns and initiatives, and UX developers to increase the promotion of normalized interactions, both physically and digitally between young people with and without disabilities [32]. A second recommendation that is key to HCI designers and accessibility researchers, is linked to the importance of reimagine the design of AT in a way that is visible rather than unobtrusive, but that also helps to highlight the capabilities of individuals rather than their limitations What difference does tech make [37]. Finally, from our conversations with young people in Kenya it clearly emerged that many felt that some of the most persistent barriers faced by people with disabilities were a direct consequence of the misperceptions and incorrect beliefs held by non-disabled people. In this light, we invite HCI and accessibility researchers to reflect more broadly on how barriers to inclusion should be deconstructed and who holds the responsibility to do so. Ultimately, although AAT projects should always be shaped by people with disabilities, they do not necessarily target them [37].

4.5.2   TAKING AN ABC APPROACH

Working with governments or organizations to develop applied research agendas can help elucidate the opportunity for new basic research, while still developing approaches to tackle immediate problems. For example, in the many countries in the Global South it is often acknowledged that there is a severe shortage of sign language interpreters. From a basic technology research point of view, this highlights the opportunity for a challenge in this space where AI and computer vision can develop a technology-mediated experience which helps to fill the severe lack of interpreters [167, 310]. This might have additional benefits such as providing interpretation in different languages and dialects and offering translation between them. However, despite the excellent and extensive work of many researchers in the space, available solutions are still not available for deployment, largely due to some of the complexities of sign language such as the need to capture the interaction between hands movements and facial expressions. As basic research advances, applied researchers have developed solutions to tackle the problem of lack of interpreters by increasing the resources available. For example, we see the emergence of Bleetch (https://www.bleetech.in/) in India, which started as a community-driven, mobile application sign language a and now hosts a range of digital interventions for deaf people. They are incubated and accelerated by the AssisTech Foundation labs (https://atflabs.org/startups/).

4.5.3   EXPLORE RADICALLY DIFFERENT INTERACTIONS

Radically different interactions in accessibility research in the Global South can occur both due to the characteristics of the interaction in itself, or thanks to radical adaptation to local context. Ultimately, they could help increase the reach of AT and other accessible technologies, leapfrogging innovations while remaining aware of the characteristics of existing infrastructure. One example of this is the wealth of research on mobile phone-based technologies addressing the needs of people with disabilities living in the Global South. In most of the Global North, mobile innovations began to emerge that build on the significant developments of technology such as computers and laptops. These infrastructural links still remain strong and create the need for systems to work across different platforms and modalities. This is not necessarily the case in much of the Global South where penetration rates of laptops and computers have always been relatively low, and the technological infrastructure is almost exclusively built around mobile technologies. Projects such as Enable Vaani and Sangeet Swara, or the mobile banking revolution in Kenya spearheaded by the Safaricom M-PESA service, represent perfect examples of this [50]. To truly explore the potential of mobile-based technologies to make an impact on the lives of people with disabilities, the call for the second cohort of the Innovate Now Accelerator, Africa's first Accelerator focused specifically on AT, was dedicated exclusively to startups who were leveraging mobile phones as part of their innovations. The five ventures that were accelerated included a variety of services from Lugha Ishara', a company providing online lessons and animations to teach sign language to preschoolers and their parents helping them to learn together and find better ways to communicate with each other, to Mpost, a patented technology enabling people with disabilities to turn their mobile phones in a unique postal address allowing them to receive letters and deliveries in a way that is more easily accessible. You can check out the Innovate Now website (https://atinnovatenow.com/) to discover all the ventures that have been supported since its launch in 2019.

Radically different interactions can also occur as we subvert expectations around the goal of the AAT such as illustrated in the case study about Ludic Design.

Case Study: Computational Thinking for Children in Schools for the Blind

Manohar Swaminathan, Microsoft Research, Bangalore India, Supriya Dey, Vision Empower Trust, Bangalore, India

The use of a novel, tangible, programming environment, CodeJumper, in combination with the new methodology of Ludic Design for Accessibility to bring computational thinking curriculum within reach of children in schools for the blind in India. The work was done by a collaborative research effort between Microsoft Research India and Vision Empower Trust, a disabled persons organization in Bangalore India.

The problem: A vast majority of children who are blind in India go to schools for the blind, where a significant percentage of teachers are also blind. Due to a combination of many factors including low resources, reduced expectation placed on such children, along with channeling them to stereotyped career paths, the children are denied STEM opportunities and are given a very basic introduction to computing, but in later grades. Given the widespread acceptance of computational thinking as a basic knowledge component starting from grade 1 in mainstream schools, our ambitious goal is to introduce accessible computational thinking curriculum along with supporting resources in schools for the blind in India.

Radically Different Interactions: The basic tool we used is the tangible programming system, originally called Project Torino, now available as a commercial product, CodeJumper, which was developed by Microsoft Research Cambridge [270]. Codejumper has been successfully used to teach the CT curriculum to children with vision impairments in integrated schools in the UK. The major challenge is to see if CodeJumper could be introduced to children who are blind in India, given the vastly different environments in the schools here. We used a radically different approach, by following the methodology of Ludic Design for Accessibility [378]. Essentially, the Ludic Design approach keeps play and playfulness at the center while ensuring that the intended skills are picked up as a side effect by extended and joyful play. CodeJumper was introduced to the children as a toy for creating stories and music and they played with the Codejumper while the facilitator played the role of an experience player helping the children when asked for and giving hints to direct the play to fully explore the toy. With two children playing together as a team on an average of about 8 one-hour sessions all 12 children in the study demonstrated a grasp of the same basic concepts in computational thinking as was acquired by the study conducted in the UK, using traditional teaching methods [188]. Play, by its unstructured and participatory approach with agency firmly with the players (the children), appears to be a powerful tool to overcome many of the systemic limitations in schools for the blind, including the shortage of teachers with training in computational thinking.

Figure 4.5: Visually impaired children playing with the Codejumper kit as part of the study conducted in India.

4.5.4   CO-CREATE RESEARCH

When we think about co-creation of DIX in the Global South we are not simply talking about the co-creation of ATs or innovative mobile solutions with users, but of co-creation of research with local communities and local researchers and practitioners. At the beginning of the chapter, we discuss the huge disparity of research outputs between Global North and Global South, indicating that strong elements of colonialism still exist in all research fields, including accessibility research [145]. The scarce presence of accessibility research outputs from Global South scholars in major HCI venues is primarily attributable to the lack of opportunities available to researchers due to lack of appropriate funding, unavailability of training and mentoring programs for young researchers who might have limited experiences publishing their findings (a notable exception to this is the ASSETS Mentoring Program where more seasoned researchers advise students and younger scholars on how to best prepare their papers for the conference submission process), language barriers, and the general elitism which is common in much of the academic and publishing word.

To better support the engagement of scholars, practitioners, and community researchers working on accessibility and AT research in the Global South, we organized a workshop at the 2021 CHI conference with the title "Disability Design and Innovation in Low Resource Settings: Addressing Inequality Through HCI" [265]. The aim of the workshop was to kickstart a community of researchers and practitioners working or interested to work in the areas of technology, disability, and international development where members could learn and support each other, ultimately developing better collaborations between countries. The workshop was attended by over 30 participants from multiple countries from Latin America, the United States, Europe, Africa, and South Asia and contributions made by participants are freely available on the workshop website at https://www.disabilityinnovation.com/projects/chi2021. The community is still vibrant and active and if you are interested in joining you can contact us through the website. Thanks to the initial connections developed through the workshop, we continue to support each other by organizing informal workshops, collaborating on funding proposals and continuing to raise awareness within the community including a new panel discussion on Negotiating Challenges for Accessibility Research in the Global South at the 10th Latin American Conference on Human-Computer Interaction [472].

4.5.5   ENGAGE IN VALUABLE AND USEFUL RESEARCH

In Chapter 3, we highlight how as HCI, accessibility, and AT researchers it is important that we focus on developing technologies that are not only useful to the individual, but also valuable to society and the whole system, be it healthcare, education, or others, in which these technologies are going to be embedded. We believe that the concept of value is particularly relevant when it comes to research being carried out in the Global South. Hence, this dimension of DIX becomes extremely important, especially as material resources can be scarce in many of these contexts [223]. However, a key point of this dimension is to ensure that the values we deliver on match the priorities of the communities we worked with, rather than our own [223]. As we mentioned before, at the time of writing this book, both authors are white women working for a UK-based university. As such, we are well aware that one of the ways in which research impact is measured at Western institutions is through publications, grants awarded, public engagement events, and similar. But what counts as impact for the people we work with on the ground? Engaging in open and honest conversations about this with local researchers and participants is essential to conduct research that adds value to communities rather than simply collecting the data we need to produce more publications. In our work in Kibera we focused on capacity building of local community researchers, adopting a handover approach that allows for increased agency and empowerment [35], whereas on our project on digital manufacturing of wheelchairs in rural Kenya we promoted the development of service delivery systems that put wheelchair users at the center of the provision process [34]. Ultimately, there is no silver bullet for how we can ensure that our research around AT and accessibility is valuable to communities in the Global South. What is required to achieve this are equal measures of collaboration, dialogue, and commitment from all parties involved.

4.5.6   FOCUS ON OPEN AND SCALABLE INNOVATIONS

When it comes to ensuring maximum access to technology, healthcare products, and most other forms of innovation in the Global South, openness and scalability go hand in hand. But, as we mentioned in Chapter 2, scalability is not just about size and numbers. In 2020 and 2021, we witnessed huge debates about the unfairness of "globalized capitalist systems" that further the inequality between Global North and Global South from patented vaccines for COVID-19 [143] to disruptions of supply chains that cause huge shortage of goods and services in more vulnerable economies [243]. Applying DIX to accessibility and AT research and innovation in the Global South means remaining mindful of what are the resources, both tangible and intangible, available to different communities. One way in which we have tried to put this in practice is through the creation of the InnovationAction network, an initiative from a consortium of global partners dedicated to tackling some of the most pressing social challenges through collaborative efforts. A significant part of the work delivered by the InnovationAction initiative focuses on mapping existing resources, manufacturing centers, service providers, and innovators in different parts of the world, promoting the creation of linkages between different organizations that can work together to address local and global challenges. Thanks to the flexibility of the approach, we have been able to work on different challenges from strengthening networks for AT provision in Kenya, to mapping oxygen supplies for ventilators in Africa and supporting distributed manufacturing networks for local production of goods in Nepal. For example, to map the availability of oxygen supply in Africa we combined both existing datasets with primary data collected directly from providers to show where oxygen manufacturers and distributors are located across the continent, and what type of oxygen they supply (gaseous or liquid). To strengthen existing networks of AT systems in Kenya we are working directly with stakeholders from government organization, private businesses, NGOs, DPOs, and healthcare institutions to collect data about where they work, the services they provide and who they collaborate with. This helps us understand both strengths and weaknesses of the current systems, suggesting strategies for improvement, but also create visual representation that can help people who are trying to access the AT system to figure out who they can approach depending on their location and needs. You can find more information about the various projects undertaken at https://innovationaction.org/, or by listening to the dedicated podcast Innovation Action Insights where you can listen to some of the stories directly from the innovators and researchers themselves https://innovationaction.org/podcasts/.

4.6   CONCLUSION

In this chapter we looked at the research, both within and beyond HCI, around disability, ATs, and accessibility in the Global South and shared our experiences to show how the application of the five DIX principles can help to maximize the impact of our work. In the next chapter, we'll take a similar journey focused on two of the most prominent domains of research for AT and accessibility: Education and Employment.

CHAPTER 5

Exploring Different Settings: DIX in Education and Employment

When we were examining existing literature to identify main topics of interest at the intersection of disability, AT and accessibility research, work and education emerged as the two areas that gathered significantly more attention from researchers and designers compared to others. A series of quick searches of the ACM digital library revealed that the combination of keywords "disability AND employment" produced 13,927 results and "disability AND education" generated 9,021 articles, whereas "disability AND health" resulted in 6,867 publications and "disability AND transport" found only 4,171 potentially relevant articles.

This focus on education and employment should not be surprising. Maximizing the impact that AAT research has on ensuring equitable access to education and work for people with disabilities is absolutely essential to achieve disability inclusion, breaking many of the fundamental links between disability, poverty, and inequality that prevent us from reaching ambitious global targets such as the SDGs [387]. Additionally, they represent pathways to achieve one's aspirations, improving socio-economic conditions and reducing inequalities [248, 337]. Furthermore, people with disabilities are much more likely to interact with technology directly in the context of work or educational settings in comparison to healthcare or transport, where the use of technology might be mediated or used by healthcare professionals or transport policy makers [264, 313]. Finally, as we saw in Chapter 1, early research in AAT was focused on the workplace in keeping with the trends of ergonomics at the time. The range of research in the area of employment and education, taken together, demonstrates a persistent effort by researchers and designers toward the improvement of opportunities for people with disabilities. However, despite these efforts and with the increased availability of AT and accessible technologies, access to education and work are still extremely problematic for many people with disabilities [172, 399].

In 2018, an analysis of data from 49 countries from 6 different world regions (Sub-Saharan Africa, Europe and the United States, Northern and Central Asia, South-East Asia and Latin America) showed youth with disabilities between the ages of 15 and 29 were consistently less likely to have ever attended school [398]. As expected, in most countries of the Global South the educational gap is larger when compared to the gap in the Global North. In Cambodia, for example, half of children with disabilities are not in school, whereas only 1 in 14 children without disabilities have never enrolled in primary schools [398]. Similar gaps persist into adulthood with literacy rates being significantly lower for most people with disabilities compared to their peers without disabilities. In Indonesia, only 7% of adults without disabilities lack basic literacy skills, whereas the rate increases to 52% for adults with disabilities [398]. In the UK, the disability employment gap continues to be approximately a third despite multiple governments attempting to close this [284], which has been one of the driving forces behind the recently launched Disability Strategy [396]. Globally, the picture is bleak for employment opportunities for people with disabilities. A global analysis on disability and employment published by the International Labor Organization (ILO) on December 3, 2020 for the International Day of Persons with Disabilities showed the employment to population ratio for people with disabilities is significantly worse than for their non-disabled counterparts with gaps ranging from 1–55% across different countries [448].

Access to appropriate ATs and accessible Educational Technologies is believed to be essential to ensure better access to education for many learners with disabilities worldwide. For example, a recent study by McNicholl et al. [255] showed how, among 111 college students with disabilities, individuals who felt that their AT needs had been fully met by the institutions where they studied were more likely to report: increased educational engagement, wellbeing, and academic self-efficacy. The first overarching aim of accessible education technologies is to enable learning, which can then be translated into greater learning outcomes and other indirect benefits such as social capital, learning outcomes, and second is how they can help translate that learning into benefits such as social capital [9, 139]. However, several authors have found that the inequalities in access to technology, also known as the digital divide, reduce the positive impact that AT and EdTech have on life outcomes for persons with disabilities [9].

Similar issues exist in relation to the role of technology in facilitating access to work for people with disabilities. This has become an important issue in the rise of 21st century gig-economy jobs. Zyskowski et al. and Vashistha, Sethi, and Anderson show how both mainstream and specifically designed digital platforms enabling crowdwork can enable people with disabilities to engage in work activities from their own homes and according to their own schedules, which can open up more accessible opportunities compared to traditional work environments [407, 447]. Unfortunately, many of the tasks which are continuously posted on crowdwork platforms are not accessible to people with disabilities in the first place [379]. Moreover, the inability to signal one's disability to obtain reasonable adjustments or the time pressure associated with the completion of many tasks, can cause significant anxieties to people with disabilities who regularly complete work on the Amazon Mechanical Turk [400]. Ultimately, the poorly regulated nature of many of the jobs linked to the so-called "digital gig economy," which includes crowdwork, has created significant concerns about the protection of workers' rights, which might put people with disabilities at further risk of being exploited [169].

Although the contexts of work and education are different in certain respects, we decided to look at these two research areas in combination as we believe that there is a great degree of overlap between the insights, challenges, and successful strategies for impactful AAT research across these two domains. Furthermore, previous research has shown strong cascading effects between education and employment demonstrating how tackling the barriers that prevent access to education can increase chances of employment for people with disabilities [220]. For example, being able to see and interact with positive role models with disabilities in the context of employment can motivate youth with disabilities to pursue further education, advocate for oneself, and even inspire others in turn, creating a positive feedback loop that promotes inclusion at both levels [329]. With this in mind, we have divided this chapter into two separate, but connected sections, that examine key AAT research around education and employment looking at (1) both the work done specifically around the technology researched and designed by HCI researchers, and (2) the research focusing on broader systems and policy considerations that could affect the successful implementation in practice. Based on this analysis we identify opportunities where the DIX framework could be leveraged to engage researchers in capturing the different levels of complexity that shape how people with disabilities can take advantage of technology in different education and work settings.

5.1 TECHNOLOGIES FOR INCLUSIVE LEARNING EXPERIENCES

In the discussion concerning AAT for learning, it is necessary to set boundaries around what is and is not included in this category. For policy and provision purposes, we would argue for the use of the broadest definition possible. One that includes mainstream, accessible or purposefully designed educational technologies and adapted teaching and learning materials for individuals with disabilities alongside AT that make it possible for people with disabilities to engage in education. For example, a wheelchair that allows a child with a disability to reach school and participate in classroom activities with their peers, or a hearing aid that allows a hearing-impaired child to listen to a teacher should both be considered by providers as essential AATs for education [114]. However, for the purpose of specificity, throughout the rest of the chapter we will focus exclusively on mainstream and accessible ICTs that have a direct impact on learning outcomes of an individual.

When thinking about education most of us are likely to picture a formal environment, like a classroom in a school, university, or another similar institution, with teachers, instructors, or facilitators and where learning is directed by a curriculum that is specific for a particular course or subject, and knowledge evaluated using standardized tests and exams. However, education, and learning in general, are lifelong processes that can take place anywhere (at home, in school or in the community); with or without facilitation or supervision from teachers and educators; individually or as part of a group; and either sporadically or along a more defined learning program [43, 56]. Some of these changes to the more traditional concept of education have been triggered, or at least amplified by technology. The digital revolution has brought us anything from e-learning platforms and Massive Open Online Courses (MOOCs) to serious games and extended reality (XR), which are now used in a variety of educational contexts [99]. Furthermore, COVID-19 has accelerated the use of digital and distributed learning through the Internet. As there is no single way to classify different AATs for education based on context, subject or age of learners, in the following sections we will give an overview of how HCI researchers have explored the use of different technologies in formal and informal contexts.

5.1.1   DEVELOPING NOVEL EDUCATIONAL TECHNOLOGIES FOR THE CLASSROOM

HCI researchers have investigated the potential impact of educational technologies to improve learning outcomes of students with disabilities at all levels of the education pathway, from primary school to graduate students, examining both face-to-face and remote learning approaches [71, 193, 260, 279, 444]. One area of particular interest for many has been the promotion of digital fluency and basic computing education among young children with disabilities, particularly children with visual or learning disabilities [225, 270, 305, 324]. This high level of interest is unsurprising for several reasons. First, in the last decade several reports from various countries around the world have highlighted the low numbers and lack of diversity among students and professionals in the areas of computer science and technology [324, 372, 391]. Second, most mainstream platforms and toolkits such as Scratch by MIT or the Microsoft's game development platform called KODU heavily rely on graphical user interfaces that are not accessible to young visually impaired students who might not yet be proficient in using a screen reader and produce intangible outputs that might not be as clear and engaging for students who have learning disabilities [225, 270]. Third, computing education and digital fluency are matters which are close to heart for many HCI researchers and professionals who believe that promoting digital fluency for all will help to democratize access to technology, enabling individuals to become empowered actors rather than passive consumers of technology [224].

The approach used by most researchers seeking to develop accessible computing toolkits for young learners has been through the use of tangible user interfaces (TUIs), physical objects that children can manipulate and arrange to create programming instructions [270]. This strategy has proven quite popular as TUIs have been shown to be more accessible and enjoyable for young children and promote collaboration more effectively [334]. One of the most successful examples of accessible computational toolkits that leveraged TUIs is Torino developed by Microsoft Research (note that the toolkit was subsequently renamed CodeJumper ahead of its release) [270]. The Torino toolkit, which was designed through an iterative and participatory design session, leverages the use of physical beads recognizable by sight or touch, that can be combined through a series of cables. Individual beads represent simple sound-based programming instructions such as play, pause and repeat, and by connecting multiple beads together children are able to create songs, melodies, and stories that allow them to explore basic computational concepts (such as variables, loops, sequences, and operators) and practices (such as experimenting and iteration or testing and debugging) [64, 270, 390]. Figure 5.1 shows an example of a simple programming structure created using Torino's beads. A noteworthy feature of Torino is that its multiple affordances which are both visual and tactile, make it suitable for being used by children with different levels of visual ability, promoting collaboration and inclusive play [270, 390]. This feature is particularly important as previous research in mainstream UK classrooms has shown that the technology used by visually impaired children often creates a "teaching assistant bubble" that sees them engaging primarily with their dedicated teaching assistants and being excluded from most classroom activities [259].

Figure 5.1: Jumpcoder (formally Torino).

Torino is not the only inclusive computational toolkit leveraging the use of TUIs to promote accessible digital fluency education for children with mixed visual abilities and other researchers, including ourselves, have chosen to adopt different strategies such as preferring controllable moving robots as an output [6], enabling learners to create customizable programming instructions to allow for more individual expression [218], or advocating for the use of simpler and open source designs of programming blocks that could be easily fabricated by learners [33]. However, to our knowledge Torino was the only computational toolkit specifically built to be used in the context of a formal computing classroom and featuring a series of activities that matched the UK and Australian primary school computing curricula [270]. Large-scale testing was carried out across 24 schools in the UK for a period of 3 months and found there is great potential for practical implementation of Torino in UK schools [269]. This was despite some difficulties with the implementation including non-specialist teachers having low levels of confidence, which prevented them from developing new activities beyond the pre-made materials provided by researchers, and some resistance to encouraging collaborative play between visually impaired and sighted children [269]. Finally, Torino has also undergone some preliminary evaluations with visually impaired children attending specialist schools in India which highlighted that the toolkit has the potential to be contextually adapted to create engaging activities for young learners from different socio-cultural backgrounds [187].

We were unable to find a good example of educational development for autistic children or adults which made use of the double-emapthy paradigm [263] which states that not only do autistic people find it difficult to empathize with allistic (i.e., non-autistic) people, but allistic people also struggle to empathize with autistic people. This is despite the multiple studies which develop technology interventions to aid academic achievement for autistic people. As we pointed out in Chapter 3, these interventions are often targeted at normalizing the behavior of the autistic person, rather than taking a more complete user-centered and systems approach to the situation. In fact, what we find across HCI is surprising—the majority of studies are situated around a medical rather than social model of disability. A case in point is research toward people who are autistic. We use the term "toward" specifically as frequently it has been demonstrated that the research is more aimed toward normalizing social interactions between autistic and allistic (people who are not autistic) people. This dynamic and explanations for it are excellently developed in a recent review by Spiel and colleagues into the purposes of technologies for autistic children. It explored the relationship between power within the study design and agency of the autistic child [362]. It starts with a review of the medical, social, and alternative models of autism. The World Health Organization's diagnosis definition specifically makes note of deficits within the autistic person's abilities to "initiate and sustain reciprocal social interaction and social communication," it further instructs to look for "a range of restricted, repetitive, and inflexible patterns of behavior and interests." In their review of the literature the authors found this definition of autism prevailed, resulting in othering of the children. The authors describe how otherling in and of itself is not necessarily bad practice, segmenting groups can be positive. However, within the corpus the prevailing view of autistic children was one of deficiency and less than allistic peers [362]. Within the review of 185 papers, 25% had a focus on education. However, the technologies were predominantly designed for others in the ecosystem of learning—teachers, parents, even allistic learners, and not directly for the autistic children [ibid.]. The authors conclude that technologies have been designed for the carers to set the topic and chose the when, how and where of interaction (ibid.). Although this might seem similar to the design of curriculum-based technology for allistic children, the particular power dynamics which autistic children face exacerbate the issue [ibid.]. More generally the paper concludes that autistic children are excluded from expressing agency in defining what types of technology are suitable for them; instead, the allistic adults define the needs for the technology [ibid.]. There are, however, some cases where a non-medicalized model has been used. In these instances, researchers have tended toward the alternative approach to autism definition by De Jaegher [103]. The review highlights a range of published guides and examples which build on this perspective to enable participatory design with autistic people including Spiel et al.'s guide to participatory design with autistic children [365], first-person experiences elicitation [214], and co-created stories [336]. A useful example of co-design of technologies with autistic children is and although the technologies developed were for wellbeing support a similar methodology could be used for future co-designed autistic educational technologies

Rather than developing new technologies for classrooms featuring students with disabilities, some researchers have focused on evaluating the introduction of mainstream and specialized technologies to improve educational outcomes and promote specific pedagogical approaches [5, 260, 283, 413]. Unfortunately, many of these studies are of relatively short in duration and only take place in a limited number of schools. For instance, Abiatal and Howard [5] looked at the impact of a free online application in a school for deaf students in Namibia to improve deaf children's learning outcomes in mathematics leveraging constructivists approaches. After 2 weeks of use the authors measured a significant increase in students' test scores for both multiplication and division, furthermore teachers expressed overall positive opinions on the use of the platform [5]. Although these results are encouraging, the short duration of the study makes it hard to judge if implementation of this technology for longer periods of time would be feasible or if the benefits outlived the duration of the study. On the other hand, Norrie et al. [283] was able to carry out a five-month ethnographic study to explore the facilitators and barriers experienced in relation to AAC technology use in a specialist school. In this case, the long duration of the study and the variety of methods used, which included classroom observations, interviews and members check (i.e., a form of participant engagement in qualitative research that is used to confirm the correct interpretation of the data) allowed the authors to paint a detailed pictures of different elements which facilitate and hinder the adoption and impact of AAC technologies. Facilitators included the importance of strong motivation among the stakeholders that surround the child with disabilities, and barriers included difficulties that arose as a result of the fast pace of change in technology [283]. The study is a great example of a detailed, long duration and large pupil size study—it involved 180 pupils. However, as is the nature of ethnographic studies, it was limited to a single site in the UK and so findings are not necessarily applicable beyond this setting [283].

Integrating new or existing technologies in the classroom can always be challenging, but these challenges are amplified when teaching resources are already over-stretched such as classrooms with a high staff to student ratio, which contains multiple learning needs [26, 129, 191, 332]. Infrastructural issues can also increase challenges. For example, to understand the barriers and facilitators to introducing the use of serious digital games in schools for visually impaired children in India [189] conducted co-design workshops and interviews with teachers working across primary and secondary schools. Findings highlight how despite the teacher's enthusiasm and willingness to use accessible digital games within their classes, infrastructural barriers ranging from limited and outdated hardware, lack of internet connectivity, difficulties with installation and maintenance, insufficient digital skills and incompatibility with current educational curriculum significantly hampered the feasibility of implementing these games in the class [189]. Although teachers identified the need for some technical and thematic modifications to the games to ensure accessibility and context appropriateness, the majority of the limitations required systemic rather than technical intervention [189]. This highlights the need for systems thinking and a broader understanding of the context when designing interventions.

Most of the studies we have examined so far have focused on the development or implementation of technology in formal classroom environments, and particularly with learners of a relatively young age and studying at primary or secondary level. However, as mentioned before, older learners who are enrolled in higher education or who engage in remote learning, due to personal choices or as a result of external situations such as the COVID-19 pandemic, might have different needs and preferences from younger students. Furthermore, the situations encountered by more independent or remote learners are significantly different from the ones of learners sitting in primary or secondary school classrooms.

5.1.2 DISABILITY AND TECHNOLOGY USE IN HIGHER EDUCATION

Higher education environments are characterized by significantly more flexibility compared to primary and secondary school classrooms. Sure, students are still expected to attend classes, complete coursework, and undertake exams, but generally they have a lot more freedom when it comes to choosing subjects and organizing their own studies. Moreover, many students will also move away from their family homes for the first time, living in university halls, shared houses, or other kinds of accommodations. This is, of course, extremely exciting and represents a fundamental experience for many young adults. However, the less structured environment and the challenges of adjusting to independent and shared living can create difficulties for many students. Students with disabilities who enroll in higher education might encounter additional challenges due to physical and social environments which are rarely fully accessible [430]. AATs play a crucial role in facilitating life and learning for university students with disabilities and, due to the changing context and educational demands, it needs to adapt to meet the needs of the users.

A recent report by Global Disability Innovation Hub (GDI Hub) and Snowdon Trust [141] explored students with disability needs within higher education in the UK and the impact of the COVID-19 pandemic had had on study and learning practices. A survey was developed across multiple stakeholders targeting disabled undergraduate and postgraduate students in the UK, followed by interviews with eight disabled students. The report finds assistive technology currently does not meet student needs due to cost, delays in access and a lack of training in how to use technology when it is provided. Furthermore, 87% of learners subjectively reported feeling their disability created financial challenges which they perceived as not being felt by their non-disabled peers.

Financial support is provided in the UK, however 41% of respondents reported needing additional support to navigate this process of funding application. Financial stress was made worse during COVID-19, people's experiences within higher education led over half (68%) of respondents to believe there would be inclusivity challenges when they entered the workplace. To overcome these financial difficulties the report recommends a more streamlined approach to applying for financial assistance alongside affordable accessible accommodation and timely access to AT which comes with training as needed.

The above report focused on higher education more generally. However, similar challenges were found in a study of doctoral Ph.D. students. Shinohara and colleagues [348] interviewed 19 current and former doctoral students in computer science who were visually or hearing impaired they discovered that accessibility challenges affected almost any aspect of students' life from attending lectures, conducting research, writing papers, and accessing presentations. In contrast to a traditional primary or secondary school classroom environment, where more responsibility is placed on teachers to find and tackle access problems, in graduate school students had to consistently fight and advocate for themselves in order to be granted necessary accommodation which should be part of their basic rights [348]. An added difficulty was represented by the need to convey the difference between accessibility problems and general difficulty which was considered by instructors as simply part of a graduate student program [ibid.]. In many cases, technology was inadequate for the purpose of which it was deployed, for example using live captioning during group meetings was often awkward for hearing impaired participants who had to divide their attention between speakers, captions, and any visual material used for presentations, with the added difficulty of captions being incorrect or simply delayed, which can make following a meeting very difficult and actively participating in it almost impossible [ibid.]. Other technologies, like reference managers, were simply not accessible which significantly slowed down participants when they were working on essential tasks like writing papers, assignments, and even their dissertation [348].

The trio-Ethnography by Jain, Potluri, and Sharif [193] identified very similar issues with accessibility and the use of technology in the context of doctoral school studies. Moreover, the authors highlight how the use of technology is unlikely to completely bridge accessibility gaps. For example, the provision of accessible slides before a presentation does not make up for an inaccessible presentation style where the lecturer keeps making visual references to particular features of the slides if attendees are visually impaired [193]. Similarly, technology failures, which happen more regularly than we might realize, can create significant challenges, especially in time sensitive situations such as when an important deadline for a paper is looming [ibid.]. Finally, two individuals with disabilities might have very different preferences and access requirements, this is particularly true for people with different impairments. However, there can be a prevailing attitude of designing solutions for an impairment group, rather than for individual abilities and preferences. Furthermore, not all access needs are compatible with one another—accommodations and technologies that address the access needs of one individual might create additional challenges for others, creating potential access conflicts that need to be negotiated—[ibid.] an example of wickedness within this space.

We don't want to appear too despondent in the outlook for technology to aid education. Despite its limitations and imperfections, technology represents a crucial tool for students with disabilities in higher education, not only as a personal tool to bridge access gaps, but also as a shared tool that can be used to navigate access challenges as a shared experience with peers [288]. In his paper analyzing the impact of technology in supporting the transition of students with visual impairment in higher education, Pacheco [288] identifies seven roles for digital technologies: enabling vision compensation, accessing information, facilitating communication, establishing, and sustaining support, assisting learning, increasing collaboration, and achieving social connection and participation. Throughout these roles technology becomes an enabler not just for learning and individual support, but also for building social relationships and human support systems that are key to one's educational experiences.

The importance of technology for connecting with communities that can help to bridge accessibility challenges in higher education was also highlighted by Vashistha et al. [404]. This interview study which involved students, teachers, and educational content producers in India explored how visually impaired students used different devices to access, create and share educational material [404]. Common uses included consuming educational content in audio or Braille form, reaching out to classmates or teachers to ask questions, but also recording notes, reading sessions or instructions [ibid.]. As access to audiobooks was often limited, many participants were also used to transferring relevant audio files to each other using various practices that were influenced by their own level of digital skills and the features of the devices in question [ibid.]. Finally, participants used their personal devices and resources to create accessible audio content that they could share with others, going as far as leveraging their own personal connections or pooling funds to hire readers that could potentially help to generate accessible material that could benefit themselves and others [404].

Deaf and Hard of Hearing (DHH) students are often under-served and under-represented in education. However, relatively simple technology interventions can aid learning. For example, highlighting key words during captioned videos for DHH learners [199]. Two technology advances have the potential to improve the learning experiences of DHH students, namely sign language recognition and Automated Speech Recognition (ASR). Even at the current levels of accuracy ASR has been found to be beneficial for DHH students in higher educational classes [74]. The possible advantages of sign language recognition, generation, and translation have recently been explored through an interdisciplinary lens [61] Advantages of automatic sign language recognition mentioned by the authors which would be beneficial to educational settings include automatic transcription of signed content to enable indexing and searching of videos and real-time interpretation without the need of a human interpreter [61]. It could also allow translation between sign languages to enable learners to connect and discuss globally. The result of the workshops to explore the future of automated sign language by Bragg and colleagues results in a call to action broken into five parts: (1) involve deaf team members throughout the design process; (2) focus on real-world applications; (3) develop user-interface guidelines for sign-language systems; (4) create larger, more representative, public video datasets; and (5) standardize the annotation system and develop software for annotation support. One would imagine a similar set of calls to action would be present or automated speech recognition systems to aid DHH learners.

Having explored the area of higher education with all its barriers and enablers, we now move to technology use in remote education.

5.1.3   THE USE OF TECHNOLOGY FOR REMOTE EDUCATION. IMPLICATIONS FOR INCLUSION

Arguably, the importance of technology in the context of education has never been as important as it has become since the start of the COVID-19 pandemic [303]. Overnight, most schools, universities and other educational institutions across the world shut their doors to students and switched to remote learning leveraging tools ranging from dedicated learning platforms to video conferencing software, messaging applications and even remote lessons delivered through radios and TVs. These transitions were largely unplanned and, in the rush, to kickstart remote education programs as soon as possible, concerns emerged including: quality of remote learning, teachers preparedness, mental health implications for learners and educators, student engagement, role of parent x in supporting education, and impact on academic performance and students' self-efficacy [10, 123, 168, 298].

Arguably, the switch to remote education has brought both benefits and challenges to all students at all levels of the education pathways [299]. However, for students with disabilities both challenges and benefits were somehow amplified. On the one hand, the move to remote learning opened the door to more inclusive education for students with disabilities who had previously struggled to attend schools and universities in person. At the same time, many of the platforms, tools and educational resources used for remote learning were inaccessible to students with disabilities who struggled to get support from educators access essential AATs, that were normally located in schools and universities or gain access to disability services more generally [257, 330, 357]. When Gleason and colleagues analyzed the discourse around disability and remote education on Twitter between the April 6 and April 12, 2020, they identified three main themes of interest for the community: supporting social and emotional learning and wellbeing, advocacy, and critiques for available education accommodations, and resource sharing [138]. The first theme revolved around discussions between learners, parents, teachers, and therapists asking for suggestions and sharing advice and resources aimed at supporting emotional regulation, resilience, and strategies for fostering motivation and engagement as learners transitioned to a different format of education. The second theme included Tweets in which learners and their supporters' reported struggles with the inaccessibility of the many infrastructures for remote learning that were put in place by schools and universities. At the same time, disability activists criticized institutions which, until the start of the pandemic, were reluctant to meet the accommodation requests of students with disabilities but were quick to implement them once they became necessary for the majority of their students. Finally, the third theme included all Tweets that saw people sharing resources and tips in relation to educational technologies that could enable more accessible learning experiences. These suggestions encompassed advice on how teachers can easily create more accessible content using tools such as Flipgrid or Screencastify to facilitate inclusive video discussions, but also how learners could use existing tools and technologies to better access education content through applications such as Microsoft Immersive Reader which leverages AI to improve readability of documents for users with different kinds of disabilities [138].

As highlighted by Shew [347], the pandemic has also shown how disability-inclusive strategies can be more resilient to sudden changes, as demonstrated by her group's ability to seamlessly shift from in-person to remote research and collaboration, including being more accommodating toward the necessity of prioritizing wellbeing over short-term productivity which became a must in the long slog of home work during numerous lockdowns.

In many ways the pandemic had helped to accelerate disability inclusive EdTech innovation at a pace never seen before. The staggering increase in demand for inclusive video conferencing platforms has led most of the major providers such as Zoom, Google Meet, Microsoft Teams, and others to incorporate automatic captioning in most of their accounts. Investment in novel EdTech companies has also skyrocketed and considerably more attention has been paid to solutions that are accessible and able to respond to the needs of diverse learners [152, 436]. For example, the Turkish startup Otsimo that developed a platform to support education and speech therapy for kids with different kinds of learning disabilities received multiple awards and additional funding during the pandemic which enabled them to expand the content and services provided to users. Similarly, BibliU a platform focusing on the provision of textbooks and reading material in a format that is accessible to learners with diverse needs, was able to secure $10 million to increase the size of their library.

Although many of these developments are extremely positive, it is also worth remembering that this rapid scale up of technology in education is not free from risks. Without solid pedagogical bases, accessibility features included from the beginning and teaching practices that are truly inclusive, EdTech can become a way to further the digital divide and further marginalize learners with disabilities [388]. Inclusive education, remote or in-person, is ultimately more about practices and individuals than it is about technology. The three vignettes included in the paper by Ellcessor [122] perfectly illustrate how even when supposedly accessible EdTech is available, the work of access largely rests on the shoulders of learners, teachers, and parents. For example, as teaching moved from in-person to digital at the start of the pandemic, Ellcessor shows that accessibility was rarely embedded directly in the delivery of lecturers. Ellcessor goes to great lengths to find additional options that can make the content of the lecturers more accessible to students, such as sourcing an OCR to PDF converter and a third-party captioning software for videos. However, implementing these solutions requires further work from herself and her students, without any support from the institution or the primary technology provider [ibid.].

5.1.4 BEYOND FORMAL EDUCATION

Education is not only about what happens in a classroom or formal learning environment, we learn as we play games and as we visit museums and cultural attractions.

We have seen a number of recent HCI-led interventions to bring cultural experiences to people with disabilities.

Figure 5.2: Xbox adaptive video game controller for people with physical impairments and mobility issues being used to playy. Courtesy of Microsoft Corporation.

Gaming, like the Arts, offers us a wonderful design space to play in. A recent workshop [180] explored disability and gaming looking at the previous HCI work completed in serious games (e.g., [411]) bespoke games (e.g., [173]) and adaptations for accessibility to mainstream games like the new Xbox controller (Figure 5.2). The workshop position paper also covers the advances made in both academic and industry guidelines to make gaming more accessible for example the Game Accessibility Guidelines (GAG) [458]. These advances aside the workshop posed the question about how games could be better co-designed, how they could be used to tackle societal attitudes toward disability and how game adaptability can promote social inclusion [180]. The future of DIX can explore these themes in more detail and continue the discussion. Looking toward adaptable characters and environments which challenge social norms, our interactions will become increasingly across physical to virtual reality with augmented experiences in the middle. Within these we will be able to carry our companions in our virtually augmented headspace, interact with crowds of people of all abilities in the metaverse—the next generation of the Internet, where people interact through 3D avatars—and also disconnect entirely when needed.

5.2   TECHNOLOGIES SUPPORTING WORK AND ACCESS TO EMPLOYMENT FOR PEOPLE WITH DISABILITIES

The UNCRPD in Article 27 enshrines the right to work and employment for people with disabilities. This covers all aspects of work from entrepreneurship opportunities for public and private work—from retention and return-to-work programs to trade union membership. People with disabilities should have full access to employment and work opportunities. However, this is often not the case and many people with disabilities have faced discrimination and a lack of opportunity at one or more points in their lives such as when wishing to enter the workforce or embarking in entrepreneurial adventures or navigating the dynamics of an office environment [97, 339, 377].

In the last decade, technology has become an integral part of employment and work. Not only have computers, laptops, mobile phones, and a variety of electronic devices specific to different professions become increasingly more relevant, but general and dedicated software applications form the backbone of most industry in the secondary and tertiary sectors [84, 148]. Moreover, most of the communication that takes place across employers, employees, clients, and other stakeholders happens through a variety of digital channels which change depending on organizational preferences and situational requirements [370, 394]. As always, technology can represent both an asset or a barrier to the working life of people with disabilities and its impact is influenced by many personal, societal, and technical factors [459]. In the following sections we take a closer look at the HCI research around the impact of technology on both the ability of people with disabilities to enter the workforce and the working life of individuals already in employment.

5.2.1   THE IMPACT OF TECHNOLOGY ON ACCESS TO EMPLOYMENT FOR PEOPLE WITH DISABILITIES

Nowadays, most pathways to employment are somehow mediated by technology, from job searches, to CV writing and job application completion; from interviewing and sometimes even onboarding, all these steps may be mediated by technology. In 2012, Lazar, Olalere, and Wentz [221] conducted an evaluation of how usable and accessible job application websites used by a variety of companies in eight U.S. states were to prospective job applicants with visual impairment. The study highlights several accessibility barriers specific to screen reader users and many usability issues that could potentially create problems to users with or without disabilities. Inaccessible experiences started from the job search page which required the use of a mouse and pointer and included forms that lack specificity and did not provide feedback for data entry problems, or links that didn't contain any information to enable screen reader users to differentiate between them [221].

The study by Lazar and colleagues was carried out almost a decade ago and many of us would reasonably expect that the situation would have significantly improved. Unfortunately, studies of similar nature carried out in 2017 [150] and 2020 [104] highlighted many of the same issues. Moreover, Grussenmeyer and colleagues [150] pointed out how visually impaired job seekers also needed to deal with further accessibility challenges with other essential tasks such as writing CVs, and job interviews or coding tests where accommodations were not provided at all, or provided in a way that put the participants at severe disadvantage such as people being assigned a non-specialist human reader instead of large print text and magnification software for a test on advanced mathematics.

HCI researchers have sought new ways in which novel technologies could help to reduce some of the accessibility barriers embedded in job seeking and application processes. Dillahunt et al. [110] developed ten design concepts that aimed to support underserved job seekers, which included people with disabilities. These applications addressed different worker's needs. For example, enabling freelancers to better gather and present feedback and testimonials among previous customers to promote themselves and support new work applications, or providing better employment opportunity matches based on prior experience and skills [110]. A second interface that has been developed was by Hartholt and colleagues [166], who developed a virtual reality-based training system that could support autistic people, veterans, and former convicts dealing with the job application process. The system includes different fictional interviewers supporting three conversational modes reflected in style of conversation and body language [ibid.]. However, this virtual reality interface assumes and expects people to learn job application skills that are typical, instead of addressing non-inclusive job application processes and ableist expectations of style of conversations and body language, which are particularly damaging for autistic individuals. AAC devices are often used by autistic people to aid their communication, this area is often under-researched, with a focus on speech rather than communication; a recent study argues for a stronger focus on communication and on the effectiveness of AAC for autistic adults is needed [445], and could support the future of work for autistic adults.

A majority of these types of interventions are tailored to the Global North. In the Global South, numerous studies have shown how the use of mobile phones can represent an essential tool for accessing both formal and informal employment [31, 192, 291]. Through our photovoice study involving people with disability in Kenya and Bangladesh, participants documented numerous practices showing how thanks to mobile phone use they were able to access financial services that allow them to support their own businesses, connect and manage customers, link to potential employers, and even found their own ventures [192]. However, as highlighted through the critical realist study by Iliya and Ononiwu [186], the extent to which people with disabilities are able to leverage mobile technologies to access employment opportunities is dependent on contextual factors such as one's level of digital literacy, available features of the phone, characteristics of the broader mobile ecosystem, and the availability of social support.

Overall, technology does have a positive impact on the ability of people with disabilities to access work opportunities. However, poor design, inaccessible interfaces and systems, or limited digital skills can further expand the employment divide. However, one additional question we need to ask ourselves is "Once people with disabilities enter the workforce, how does technology impact their working lives?"

5.2.2   INTERACTIONS BETWEEN PEOPLE WITH DISABILITIES AND TECHNOLOGY IN THE WORKPLACE

Although the employment gap between people with and without disabilities is still significant, many people with disabilities in the world are part of the workforce, either working as self-employed individuals or as employees in different organizations [448]. Reasonable accommodations, including the provision of adequate AATs to ensure people with disabilities have equal opportunities to task and work completion, is a legal requirement for employers in most countries [51].

The availability of appropriate AATs in the workplace can have a tremendous positive impact on the capabilities, productivity, and wellbeing of employees with disabilities. When interviewing visually impaired workers in India about the impact of AAT on experiences, aspirations, and inclusion in the workplace, Pal and Lakshmanan [290] reported that participants felt that access to AAT and acquisition of digital skills had a positive impact not only on their day-to-day jobs, but also on their aspirations and ability to progress in their career. When companies were unwilling to invest in them and acquire necessary tools such as screen readers or magnification software, participants found alternative ways to access these technologies by relying on pirated copies or repeatedly installing demo versions, but this had a negative impact on their productivity [ibid.].

Even when required AATs are provided to employees, many practices that are popular in the workplace can create additional "invisible work" for people with disabilities who constantly need to find alternative strategies to access documentation or tools that are used by their colleagues [63]. Printers, scanners, office phones, and fax machines that are commonly found in millions of offices around the world lack basic accessibility features and many software tools used by companies for work-related and operational tasks from booking annual leave to filling in timesheets were not compatible with the use of screen readers [63]. Once again, visually impaired workers were often able to find their own accommodation by combining technologies in creative ways such as overlaying two pairs of headphones (one pair of earbuds covered by a pair of overhead headphones) to monitor notifications from multiple devices at once [63]. However, devising one's own accommodation required skills, time and energy that went unseen by sighted co-workers and managers [ibid.].

When it comes to the productive use of technology, many non-disabled users could definitely stand to learn more from their peers with disabilities. The analysis of interactions between blind podcasters and voice-activated personal assistants (VAPAs) showed that this particular group of users has been able to leverage VAPAs for much more significant tasks than the average playful user [4]. Podcasters leveraged third-party applications to enable their preferred VAPA to access their work calendar, organize meetings, set up reminders, and read emails creating faster and more efficient interactions. Furthermore, thanks to their extensive expertise they were also able to illustrate how new features could be beneficial for all users regardless of their visual abilities [4].

Regardless of one's level of digital skills, people with disabilities keep facing accessibility barriers in the workplace which are often linked to technology that does not match their needs or the recurrence of ableist work practices. From the interviews and survey conducted with neurodivergent software engineering professionals working at Microsoft, Morris, Begel, and Wiedermann [267] explored how despite their excellent ability to write code, identify patterns, exhibit intuitive thinking and maintain high level of focus when working on projects thanks to their different cognitive styles, participants often struggled to see their work recognized or being promoted as career progression was only possible if one was stepping into a managerial role.

What we see here then is a complex system in which when technology is provided people with disabilities thrive, and indeed go further in use cases than were perhaps originally envisioned by the developers. However, across work settings technology can be inaccessible and practices including the values placed on promotion and career progression can be ableist in design. We now turn our attention to the 4th industrial revolution and the future of work.

5.2.3   REMOTE WORK AND THE PROBLEM OF (IN)ACCESSIBILITY

The 4th industrial revolution has created a wealth of opportunities for new work arrangements that go beyond the traditional boundaries of co-located offices and workplace and the COVID-19 pandemic has further accelerated the move toward flexible or fully remote work [156]. As with education, this change had both positive and negative implications for workers with disabilities which are mediated by the accessibility or (in)accessibility of the available technologies and dominant work practices.

The 36 neurodivergent professionals interviewed by Das and colleagues reported that, on the one hand, working from home allowed them to create both physical and digital workspaces that suited their needs much better than traditional offices [101]. For example, several participants explained that they used to find their traditional open office environment distracting and anxiety producing, due to the excess sensory stimulation and the constant feeling of being on display while working. While working from home they were better able to control their environment and ensure that it was less draining and more productive for them [101]. However, working from home also meant spending significant amounts of time on video calls during which it can be challenging for neurodivergent individuals to remain concentrated, especially when other meeting attendees had a lot of background movement and noise on their video and audio feeds or if multiple notifications from the chat kept disrupting the videoconference [101, 446]. Furthermore, managing remote communication and particularly turn talking which can often be chaotic in larger video calls can be stressful for neurodivergent individuals who might feel too self-conscious to attempt to express their opinions or be unable to decipher the flow of conversation when the rules of turn talking are not explicit and people are interrupting each other [101, 446].

On the other hand, for people with limited mobility, the switch to remote work and the rise of video conferencing software meant that they were finally able to attend work meetings on an equal basis with their non-disabled colleagues without having to worry about their "unusual posture" and the use of background filters enables them to cover medical equipment that would be otherwise captured by the camera [382]. Most video conferencing software also offers visual clues to highlight who is speaking in a meeting at a particular time and this feature can be especially helpful for individuals with hearing impairment, deaf workers and sign language interpreters [382]. Interestingly, the same feature can also create issues when a Deaf person speaks through their interpreter, as the software will detect the interpreter through the microphone and would spotlight their video rather than the person who is actually speaking [382].

Figure 5.3: Example set-up for a deaf person joining a video conferencing call.

Conflicts between multiple video or audio streams can also be extremely problematic for workers with disabilities. For example, attempting to follow a presentation where the speaker is talking and at the same time, the screen reader is reading the slides used by the presenter can be confusing for a visually impaired person [382]. Similarly, hearing impaired individuals often need to integrate and manage several visual channels at the same time during a meeting. As shown in Figure 5.3, these might include presenter's slide, video of the presenter, live captioning streams, and the video of the interpreter, requiring not only high degrees of attention, but also sufficient space on the screen, or necessitating the need to negotiate multiple devices to be able to look at all this information at the same time [382]. Finally, common practices in remote meetings such as screen sharing could create additional challenges to people with disabilities due to incompatibility with essential tools such as magnification software, minimization of participants' videos which include the sign language interpreter, and challenging controls with alternative interfaces such as voice commands [382].

Ultimately, and in contrast with education, the move from in-person to remote work seems to have more benefits than drawbacks for people with disabilities and in part this is linked to the wide variety of AATs which are available to people. However, problems linked to the integration of multiple programs and devices combined with practices and expectations that are still, if not actively ableist, at least inadvertently so, can create significant accessibility challenges that hinder productivity, cause stress and damage the wellbeing of workers with disabilities.

Case Study: Enabling Access to Quality, Inclusive Education for Learners with Visual Impairment in Africa
Author, Kilimanjaro Blind Trust Africa

KBTA's Commitment: Kilimanjaro Blind Trust Africa (KBTA) a charitable trust based in Nairobi, Kenya works in five countries of East Africa and Malawi to promote inclusion of learners with visual impairments (VI) by providing digital, multifunctional Braille assistive devices with full-service support to ensure that every VI learner has a functioning device. The Orbit Reader 20 is a Braille note-taker and book reader accompanied by mobile applications that have enabled VI learners in Africa to access quality education in inclusive schools. KB-TA's ambitious target is to distribute 3,000 devices across the 5 countries.

Innovation of the ORBIT Project: In Africa, poverty is linked to disability. There is no inclusion without access to quality education. The VI learners in Africa are passive learners in the classroom without appropriate assistive devices. The public institutions are cash strapped and cannot provide the technology needed for access to digital literacy/skills or even STEM subjects that can give them career choices and access to relevant employment.

KBTA sought out affordable digital Braille technology in 2018 from U.S. innovators called the Orbit Reader 20 (OR20). Their innovative strategy worked to cover entire class cohorts across all the schools, in order to ensure uniformity. Working with governments and their agencies, KBTA delivered the OR20 to learners across approximately 100 schools and 1,000 plus learners in inclusive classrooms across 5 countries, starting the process in primary followed by secondary schools and finally institutions of higher learning such as Universities, TVET institutions, and teacher training colleges.

KBTA also ensured that the OR20 were:

- loaded with the digital Braille curriculum content and other reading material;
- the teachers in each institution were trained while working with the school management to ensure proper use and security of the Orbit Readers;
- KBTA also trained school-based technicians, a concept developed internally to support continuity of use;
- providing spare parts;
- continuously supporting the schools to adequately support the VI learners; and
- KBTA has been able to enhance access to digital literacy/skills for VI learners, in order to take the next step toward career selection, employability skills and employment.

The Impact on VI Learners and Progressing Toward Employability: The OR20 has literally transformed access to education for the VI learners in five African countries. It has changed the way teachers in overcrowded, inclusive classrooms are able to support the VI learner. The learners are able to participate easily in classroom assessments and tests, take notes, and get responses to their queries from teachers by using the mobile applications, which also support those with hearing impairments. The VI learner has improved reading skills through access to story books and other learning material of interest. The VI teachers are able to prepare for and teach their classes without having to depend on transcribers. KBTA is now working to provide access to STEM subjects and computer sciences which the learners were unable to access. Progress is thus rapidly taking place due to digital technology/innovation toward access to varied employment skills and opportunities. The OR20 has brought down the cost of educating the VI learner.

The first cohort of learners who started with the Orbit Reader in 2019 took their primary/ secondary national examinations in 2021 and registered exemplary performance compared to the previous years.

Figure 5.4: Visually impaired learners using the orbit reader (left) and a birds-eye view of orbit reader (right).

In the above case study, we see how complex, entangled challenges can be successfully met. For example the input to the Orbit Reader is Braille. Curricular and refence books are received from the government agencies and adapted info Braille readable format (BRF), these are all loaded onto the device via a memory card. Global books are also added. This is aided through the Marrakesh Treaty, which allows visually impaired users and people acting on their behalf, to make copies of copyrighted printed material without infringing on copyright. Users can type retrieve and manage their notes in Braille on the device. In rolling out the device, KBTA provided full service for the devices and training for teacher and technicians in each school. The teachers download the mobile app called TEACHER to manage their inclusive classroom. There is also a second application—COMMUNCIATOR—which translates between Braille text to voice to enable teachers who do not understand Braille to interact with learners in a meaningful way. The applications are free, while the device costs $700. Currently, KBTA absorb all training costs and repair costs. They report (via email exchanges) that breakages while rare occur mainly due to dust and dirty hands when using the device. This demonstrates the necessity of focusing on the full system, including repair and training, and not only the product development itself.

5.3   THE ROLE OF DIX IN EDUCATION AND EMPLOYMENT

5.3.1   ACKNOWLEDGE THE WICKED PROBLEM

Many of the problems of access to employment and education opportunities for people with disabilities sit beyond the remit of HCI researchers, however, in understanding the types of data needed for policy and for example knowing that there are policies and targets for employment of people with disabilities can help us to orientate our thinking.

In the context of education, we might be tempted to focus our intervention on designing a new technology which can support the learning of a child with disabilities in a particular subject or toward a specific set of skills. However, in our design efforts we need to be mindful of how this new technology will influence the child's experience within the classroom environment, not only in relation to their individualized learning, but also considering the relationships with peers. For example, to explore how educational technologies can affect the experience of inclusion of children with visual impairment within the classroom Metatla and Cullen engaged children with mixed visual abilities and educators in the co-design of novel inclusive technologies for the classroom. As a result of this cooperative effort the authors highlighted how one of the key aspects to consider for technologies that wish to promote inclusive experience is to reduce the disconnects of space, language, and materials that often contribute to the creation of a "teaching bubble" which separates the visually impaired child from their peers. All the technology prototypes designed by the groups of participants leveraged different strategies to achieve this from focusing on sharing experiences to augmenting the existing environment to provide important information or combining multisensory feedback to maximize accessibility for all.

This study highlights how to really promote the inclusion of people with disabilities in education or employment. We cannot merely focus on developing technologies that support the completion of certain tasks or the learning of specific contexts. Both work and education take place within a complex socio-cultural environment that needs to be considered to maximize the positive impact of technology.

We sought to have more examples in this chapter of technologies that support neurodivergent people. However, in our search we found relatively few studies which had embraced the design of technology with this population from a social disability stance. Therefore, we choose this point to reflect on neurodiversity with a case study and definitions of key terms in the hope it will engage more research in this space.

Neurodiversity and Disability—Reflections
Dafne Zuleima Morgado Ramirez, Global Disability Innovation Hub and UCLIC

There is a prevailing controversy about how to use the term neurodiversity [354] and what it means. Neurodiversity refers to both strengths and disability. Misinterpretations of the term neurodiversity enable distorted and over-simplified arguments [27, 58]. The act of valuing neurological differences or complementary cognition [386] is about acknowledging and accepting disability and ability of human beings [25, 201]. Thus, dedicating time to understand the origin and use of terms used by neurodivergent [354] people, along understanding their experiences, should be a standard procedure for anyone designing interactions with and for neurodivergent people. It is estimated that a quarter of the world population is neurodivergent. For instance, between 5% and 20% of the world has dyslexia, 6% have ADHD/ADD and 2% are autistic [47]. Similarly, in the recent #WeThe15 campaign it was highlighted that approximately a quarter of the world population has a disability [460]. Coincidence? Moreover, it was recently suggested that the human species has adapted and evolved cognitively, analogous to evolution at the genetic level, thus we complement each other through cognitive specializations and effective collaboration [386]. That is, the human species neurodiversity is a result of evolution, and we are meant to work together leveraging our different cognitive abilities. Yet, humans have created cultural systems and practices that undermine our complementary cognitive capacity as a species [157], such as diagnostic labels for learning and neurodevelopmental disorders and neurotypical expectations. Thus, we must ask, is disability/ neurodivergence what we are looking at? Or, is complementary evolutionary cognition? Or, is it complementary cognition and we must acknowledge that cognitive difference has strengths and disabilities? And, thus, the neurodiversity concept helps us to capture well the complementary cognition and disability.

Terminology is critical and so I provide some key definitions to aid future researchers.

Complementary Cognition: Theory that the human species adapts and evolves through a collaborative system of collective cognitive search. It is a consequence of individual neurocognitive specialization. The theory implies that the neurocognitive capabilities of individuals differ and these support search and the balance of information search toward efficiency [1].

Neurodivergence: Neurologically different to 75% of the human species typical neurology. An individual can be neurodivergent.

Neurotypical: Neurologically typical compared to the quarter of the human species that is neurodivergent. An individual can be neurotypical.

Neurodiversity: Neurological diversity. Neurological refers to the nervous systema and diversity refers to the variety and variability of life. The human species is neurodiverse. One can refer to a species as neurodiverse but not to an individual as neurodiverse. An individual would be either neurotypical or neurodivergent.

5.3.2   TAKING AN ABC APPROACH

As we have seen in the educational research thus far there are few studies which have developed the depth and length of study which would enable us to then see opportunities for new technologies. We therefore see an opportunity for HCI researchers to develop longer and more intricate mixed-method studies which then help to show ways that ethnology can scaffold and expand learning opportunities for people with disabilities. While basic research can be used to unpack the details of interactions between the user and the technology used to complete a particular task in the class, at home or in the workplace, applied research can investigate how the use of these technologies integrate within school curricula or existing work practices.

5.3.3 EXPLORE RADICALLY DIFFERENT INTERACTIONS

One emerging area of radically different approach to education is one where education is seen more as a service, potentially accessible through an ecosystem of devices and materials. This would allow people in middle-income countries to access a variety of learning materials both at home and in the school setting.

Radically different interactions are emerging in the way in which we develop employment opportunities for people with disabilities. However, these can be expanded further through the use of more integrated, augmented, and extended reality. For example, future technologies could look to enable non-speaking autistic individuals to communication a form they wish, not in a neuro-typical way, or technology which would enable an easier and more enjoyable driving experience for autistic people.

5.3.4 CO-CREATE SOLUTIONS

Solutions which are co-created across a wide range of actors are better able to be incorporated into classrooms and curricula and are also able to be appropriate to the context. We have seen a large number of solutions applicable to the coding education. This could be expanded further into STEM and other areas, where we help to apply our approach to the broader remit of education.

5.3.5 ENGAGE IN VALUABLE AND USEFUL RESEARCH

It is clear that education and employment is of the utmost value to people with disabilities, however, what appears lacking is our ability as HCI researchers to demonstrate the value in our technological solutions to enhance learning outcomes and offer enhanced opportunity for people with disabilities.

5.3.6 FOCUS ON OPEN AND SCALABLE INNOVATIONS

Open and scalable approaches to employment can be made simply by designing inclusive hiring policies. An exemplar here is the Microsoft neurodiversity hiring program [461] which has a number of stages. First, a neurodiverse applicant applies and is their technical skills and qualifications are assessed against the requirements of open roles [461]. If there is a match between skill set and requirements the applicant is invited to complete and online technical assessment. If the assessment goes well the applicant is invited to a hiring event. This takes place over several days and allows the applicant to work on technical kills, team building and interview preparation, including meeting the interview team in both formal and informal settings [461]. Based on the applicant's skills assessment and interviewer feedback the applicant is hired or not.

5.4   CONCLUSION

Through this chapter we have explored DIX in relation to education and employment. In doing this we have seen how technologies are now frequently co-designed for learners with visible disabilities but that medical models of understanding autism prevail resulting in a lack of learner agency. The COVID-19 pandemic and subsequent increase in working from home has offered an opportunity for increased inclusion in many instances. This may go some way to increasing closing the disability employment gap. However, it is probable that investment in awareness of diverse employment practices such as Microsoft's neurodiverse hiring process is needed alongside increased funding for and availability of AT.

CHAPTER 6

Exploring Different Settings: DIX in Health and Healthcare

In this chapter we explore the setting of health, this covers healthcare as well as illness which can affect the health of an individual. We start the chapter by exploring the value of health within society, to understand how its conceptualization might affect the development and diffusion of technology to support the health of people with disabilities. We then take a quick look at digital health interventions and move onto unpack some of the arguments about healthy aging, assisted living and the overlaps and contrast between aging and disability. Afterward, we look more closely at the links between mental health, disability, and the role of technology in supporting psychological wellbeing. We then move to understand some of the nuances and interactions between assistive products and the provision of healthcare services by exploring the definition of AT as formulated by the World Health Organization. Finally, we bring an example of how the DIX framework can be applied to research in health and healthcare services by analyzing the role of data population level screening to connect functional assessment to the estimation of AT need and support provision.

6.1 THE VALUE OF HEALTH

As HCI researchers we are fluent in understanding, measuring, and describing the usefulness of products for the individual. We are less proficient at describing their value to society. We must realize we are innovating and designing in a world of limited resources. Healthcare expenses are a considerable proposition of a country's spending. High-income countries with ageing populations and rising non-communicable diseases are spending almost 20% of their gross domestic product (GDP) on healthcare [170]. With such high spending, how can we ensure a new technology makes it into healthcare? One of the ways in which this can be done by assessing the impact of the technology through a health technology assessment (HTA), which is defined as "a multidisciplinary process that uses explicit methods to determine the value of a health technology at different points in its lifecycle. The purpose is to inform decision-making in order to promote an equitable, efficient, and high-quality health system" [287]. Assessment should cover a wide range of factors: clinical effectiveness, safety, costs and economic implications, ethical, social, cultural, and legal issues, organizational and environmental aspects, as well as wider implications for the patient, relatives, care-givers, and the population, however, too often due to time pressures and data issues, only financial and medical information get reviewed [287]. Therefore, as designers we need to be cognizant of the making the medical and financial case, or lobbying hard for the other components to be included in the HTA for our technology.

There are now wider efforts to generate evidence for the value of assistive products more generally, to help raise their profile and make it easier to make the financial case for investment both for the purchasers and investors. For example, using a simple return on investment model, traditional assistive technology is found to provide a 9:1 return—so for each dollar spent, 9 are saved [18]. However, this analysis looks only at the level of the user and not the wider innovation landscape. It measures, for example, reductions in social welfare payments and higher income tax returns due to employability of a person with an assistive technology, but does not look at the wider innovation returns, which could for example include the generation of fundamental new scientific advances and jobs where people are designing for disability inclusions [335].

It might seem that the above economic evaluations are beyond the scope of a HCI researcher. However, we must ask ourselves in a world of limited resources, each of us with limited time and energy available to develop new technology, do we not want to ultimately see our designs reach the people who need it most? To achieve this, we must begin to think beyond our traditional methods and seek to understand the wider system nature of the technology we are designing. We can also though look to develop tools which influence the capture of wider experiences of a technology. How, for example, could we develop technologies to better capture carer and user experiences which could then be translated into the language specific to HTA evaluations? Inspiration can be taken from studies such as that from Honary et al. [182], who describe the design of a series of video stories based on the lived experience of people who live with and are affected by severe mental illness. Their study produced relatable and empathic digital content, however, could these outcomes be built upon leveraging an approach that helps to incorporate and enumerate the wider impacts of technology? Furthermore, there is a movement to base healthcare technology assessment directly at the hospital level [182] that would make our work as HCI researchers and designers more easy to integrate into practice. As researcher and designers, we also have experience in developing digital health solutions which have scaled well and therefore passed the HTA test from which we can draw experience and inspiration.

Of course, not all of healthcare is provided through formal services. As individuals, we are each responsible for maintaining our health and there is now a growing number of technologies to help us self-manage components of our wellbeing. Much of this work is based on measuring data and helping us to manage or change our behaviors as a result [216]. We saw examples of this in Chapter 3 with the case study on physiological computing. There has also been recent work to measure and make sense of data relating to self-tracking to manage conditions which HCI researchers sometimes term "serious mental illness." One such study is from Snyder et al. [216], which focuses on the design of data visualizations which are useful and valued by people who have bipolar disorder. They found a key aim of self-tacking for people with bipolar disorder was to reconcile their internal self-view with the external reflections of their behavior, as well as measuring the cycles of depression and mania which they experienced. Therefore, the data was valuable both in tracking and explaining behavior [ibid.].

As we grow our approach to measuring value and usefulness, we can also get better at explaining this wider value to people who make the big decisions on procurement and provision. To do this we could leverage collaborative mission-led approaches that enable the creation of broad agendas of AT innovation for health, capitalizing on the collective interest of different actors including government, NGOs, industry, AT users, and the charity sector to tackle key healthcare challenges, framing AT access as key to achieving wider goals and building on the complementary role of different actors [7]. Now that we have explored this wider picture we move onto healthy aging and assisted living.

6.2   AGING AS DISABILITY?

I (Cathy Holloway) recently visited my parents and, while sitting in my campervan in the driveway (isolating as it is required for COVID-safe travels), I could easily hear them conversing in their bedroom, through a closed window and a van wall. This is because they can't hear well. When I mention that they could benefit from hearing aids, they do not believe me. Both wear eyeglasses happily. Neither will wear or even entertain the idea of hearing aids. This is not a unique story; we are sure many people who read this with parents over the age of 70 or so will be able to relate and previous research had documented significant reluctance toward hearing aids by many elderly individuals [326]. Similar examples are often found with people as they age not wishing to use a mobility scooter or wheelchair, but if temporarily injured with a broken leg would be happy to use either.

Why is this? It has much to do with the identity of a person who is aging and their view of disability. The *World Report on Disability* starts Chapter 1 with:

> *"Disability is part of the human condition. Almost everyone will be temporarily or permanently impaired at some point in life, and those who survive to old age will experience increasing difficulties in functioning. Every epoch has faced the moral and political issue of how best to include and support people with disabilities. This issue will become more acute as the demographics of societies change and more people live to an old age* [226].*"*

Given this definition, my parents are disabled, but they don't think so. Their opinion matters and doesn't at all. Their opinion doesn't change the facts—their hearing is declining, they cannot change that by wishing it were different and by not accepting this reality they and many others lose out on the ability to hear, which is also linked to cognitive decline. From our point of view as HCI researchers, this matters for two reasons. First, we might develop technology which people won't use due to their own internalized stigma (ableism knows no bounds!). Then knowing this we are better able to design for people who identify as disabled person/a person with disability (depending on where they live) as well as those who don't but who would benefit from the technology. Second, the aging population is responsible for a much larger proportion of the society living more of their life as a person with impairment. This second point is costly at a society level—remember the 20% of GDO figure. This is driving investment into research and technology development to help people age well. Of course, much of this is baked into a neoliberal politics where "well" is seen as not costing money from the state (or less money) and continuing to provide benefit to society in terms of economic output (direct—continue to work, or indirect, continue to care for grandchildren). However, we do not need to only design for such measures we can leverage designing for phycological wellbeing, and work across generations to develop better community value-led definitions of well ness for our work. We should though always remain cognizant of the wider drivers if only to secure the funding necessary to drive change. One such lever we can use to fund innovation is the aging and digital agenda which is so strong the WHO has now launched a new initiative to support its development.

6.2.1   AGING AND DIGITAL

The WHO recently launched a new agenda from their AT team called DATA—Digital and Assistive Technologies for Ageing [209]. DATA seeks to encourage the "development, synthesis and use of solutions that promote access to affordable, quality, digital and assistive technologies for people with impairment or decline in physical or mental capacity, with a particular focus on older people" [209]. This follows the successful Global Cooperation on Assistive Technology (GATE) which has helped drive the AT agenda within WHO. The launch of DATA acknowledges two important areas: the rise of digital technology as a mediator of healthcare and a healthcare tool, and the significant number of older people in the population which drives the need for improved technology for assisted living. In this new agenda, AT is seen as a mediator to help people in their everyday lives, especially as functions decline due to the ageing process. This concept of assisted living is becoming increasingly important to population health and is driven in part by the greater affordability and usability of digital devices which are becoming increasingly ubiquitous [209]. Digital interactions are seen as essential to underpinning the assisted living agenda. A number of examples of digitally powered assisted living solutions are given in this *Lancet* paper from virtual or augmented games to help people with dementia to navigate through familiar but forgotten, or indeed completely new living spaces to companion robots [209]. This association of digital health and ageing is yet to grip HCI—a search of the ACM library of *Ageing* and *Digital Health* found 352 results, one of which was *DigiTAI: The 1st International Workshop on Digital Health Systems for the Aging Population*, demonstrating this nascent but growing HCI agenda. "Assisted living" across full texts produced 1,234 results.

While people age is important, people tend to wish to stay in their homes for as long as possible—they have invested a lot of money toward their home, created a style and functionality of space they enjoy and invested in their community. Aging in place seeks to empower older adults to remain independent in their own residences for longer [78]. For this to be possible, people need to perform acts of self-care and health monitoring generating data which can be shared with health care professionals and caregivers. This results in a trade-off between assistance and independence [78]. In a recent study which looked at the needs of older adults living in retirement communities—where there was a level of assistance given by technology and carers to help support independent living—found there was a need for understanding the deep sociotechnical systems in which assisted living technologies are used [77, 147]. Furthermore, there is a need for designers to understand the emotional response to monitoring and sharing monitored data by older adults [78]. They reflect that there is meaning attached to this data, the meaning is a measurement of their ability, and this is directly related to their ability to remain independent. Declining abilities may mean a person needs to leave their home, and move into a nursing home, something which people wish to avoid. Their findings relate to previous work which has shown a link between the meaning of data and use of a system [11, 144]. Older adults also demonstrated abandonment of technology which they found stigmatizing. Finally, the authors make the interesting point that perhaps as designers we could look toward monitoring instances which have more positive connotations as way of increasing adherence and positive connection [78].

A second element of digital and ageing is the use of Interactive Digital Health Interventions (DHIs), which are interventions that improve health more broadly and are delivered digitally [118]. DHIs are designed collaboratively across interdisciplinary teams from HCI (including software engineering) and health (including people in biomedical sciences and psychologists). DHIs have traditionally been developed through clinical environments and care pathways and have therefore been evaluated accordingly drawing heavily on these evaluation methods. In a recent publication which explored lessons learned from interdisciplinary research on DHIs, Blandford et al. [54] explain how this clinical derivation has led to the view among health researchers and policy makers that development of a DHI is a one-off cycle which results in a product which should then be evaluated for effectiveness through a randomized control trial (RCT). This is despite research demonstrating the power of and need to iteratively design (e.g., Klasanja et al. [216] and Yardley et al. [437]). The authors also highlight the issues inherent in working across disciplines when developing DHIs with an exploration of the separate understandings of the term "implementation." For HCI researchers this means the development of the solution; for health there is a science of implementation which is known to overcome the second translation gap and get the DHI into practice. Blandford et al. [54] urge us toward a common understanding of both perspectives, and indeed for HCI researchers this could be a useful endeavor as in understanding the second translation gap and researching around this area we would be able to close a loop within the ABC approach to research; researching the applied problem—implementation into practice, to help derive new basic research questions for future DHI's.

The seven lessons proposed by Blandford et al. demonstrate the differences between HCI and Health. Within HCI establishing the state of the art is usually done in a more opportunistic way, as researchers gather and organize relevant literature to support the exploration of a particular research question. Development lifecycles are usually based on an iterative approach that leverages evaluation of new artifacts to unearth more opportunities for other novel technologies and inter-actions. Methodologically we design iteratively, and end users are our primary experts. We focus on developing computer systems and implement before evaluation; our methodologies are adapted from many disciplines, and we have an ethical practice derived from individual rights. Finally, our publications focus on basic research and credible papers are between 6,000 and 10,000 words. In contrast within health the state of the art is systematically assessed. Lifecycles are iterative but focus on impact from development to large-scale implementation, clinicians are often the primary experts, and implementation has a heavy focus on large-scale roll out. Evaluation is dominated by RCTs and focuses on effects of interventions; ethical practices are highly regulated and focus on preventing harm. Finally, results can be presented in several ways from case notes to opinion pieces with most papers under 4,000 words [54]. In preparing this contrast Blandford also develops the necessary elements of successful DHI development—it must satisfy both communities; and when this happens more patients are better served. From a DIX perspective, this speaks to value and usefulness, co-creation of solutions with all stakeholders, and open and scalable solutions. These are also necessary in the third element we felt worthy of discussing in this section—Telehealth.

Telehealth is the provision and management of healthcare in which individuals and their families manage aspects of their care with remote support from healthcare professionals [55]. A recent cross-sectional analysis of telehealth in a single U.S. institution found an increased number of telehealth appointments as people aged, however the likelihood of full audio-visual encounters decreased for people over the age of 45 and then again for over the age of 65 and instead relied on audio only [304], pointing to a lack of infrastructure and accessibility of services. These challenges and opportunities telehealth during and beyond the pandemic were explored more generally in a recent *Lancet* commentary [55]. In this review the authors note how the pandemic has forced healthcare providers and individuals to turn toward telehealth practices to reduce physical contact within workplace settings [55]. The authors highlight how this offers the opportunities for tele-health from wearables for remote monitoring of patient symptoms to remote consultations via text messages. However, they also note the risks inherent in telehealth. Telehealth requires a level of digital infrastructure and literacy which may not be equally present in a community. A recent re-view of assistive technology services found that COVID-19 disrupted the delivery of AT services, primarily due to infection control measures resulting in lack of provider availability and diminished one-to-one services [359]. The under-investment in telehealth and in the ability of people to use telehealth services was outlined in this COVID-19 AT study which concluded a need for stronger user-centered development of funding policies and infrastructures that are more sustainable and resilient alongside the development of best practices for remote service delivery; robust and accessible tools and systems [359].

The recognition for more robust and inclusive telehealth services is an opportunity for HCI more broadly, and DIX specifically in ensuring these services are accessible to all people regardless of ability. Developing solutions which cater to older populations will be critical to the success of future interventions.

6.3 ASSISTIVE TECHNOLOGY IN HEALTH SYSTEMS AS A COMBINATION OF PRODUCTS AND SERVICES

We now move to "technology" as defined by the WHO, because in collaboration with health professionals and policy makers we need to understand their language in the assistive product and service space. Traditionally assistive products (wheelchairs, pill organizers, hearing aids, etc.) were provided to people through clinical or educational settings with specialists assessing the user, selecting the product, and then providing training for use. This service, combined with the products and the policy and provision systems are together termed "technology."

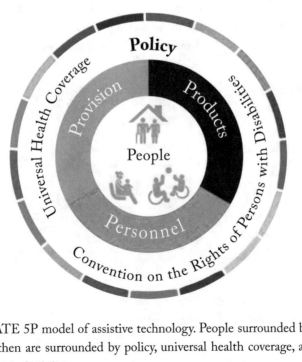

Figure 6.1: WHO GATE 5P model of assistive technology. People surrounded by products, personnel, and provision, which then are surrounded by policy, universal health coverage, and the convention on the rights of persons with disabilities.

To improve access to AT the WHO's flagship program—the Global Cooperation on Assistive Technology (GATE) has developed the people-centered, AT framework which describes the need to improve access across 5P's framework [209]. This framework, which we briefly introduced in Chapter 2, is drawn from the UNCRPD and is reproduced in Figure 6.1. At the center are the people who use the AT and their support network. To ensure people get access to AT it is also critical to have global and national policy, with associated data collection and financing structures to ensure makes high-quality AT is affordable to all citizens [462]. One important way to do that is Universal Health Coverage (UHC), which is increasingly considering AT. Such a policy must be person centric. A person-centered approach—in keeping with a human rights-based approach—is essential to ensuring products match user-needs and are used [107].

The GATE exists to advocate for and provide evidence to advance AT provision globally, and specifically through Universal Health Care. One of the first initiatives of GATE was to advance the Assistive Technology priority Assistive Product List (APL) which is equivalent to the WHOs essential medicines list [416]. The list was the starting point of GATE attempting to standardize what Nation states should provide as a base minimum for its citizens living with disabilities to fulfil their human rights. Moreover, the APL has also been instrumental in producing guidance in areas such as wheelchair services in low resource settings—[463]. These guidelines were set via consensus to prevent inferior quality products being given to people (e.g., devices which were dangerous, would break easily, or were given with little or no training rendering them all but useless). The 5Ps map shown in Figure 6.2 shows the identified list of barriers that prevent the successful scaling of assistive technology.

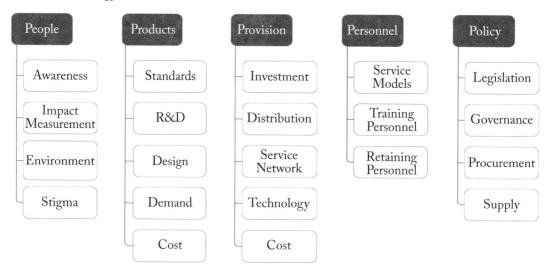

Figure 6.2: Barriers for AT provision across the WHO's 5Ps, taken from Holloway et al. 2018 [179].

Assistive products and services are themselves healthcare technologies and, as Blandford so eloquently captured, there is a paradox in healthcare technologies, where those which seem to scale are often difficult to use, whereas more user-friendly, innovative interaction technologies often struggle to scale up to be fully inclusive [55]. Assistive products and services are, in many ways, affected by the same issues. Why is this? A clue lies in the complexity of healthcare systems which are highly regulated and require approaches that go beyond the focus on user centered and iterative methods employed in HCI research [240]. Through the comparison of approaches between HCI and healthcare technology research, Blandford concludes the following relevant insights [55]: (1) the scale and complexity of health is a challenge for HCI; (2) to have impact at scale HCI needs to work across disciplines; (3) health and wellbeing technologies need to fit both the individual and care contexts; (4) there is a role for digital interfaces as a mediator between the technology and the individual; and (5) the role of data across its lifecycle to help from an individual to a population level. These insights apply equally to DIX and health.

Assistive products and services are increasingly leveraging digital interactions in many fundamental areas, so much so that the WHO has explicitly mentioned digital in the launch of its latest initiative DATA—Digital and Assistive Technologies for Ageing [209]. This acknowledges the increasingly blurred divide between what is an accessible technology and an assistive product. Given this increasingly blurred boundaries which also lie between accessible and ATs on one side, and the rise of emerging technologies which augment and push the limits of human ability on the other (see some of the examples of Radically Different interactions we made in Chapter 3), there is a need for HCI professionals to understand the world of assistive products and healthcare, so that they can more easily work across interdisciplinary teams.

As mentioned earlier, The WHO has developed a priority assistive product list (APL) to help guide countries on which technologies should be made available to all citizens. They undertook this process to mirror the Essential Medicines List, which was developed to help countries prioritize medicines which are essential to the health of a nation, thereby focusing demand on these products and subsequently lowering the cost of items as countries would secure budgets and procure larger quantities of medicines on the list. The essential medicines list has been highly successful [17].

The assistive products which made it onto the APL are shown in Table 6.1. In this table we have divided products into those which still remain primarily assistive products (such as a wheelchair), and ones which have, since the list was created in 2006, been partially met by accessible solutions, i.e., solutions that are available from outside specific healthcare provision (such as a screen reader). This demonstrates the shift from assistive technology to accessible technologies.

Table 6.1: WHO APL digital products divided into those which remain APs and those which since 2006 have been partially met by accessible solutions (note we have not mapped global positioning systems as this is a fundamental technology, and where a product cuts across domains we have included it twice)

Domain	Assistive Products	Partially Met by Accessible Solutions
Vision	Braille displays Braillers (writing) Deafblind communicators	Audio players with DAISY capability Keyboard and mouse emulation software Magnifiers, digital hand-held Screen readers Travel aids, portable Watches, talking/touching
Hearing	Deafblind communicators Hearing loops/FM systems	Closed captioning displays Hearing aids (digital) and batteries Video communication devices
Mobility	Fall detectors	Keyboard and mouse emulation software
Communication	Personal emergency alarm systems	Communication software Gesture to voice technology Personal digital assistant (PDA) Recorders Simplified mobile phones Video communication devices
Cognitive	Time management products	Watches, talking/touching

6.4   FROM THE WHO TO HCI

In the future we see many more traditional AT types being replaced, in part or in full, by mainstream technology which are accessible and more useable by everyone or by technologies that merge characteristics of both mainstream and specialized assistive devices. HCI has already started to develop these technologies. Some examples of this is the integration of wearable technology in traditional wheelchairs, which have evolved into "chairables" devices transforming the input and output modalities of powered wheelchairs [83]. Another example has emerged through the development of "Ultimate Prosthetic Wearables" as prosthetic limbs have been connected to the Internet of Personal health [422]. These demonstrate a convergence between AT and mainstream emerging inclusive technology.

The DIY-AT movement has also demonstrated the HCI-style take on digital fabrication in health which encompasses empowerment, user choice, and acceptability and ultimately shows a shift in power from the designer toward the user. In 2010, at Nordic CHI, Kuznestov and Paulos [219] explored the rise of the Expert Amateur in DIY projects, Communities, and Cultures. Shortly after this call-to-action Hurst and Tobias [185] explored the empowerment of individuals through DIY-AT. Through case study examples they note how the increased control over design combined with user passion and a need to control costs drive engagement of users in DIY-AT [219]. Hurst evolved this thinking with Kane in 2013 [184], setting out a position paper on DIY AT which combined rapid prototyping and online communities as core parts of this new approach to AT design and manufacture. The first allowing rapid realization of ideas, the second allowing ease of sharing ideas and connecting to expertise and advice. Since then, a number of case study examples have emerged, for example Buehler et al. developed 3D-oriented grips for accessibility and Hamidi et al. and developed a communication board by a "citizen designer" [159].

Digital fabrication has also been used by Hofmann and colleagues to explore the requirements for a prototyping methodology for upper-limb prosthetic users [176]. The nuance here is the use of 3D printing and playful prototyping as a method rather than the end result, allowing us as HCI researchers to use digital fabrication and crafting methods to explore the possible [219]. This playful approach is perhaps in contrast with the more serious methods of design used within medical practice. These tensions between the "do not harm" approach of clinicians, and the do something better than before approach of makers was explored by Hofmann and colleagues using the case of upper limb prosthetics [175]. The tension was multi-layered—makers appeared chaotic and trying to fix a multitude of AT problems with the promise of digital fabrication when viewed by clinicians. The prosthetists who took part in the study were very concerned about end effectors of prosthetics causing death when applied to high-risk situations, like a device that enables a person to surf while at the same time wishing the end effector to be the main focus of maker activity—leaving the socket, which is the section of the prostheses that interfaces with the residual limb of the user, for more experienced experts. The skin-prosthesis interface is a very complicated area which gets hot and sweaty and can cause skin damage and fit issues for prosthesis users [423]. One of the ideas that emerged from Hofmann's study [175] was to embed sensors within prosthetic devices through digital manufacture was one area prosthetists felt there were good opportunities for collaboration, especially to aid monitoring and reducing abandonment issues. Interestingly, another recent study trialed the use of wearable sensors to monitor thermal comfort, demonstrating it was possible to measure thermal comfort in-the-wild [423].

We end this section with a brief look at function and value. The WHO developed the International Classification of Functioning (ICF) to apply the bio-phyco-social model of disability within health and healthcare. This focus on functioning is a crucial design principle within the clinical space. Improving functioning is the key aim and driver. However, in HCI research we are seeing an emergence of broader concepts such as usefulness and value, which are differently stated by the users. Bennett, for example, has shown that prostheses users valued their upper-limbs, which were designed and manufactured locally with makers, even when they functionally failed [39]. The users were accepting toward failure because they cared about the positive impact the community-led culture was having, and the feeling of community that the making of these devices was helping to build. These benefits may seem paradoxical compared to the "normal" prioritization of function [39]. However, these findings are also supported in a recent study of digital manufacture of wheelchairs in Kenya—being locally produced, with direct inputs of the users, induced values of agency, empowerment ,and self-expression which went beyond the function of the wheelchair. These tensions will continue as HCI designers we will continue to use new technologies to open dialogue, create methods of discovery and new interaction experiences for people with assistive devices. We now turn toward how we promote psychological wellbeing within the DIX framework.

6.5   PROMOTING PSYCHOLOGICAL WELLBEING

Mental illness is a global challenge. Globally, more than 264 million people live with depression. Another 45 million people are bipolar and 20 million people globally have schizophrenia [195]. Nearly all people affected by emergencies, such as conflicts and natural disasters, will experience psychological distress and 22% of people living in a conflict will have one of depression, anxiety, post-traumatic stress disorder, bipolar disorder, or schizophrenia [418]. Within a technology context, we are now seeing new ways of detecting people's mood, for example social media posts are a good indicator more broadly of a person's mood [142] this can then be used to better monitor population health by institutes such as the U.S. Center for Disease Control [79]. Although this type of intervention can help show patterns at a population level, it is important to note that mood tracking through social media is not necessarily a positive thing. There is now the ability to measure stress from a simple smartphone camera [88] and indeed there is now a flourishing field of "mobile mental health" [286]. There is a burgeoning number of mobile applications being developed to support mental health, however, this is not matched with rigorous validation and testing of applications [286]. Some exceptions exist, such as for the newly developed m-health applications for PTSD for example. However, such examples are relatively few and far between. Furthermore, research in HCI for mental health can sometimes underplay the complexity of managing a mental health condition. Furthermore, research is often more heavily focused on the Global North, ignoring the problems faced by people in the Global South [300]. We explore these issues in turn before exploring psychological wellbeing more broadly.

Managing a mental illness is complex and people often rely on an ecosystem of technologies to support their wellness and manage their condition [72]. However, researchers often focus on a single tool or service reducing a study to a component, for example an online community or a mobile application. This fails to account for the diversity of interactions across systems, which prevail in managing a complex health condition. To help develop more comprehensive frameworks of understanding the space of mental health technology, the authors of a recent think piece therefore purpose the idea of technology ecosystems [72]. Such ecosystems would go across tool types and the social interactions which pervade these [72]. The workshop which produced the think piece dedicated significant time to research methods, acknowledging the need for mixed-methods and the need for more longitudinal studies across ecosystems rather than a temporal snapshot [72]. This thinking aligns with the DIX principles.

During the COVID-19 pandemic, a high number of COVID-19 patients had experienced high levels of post-traumatic stress symptoms and increased levels of depression. Moreover, psychiatric symptoms were present in many healthcare workers, and that the general public had reduced psychological well-being [410]. Mental ill-health is becoming so pervasive that in the United States it affects nearly half of all adults [207]. COVID-19 has also had significant impact on mental health services, with almost instantaneous switches from in-person care to technology-mediated services; which has raised challenges for both the service user and providers [72]. Challenges such as finding more difficult-to-build rapports with others or hold people accountable, were raised in a recent workshop, as well as the simple challenge of remaining attentive online [72]. The workshop concluded with a list of components of a mental health ecosystem which could be further researched by HCI community, these were: user goals, life stage, health management systems and scale [ibid.]. Discussions around scale were centered around questions examining approaches that focused on measuring individuals versus having larger units of analysis such as all platform users, or all people in a city. Developing this concept of scale within research is interesting from a DIX perspective as we might be able to use larger data sets to then provide more personalized insights while also generating data which could help service providers better provide budgets for adequate services provision for a population.

Pendse and colleagues [300] explore the challenges and opportunities for HCI for development (HCI4D) in engaging in mental health. The review demonstrates the complexity of mental health experiences in the Global South, which necessitates a nuanced approach to engagement. They demonstrate the importance of HCI4D in considering mental health and give a set of advice for best practice. Some are simply best practice for any setting, for example: the role of diagnostic interviews as the gold-standard for formally diagnosing someone with a mental illness [127] and that self-report scales can be used to understand symptoms of mental distress [105]. However, some have very specific relevance to the global South, such as: culture-based interactions which take account of cultural norms in how people might express distress and resource-based interactions which takes into consideration the role of stigma [ibid.]. Finally, they also highlight the use of the SRQ-20, a scale validated by the WHO for use in a wide variety of contexts including LMICs, which can detect psychiatric symptoms and mental distress, including potential somatic symptoms of mental illness [415].

6.6   THE ROLE OF DIX IN HEALTH

We examine the role of DIX and health through two case studies. The first looks at mobile tools which can scale to produce data actionable at multiple levels from user to population levels. The second looks at an assistive product—a new customizable active wheelchair which demonstrates an approach to co-creation, value, and usefulness upon which we can build technologies which can scale. A video of the wheelchair being used in the streets of India can be found here: Video of Neo-Fly-NeoBolt. More than ever there are opportunities for HCI researchers to partner with Health colleagues and explore new possibilities for shared goals—could we develop wearable and chairable sensors to help map the streets of India, as was demonstrated possible in a previous piece of work [86]. Could these sensors be used to give personalized feedback to wheelchair users on how to push their wheelchair to prevent upper limb injuries [85], or biofeedback to relieve stress [171] when pushing in a busy city like Delhi. All these things we know are technically possible, but are challenging to implement in practice and scale. However, if successfully scaled and implemented such solution could help relieve pressure on stretched healthcare services, could be delivered remotely and would allow the person to feel in control of their training.

Case Study AT2030: Measuring Need through Population Health Data and Screening Tools

Jamie Danemayer

The problem: Measurement of unmet need, met need, and under-met need (occurring when a person's AT is broken or inappropriate for their needs) is essential data in planning services for people with disabilities. Yet despite the tools described above, global AT need data are lacking, as identified by a background scoping review for the first WHO's and UNICEF's first World Report on Assistive Technology [98] conducted by the AT2030 program. Building on this need, a follow-up systematic review utilizing the same corpus, highlighted how functional domains are not equally represented in the literature; nearly 80% of studies identified in the systematic review inform all or in part on glasses. We have a more limited understanding of population-level need where AT need assessments, and/or the relationship between a disability and an assistive product are more complex (such as mobility or cognitive functional domains); data sets for mobility device needs, communication aids, tools to help people with autism or mental health issues are almost non-existent. Unmet need for APs was found to be high in all country income contexts, yet studies varied considerably; most studies utilizing centralized health record systems were set in high-income countries, and these data sources are not universally available. Though most studies identified in both reviews originate from LMICs, the vast majority are cross-sectional, and the evidence basis decreases rapidly when narrowing to country- or device-specific findings. This indicates our knowledge gaps are widest where coverage and access are the most limited. Large, population-based surveys can be time and resource-intensive and may not produce the timely data needed by policymakers.

Value and Usefulness, Open and Scalable: Emerging tools, based mostly on mobile phones, have been developed to support individual assistive technology need assessment. For example, Peek Vision is a smartphone-based visual acuity (VA) test, which replaces the equivalent paper-based vision assessment. However, the Peek Vision tool extends beyond screening and provides a data-driven systems approach to vision health. This allows for customizations and individualized health care plans for the user, with integrated text message reminders that have demonstrated a two-fold increase in attendance at follow-up appointments of children [327]. For healthcare providers and policy makers, Peek's data allows population-level analysis of need to identify and plan care pathways and services [266]. In the hearing domain, a similar approach is used by HearX, who are currently trialing the rollout of a smartphone-based hearing loss screening tool, an affordable hearing aid, and WhatsApp-based support tool [23]. Again, the intervention works at multiple levels and necessitates the consideration of multiple dynamics: for the user and devices, clinician and devices, and the clinician and the user. This approach also begins to look at the role of online communities, which again links back to the opportunities for HCI and health and wellbeing by Blandford [52]. Both Peek Vision and HearX produce data that is useful beyond simply growing their products and services; they can help inform policy through a nuanced understanding of population-level need.

There is then work to be done by HCI researchers with the emerging data collection tools and novel data sources to maximize learnings in this sector. How can we best aggregate and share data insights to policy makers so that they are actionable and fair? How can better integrate data-driven models of care within communities and increase provision of services? What role could communities of practice have in capturing community-level data sets? What role might there be for ubiquitous monitoring of abilities to help drive data collection? How can we turn all of the resulting information into what Rogers describes as "actionable information" [80]. A starting point for this work is the global mapping and data dashboard being created through AT2030, which will automate insights with the help of a collaboration between the UNESCO Center for AI and UCL's WHO Collaborating Center on AT based at the GDI Hub.

Case Study: The NeoFly-NeoBolt System, Enabling Seamless Indoor-Outdoor Mobility for Wheelchair Users

Sujatha Srinivasan

NeoFly is the first India-designed customizable, active wheelchair that provides comfort, superior ergonomics, maneuverability in cramped spaces, and efficient propulsion. NeoBolt is a motorized attachment that converts NeoFly into a road-worthy vehicle that can travel at a maximum speed of 25 km/hr and traverse any kind of uneven terrain normally encountered. NeoFly and NeoBolt have been commercialized by NeoMotion, a startup from the TTK Center for Rehabilitation Research and Device Development (R2D2), IIT Madras, based on the GRID collaboration model [373].

The Problem: There are over 300,000 wheelchairs sold in India per year, of which 250,000 are imported. The most commonly used wheelchair is a one-size-fits-all cheap model, which results in postural problems, restricted mobility, and low self-confidence. Traveling longer distances to participate in the community or be gainfully employed requires transfer to a tricycle, a triscooter (a modified scooter), or a car, but this is difficult to accomplish, unsafe and limiting for most wheelchair users to do independently. NeoMotion (neomotion.in) was set up with the goal of making quality mobility devices accessible and affordable to the vast majority of wheelchair users in India currently confined to their homes.

Applied and Basic Research Combined, Radically Different Interactions: Based on innovative design and robust engineering at R2D2, NeoBolt can be attached within ten seconds independently by the NeoFly user, enabling safe outdoor mobility, where the user can travel 25 km on a single charge. When the user reaches their destination, they can detach NeoBolt within seconds and continue on indoors with their NeoFly, which is designed with a small footprint for better access to cramped spaces. The original plan was to have NeoBolt attach to any wheelchair, but initial trials showed that none of the available manual wheelchairs were durable enough to handle extended outdoor mobility. This led to the design of a better wheelchair overall—NeoFly, with customizations for better fit, ergonomics, a rigid frame for active propulsion and cushion design for comfort and stability. In a country like India where infrastructural access is limiting and challenging, the NeoFly-NeoBolt system attempts to radically change the accessibility narrative by enabling greater community and economic participation.

Co-Created Solutions: NeoFly and NeoBolt were developed over three design iterations between 2016 and 2018 (see Figure 6.3). The devices were tested by 400+ wheelchair users before release, in addition to mechanical tests as per ISO 7176 standards. The inclusive design of NeoBolt accommodates Indian attire across genders. The system incorporates customization of 18 features to suit the user's health and lifestyle. The collaborative GRID model (see Figure 6.2) enabled the successful translation to market of complex hardware products for a startup with otherwise limited resources and capital.

Figure 6.3: GRID partners for NeoFly-NeoBolt development: G-grants, R-research, I-industry, D-dissemination

Value and Usefulness, Open and Scalable: Enabling a bespoke design while retaining the advantages of mass manufacturing ensures affordability. Use of the GRID model for Research, Development and Translation has helped keep the all-told price of the system under GBP 1000, less than half of the average cost of a motorized wheelchair with similar specifications. This was achieved thanks to the collaboration between funding agencies that supported the initial development, research institution that provided design expertise, users that guided the design process and industry which supported the manufacturing and distribution. An innovative process of remote assessment and fitting (called NeoFit) enables the entire customization to be done online so that the user gets a personalized system at their doorstep. EMI and credit options are available for purchase to enhance accessibility. A toolkit is shipped with each wheelchair/system, spare parts are shipped when necessary, and much of the maintenance can be done by the users themselves with video instructions/support over video calls, greatly empowering them and reducing down time. As a result, despite the pandemic, the startup has shipped over 600 units over the last year (when they began operations) across 27 states in India. An example user is Shailesh—see Figure 6.4. The goal now is to scale-up for impact not just locally, but globally.

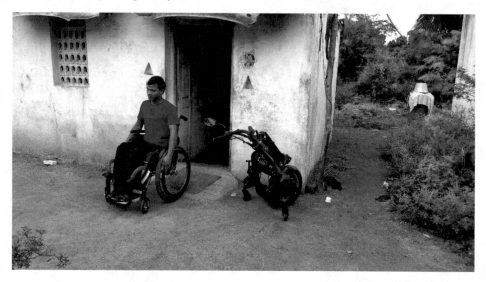

Figure 6.4: User Shailesh, hailing from a small village, is now the fastest wheelchair half-marathoner in India, on a NeoFly and uses a NeoBolt to traverse the rough terrain around him (empower in cramped spaces and rough terrain).

6.7   CONCLUSION

Through this chapter we have explored DIX in relation to health and healthcare. In doing this we have looked at how policy makers value products and services, helped to unpack the language and differences between HCI and Health, and looked to explore examples of how DIX can be used within health and healthcare. Much investment is needed to make mainstream services accessible to people with disabilities and to create AT that are able to meet the diversity of needs of people with impairment from people who are older and don't identify as disabled, to people who will need specific technology all of their lives such as hearing aids, wheelchairs, and prosthetic limbs. The opportunity for HCI designers and researchers is to become work closely with experts in the field of Health as well as with the people who can scale interventions, allowing us to be part of the basic and applied research cycles and ensuring our excellent design work is used by as many people as possible. We might also need to help make the case for AT, we are a rich source of wonderful case studies which should be known by policy makers and investors globally.

CHAPTER 7

Future Disability Interactions

The UNESCO defines Future Literacy as a universally accessible capability that "allows people to better understand the role of the future in what they see and do. Being futures literate empowers the imagination, enhances our ability to prepare, recover and invent as changes occur" [183]. At their core, the Future Literacy Laboratory and its related initiatives are built around the idea that is essential for people to be able to dream and imagine futures that can inspire hope. These aspirations for the future represent the key for acting in the present as we work to shape the future that we dream for the world [385]. We use this as inspiration as we take a crystal ball to the future of disability interactions.

We are imagining a world in which the stigma and sense of burden associated with disability is left behind, replaced with an emergence of acceptance and opportunity of multiple possibilities for each human, aided by technology. We take, in short, a utopian view. This view will see a closer collaboration between the Arts and HCI, blurring of lines across what is and isn't an assistive technology or even what is disability. Within this world, HCI will be designing disability interactions are often invisible, but also bold and brilliant when wanted.

Within our utopian new world, our ability to make sense of our world, the third paradigm of HCI, will be increasingly in collaboration with technology. Agentive technologies will help process the increasing amounts of data, multisensory experiences will be possibly equalizing and enhancing differences between individual human abilities, and we will work collaboratively with robots and intelligent machines, sharing tasks and control. Our abilities to create will become boundless, as we live and move in mixed and enhanced realities supported by agents that magnify our capabilities. As this future unfolds, it will have as much to do with how we allow it to unfold as well as how fast technology advances. How we allow it to unfold will have two parts: the **operational** and the **conceptual** [282]. In his book on agentive technology, Noessel explains how at the operational level we will be looking to apply new technologies to the right problems at the right time [282]. On the other hand, at the conceptual level, we will need to reevaluate our role in the world and our relationship to the technology we create and use [282]. If we unpack the conceptual a step further—we can imagine how we will have challenged both our identity as individuals as well as our identity as a species. Our thoughts about what is or isn't human will be challenged, and the ethics of what should be allowed to be decided by technology or human weighted and debated.

We look at this future through three emerging trends: (1) AI and agentive technologies; (2) robot-human collaborations; and (3) mixed realities. We examine these trends in the near future, to identify things we can make use of now to sculpt the steps toward fully disability-inclusive societies.

We then conclude the chapter with a peek toward the possibilities for DIX in 50–100 years times. And then we bid you goodbye and good luck on your DIX journey.

7.1 AI AND AGENTIVE TECHNOLOGIES

> *"...the conjecture that every aspect of learning or any other feature of intelligence can in principle be so precisely described that a machine can be made to simulate it"*—1956 Dartmouth Conference, the birth of Artificial Intelligence.

Artificial Intelligence was birthed in 1956 by a group of leaders who came to discuss the basic "conjecture that every aspect of learning or any other feature of intelligence can in principle be so precisely described that a machine can be made to simulate it." In the grant proposal which funded the conference the term artificial intelligence was first used [217]. Since this time, the definition has expanded to include: "computational understanding of what is commonly called intelligent behavior, and with the creation of artifacts that exhibit such behavior" [341]. Agentive technologies do not always make use of AI, but increasingly they do—and this trend is one we wish to follow.

The use cases for agentive technologies are vast. Let's start our exploration from the increasingly popular voice assistants which are now embedded into many homes, for example Amazon Alexa, or Google Home. These smart speakers wait for us to speak to them and then use our voice commands to provide a service to use. These are often in the form of information requests or simple actions like turning up or down music, making a note of something or answering a call. These types of interaction are transactional—they have a specific purpose or goal. In comparison, social conversational elements of a conversation have more to do with positive reinforcement of social bonds [92]. Generally, most people see agents as useful to help with transactional tasks [92].

Given their non-visual, hands-free interaction mode, agents are particularly useful to people with limited ability to interact via touch or sight. People who are blind or who have partial vision are exceptionally adept at using conversational agents [232]; HCI researchers have explored the usability, use cases and future of agents like these with people with and without sight. Abdolrahmani and colleagues recently completed a study which cast a glimpse to the next generation of transactional agents for both blind and non-blind people [2]. Their setting was airports. The challenges faced by all users were due to structural complexities of accessing real-time information and navigating the airport. Multimodal transactional interactions are recommended in future agents to meet the overlapping needs of blind and sighted airport users [2]. However, there will be other use cases where the social elements of conversation are also needed, for example built into companion moments. As these agents become more commonplace and are able to work for a range of abilities, we will see more use cases derived from populations of disabled people who offer unique use cases which then drive the agentive advances further than would have been necessary without designing with the inclusion of this population, in turn making the mainstream technologies more robust and accessible.

Interestingly and as an aside, airports in the UK were upgraded significantly in both technology and policy for people with disabilities in occasion of the London 2012 Olympic and Paralympic Games. Prior to 2012, wheelchair users, for example, would have to be pushed through the airport by a companion or an attendant. Of course, this was not a feasible approach during the 2012 games, could you imagine asking a Paralympian to sit still while they were pushed through an airport for their own safety?!? This was one of the many structural barriers to inclusion which were dismantled as part of the Paralympic Games and its legacy and is mentioned here to highlight how as large events such as the Olympics can be excellent places for resistance to inclusion to be tested, and technology can play a role in achieving this. Perhaps even more interesting was the need for disability-community-led innovation throughout the design of the Games, which is what managed to make it so accessible [24]. An example of this was the creation of an independent Built Environment Access Panel comprising people with different disabilities who will be in charge of reviewing all the development work in the Queen Elizabeth Olympic Park. The panel was equipped with an unprecedented veto power to ensure that they could stop any development on the ground that was deemed inaccessible to people with disabilities [ibid.].

Going back to AI, according to the newly launched International Research Center for Artificial Intelligence (IRCAI), which was setup under the auspices of UNESCO, artificial intelligence (AI) presents opportunities to both enhance AT and to improve access to AT [16]. A recent policy review from IRCAI states computational advancement in vision, speech recognition and spatial guidance will all aid new product developments [16]. However, for these to make a real impact for people with disabilities there is a need for policy makers to fully understand the scale of opportunity of both AI and AT to transform lives [16]. What this means for HCI researchers is not only is there a need to understand the user needs but also to be able to translate the opportunity right up to policy makers. This need for working across scales from the detailed design to the implementation is one of the "Eight Design Tenets for Emerging Technologies" [128].

AI is already powering a vast number of technologies for people with disability. These often rely on computational vision to identify, interpret, and transform images and visual information into speech such as Seeing AI which will interpret a variety of scenes [464]. Frequently people with disabilities are quick to adopt and use technologies to enhance their lives. However, relatively few studies have worked with people with disabilities to explore the design of emerging technologies. Those which have (e.g., [268, 35]), found there is a need to understand the social context of people's lived experience. This social context has been expressed in the desire to contribute to experience planning, realization and reflection by BPSP when reflecting on how they are currently able to interact with natural environments [28]. AI is also allowing us to better understand our mental wellbeing. Physiological computing for example is allowing us to measure stress responses using low-cost thermal cameras to monitor a person's breath [88] or even a smartphone camera [89]. This opens the door for technologies which could sense and then adapt to stress levels which would be of benefit to people with anxiety as well as people who use assistive products who may require more or less assistance due to the context.

Case Study: Google Euphonia, Supporting People with Impaired Speech to be Better Understood
Richard Cave

For people whose speech is difficult for others to understand, face-to-face communication can be very challenging. Using voice-activated technologies such as Google Assistant or Google Home can also be frustrating. These tools enable people to use their voice to adjust lighting, send a text, get directions, play music, and thousands of other uses. For people with physical or mobility limitations, using voice to better control their environment could be particularly helpful, however this technology does not work well for people with impaired speech. At the same time, voice interaction with devices is becoming ubiquitous: by 2024, it is forecast people will be able to interact with over 8.4 billion devices using their voice—larger than the world's population. As voice interaction with devices becomes more normalized, individuals with impaired speech increasingly risk being excluded from these current, commercially available technologies—even though they could benefit extensively. At a societal level, inequality in access to technology risks increasing the "digital divide," potentially increasing social exclusion. Investigation in academic and market literature showed that although many groups have tried to address this problem, limited progress has been made.

Euphonia is a Google research project and uses voice samples from many thousands of contributors who have impaired speech to train a speech recognition model, opening the possibility more equal access to voice activated technology. Additionally, Euphonia may provide near-real time transcription of impaired speech as it is spoken in daily conversation. This may support better listener understanding as a conversation unfolds.

People who live with impaired speech have been involved throughout each stage of Euphonia ideation and development to contribute their ideas, help with design, try prototypes, and give feedback on how Euphonia actually works in their daily conversations. In this way it is hoped that Euphonia will provide significant and practical benefit for people living with impaired speech in daily life.

Figure 7.1: Google Euphonia user who has ALS/MND.

As shown in the previous case study and in the numerous examples presented in this section, AI and other technologies can have a tremendously positive impact on the lives of persons with disabilities, we also need to remember that they carry inherent risks to exacerbate existing inequalities [262, 414]. In a survey exploring the awareness of AI-related ethics that involved computer science students across various U.S. programs, Williams et al. [428] highlighted how many participants had some level of awareness about risks of racist and classist bias in the context of AI, but little knowledge about ableism. Moreover, although students were able to recognize risks related to the use of biased datasets to guide AI decisions in relation to medical practice, they rarely questioned the purpose of the AI in itself, even when it was used as a tool for medical discrimination [ibid.]. Similarly, Keyes [208] explores two separate examples including the research surrounding the use of AI for autism diagnosis and the practices of companies that employ autistic people for data labeling tasks, to illustrate how the problematic aspects of these AI-related contexts come from the ideas of autistic people as either medicalized and problematic or as robot-like individuals. These misconceptions have little to do with the technology itself or the representativeness of the datasets used for specific algorithms, but lay in deep rooted ableist ideas in society itself [208]

Overall, AI has extreme potential to be a transformational force for disability inclusion, but to realize it we need to become more aware and accountable of its ability to amplify existing bias and inequalities. This requires researchers and technologists to become more inclusive in our development practices, implementing collaborative and bottom-up approaches that promote accountability and critical thinking from a wide variety of perspectives.

7.2   MULTISENSORY EXPERIENCES AND MIXED REALITIES

In Chapter 3, we explored the idea of augmenting or promoting new human abilities and the ability for devices to translate our senses. We explore this idea further here, taking it toward the augmented human.

Recent advances in sensor technology that allows us to sense smell open up possibilities for scent-assisted learning. This might seem futuristic, but this recent paper demonstrated the possibilities. Building on the work of Kaye [198], who demonstrated the ability of olfactory sensation to trigger the limbic system, which is responsible for emotional responses and memories, the researchers developed an AromaCue scent-based toolkit to help people cope with stressful situations [228]. AromaCue contains a breathing training device which mixes visual and olfactory stimuli to aid a relaxation response and a wearable scent-emitting system that sends aroma cues to simulate this conditioned (deep breathing) response [228]. The olfactory conditioning paradigm was developed and proved useful in reducing stress [228]. What if we could capture and share smells, in the way we do photos, what if smells could be added to navigation aids around cities? And what if we could translate the senses?

Though sensory substitution devices (SSDs) we have the opportunity to encode information normally associated with one sense through another sense, allowing people with sensory deficiencies to experience things which are otherwise not possible to experience. This type of work represents an opportunity to design radically different types of interaction. An example of this type of work has been undertaken by Hamilton-Fletcher et al. [160], who investigated the designs of SSDs to enable people with visual impairments to experience vision-related functions. Starting from the point of view of developing vision-substitution devices for this population, the authors are careful to explore what this means both in terms of HCI methods and also the wider conceptual problems. For example, what would people with visual impairments like to experience in terms of vision-functionality?

We now move to the world of the extended human and mixed realities. In recent work, auras have been projected into the real world to act as a communication bridge between pedestrians [443]. Building on the observation that walking with pets aid communication with strangers [435:005], the researchers build a prototype projection of a person's aura e.g., waves or bubbles which projected onto a person's feet as they walked. Auras could interact with one another when people stopped to speak, and they changed interaction dynamics between people [443]. This idea of mixed realities and connection was also explored by artist Jason Wilshire-Mills in his interactive Brave Boy Billy sculpture (see Figure 7.2), which is inspired by children who use wheelchairs experience of disability. The artwork is littered with badges which when scanned with a mobile application come alive—you can see for example dancing chromosomes flutter over Bad Boy Billy as you hear a story of how a chromosomal condition has influenced a young girl's life. The artwork was commissioned for the first Global Disability Innovation Summit held in London in 2017. During the summit the artwork inspired a conversation between one of the speakers, a young BBC producer who identifies as neurodiverse, and the artist as she realized the artwork inspired a thought—could she have dancing dinosaurs projected for her as she speaks? Why might she want it, is a dinosaur aura what she needed?, As she spoke about her many accomplishments at the BBC, she explained that carrying with her a model dinosaur was beneficial to her mental health and confidence, but by having to hold the dinosaur sometimes created difficult situations with strangers—what she would like is a dinosaur or dinosaurs to be in her reality but not necessarily in others.

Figure 7.2: "Brave boy billy," an augmented reality art piece telling young wheelchair user's stories. An example of art-inspired interactions.

Moving from mixed reality to the metaverse, we see yet more possibilities for disability interactions. The Metaverse is a shared online space, which can be on screen or in virtual reality, and incorporated 3D graphics, it was coined as a term by novelist Neal Stephenson in 1992 [360]. Recently, the hardware and software to power meteverses have gotten a new lease of life, in part due to Ariana Grande fans being able to attend a string of concerts during the summer of 2021 within multiple video games settings (Splatoon, Mario Kart, and Fortnite to name a few), rather than in a real-world stadium. The news was covered by many outlets including the New Scientist [360]. Recently, Hansen and colleagues explored the use of a metaverse delivered though a combined wheelchair platform and VR headset to allow wheelchair users to interact in virtual spaces an incorporate element of training and rehabilitation within games [163]. The researchers build their own wheelchair platform. At around the same time Invictus Active a UK-based company were growing their wheelchair fitness and health business, which has the wheelchair platform hardware perfected and uses a mobile application. However, it is yet to incorporate mixed realities though and we see great potential for collaborations in this space between HCI researchers and areas specialists such as wheelchair fitness trainers or mobility and orientation experts for people with visual impairment.

7.3   ROBOT–HUMAN COLLABORATIONS

Together AI and robots offer huge potential for powering agentive technologies and enable new levels of collaboration between human and machine, which we will explore now. This collaboration can be used to help overcome some of the societal challenges we see such as insufficient numbers of trained personnel to deliver services such as rehabilitation or sign language interpretation and given the rising societal problems of an increasingly ageing population and the associated caring responsibilities. We look at the role of AI and robotics in creating new disability interactions.

Human–robot interactions are increasingly collaborative, with boundaries being blurred between what is human and what is machine—a sort of augmented human is emerging as possible who can work collaboratively with robots. We have come a long way since Fitts explored these what Humans Are better At and Machines are Better at (HABA --MABA) when exploring effective air traffic control systems. His list—demonstrating humans' capacity for inductive reasoning vs. machines' capacity for deductive reasoning for example—has in some ways stood the test of time and in others been challenged, for example, Bainbridge [473] found automation meant people were less good at preventing problems and troubleshooting, demonstrating how when we interact with machines our abilities change over time, and with the increase of AI we will see machine capabilities change also. Making the interaction more complex and interesting.

The idea of sharing control between humans and robots is increasingly being applied to the area of disability interaction. For example, wheelchairs can now share control with their user—the user inputs a command through a joystick or another interface and sensors onboard the wheelchair calculate the proximity to an obstacle and then using probabilistic modelling the two input sources are blended into an output [440, 441]. Wheelchairs are also being programmed to be socially aware as they navigate—learning the behaviors of pedestrians and being able to copy these [196]. Shared control approaches are also being used to develop exoskeletons [81]. Outside of disability we are seeing driverless cars [42], which offer the possibility of a future of driving for people who are currently unable to drive due to sight loss for example.

A second area where we see human robot collaborations is in care, thorough socially assisted robots (SARs). As societies age there is an increasing gap in their ability to provide care to their older citizens. A recent systematic review of SARs for older people with and without dementia found robots were able to positively help people in remaining independent through assistive in basic daily activities. The reviewed robots highlighted telepresence robots, which helped people connect to family members [318] to PARO the robotic seal was also highlighted in the review for being able to elicit positive emotional responses from people [380]. Beyond specific use cases for older people, we are beginning to introduce caring robots into our lives more generally from robotic dogs for anyone to have as pets to robots, like Aibo (Figure 7.3). What will this mean for the future—will there be robotic guide dogs? And will older people of the future, who have grown up with robots integrated into their everyday, be better able to adapt to robotic care?

Figure 7.3: Aibo, Sony's robot pet dog.

A third area of robot human interactions is in extending inherent human body functions. We are now well acquainted with prosthetic devices and their ability to allow a person to complete a body function which wasn't possible without the limb. However, the future of disability interactions can reevaluate human function. Looking simply at limitations we all have and designing new abilities for everyone. Currently, we are still talking about a paradigm of disability, but the future is about ability and enhanced abilities. In this new reality, when our balance begins to fail as we age, would we simply don a tail that will help to compensate balance [144]. This is the research approach taken by Keio university in developing a [276] a robotic tail to aid balance and to alter body momentum for full-body haptic scenarios. Or, can we develop a new neck like device to enable omnidirectional observation, such as the one created in recent study exploring how to overcome human's limited range of neck motion [343].

Figure 7.4: Robotic tail produced at Keio University to aid balance.

7.4   DIX IN 2079

In 2079, one of the authors would be 100 if she were still alive, and with that in mind we take a moment to reflect on what might have been made possible. Will we have a symbiotic relationship with robots where they are pets and carers—fun and support. Will we glide from A to B alongside our auras interacting alongside others' auras? The above scenarios are possible in or before 2079. In 2079, regenerative medicine may well have cured some conditions which cause disability now, and we may find ourselves selecting which senses we wish to turn on and which we wish to dial down in a situation. All of this is possible.

However, disability interactions will not evolve in a bubble, it will evolve on planet Earth, a planet of limited resources and one with a fragile ecosystem which is at breaking point. This will lead to increased displacements of people and increased numbers of natural disasters. There is a close link to inclusion and sustainability [285] and as natural disasters increase so to do the instances of disability—people are injured and the environment more hostile so even people who could once do something are temporarily impaired by the change in circumstances. As mass displacements increase, so too will the number of people with disabilities moving across borders and needing to transport their assistive technology, their medicines, their lives. These are both challenges and opportunities for us in disability interaction. In this closing section, we choose to focus on the opportunity. First, in researching and understanding the complexities of disability interactions, we believe there is much we can help explain to other complex problems. Second, understanding this changing landscape can help us focus our design efforts toward inclusion across borders as well as across ability levels. Third, we can work toward sustainable solutions which can adapt to changing circumstances at an individual and environmental level. Perhap, for example, we can look to extended human ability to withstand impact during an earthquake, or wheelchairs which can float and propel in water, as well as travel on solid ground.

What is certain is the advance of technology, and of humankind will force us to develop new mental models, new frameworks, new theories, new tools. Disability Interactions could be extinct as a framework in this future; the concept of the range of human abilities no longer relevant or outstripped by our contrast with the technology we have created. However, something tells us this might not be the case. If it is, we hope disability interactions has helped evolve us toward a fairer world. We hope you will join us in the journey.

References

1. Ali Abdolrahmani, William Easley, Michele Williams, Stacy Branham, and Amy Hurst. 2017. Embracing errors: Examining how context of use impacts blind individuals' acceptance of navigation aid errors. *Proceedings of the 2017 CHI Conference on Human Factors in Computing Systems*, ACM, 4158–4169. DOI: 10.1145/3025453.3025528. 16, 113

2. Ali Abdolrahmani, Maya Howes Gupta, Mei-Lian Vader, Ravi Kuber, and Stacy Branham. 2021. Toward more transactional voice assistants: investigating the potential for a multimodal voice-activated indoor navigation assistant for blind and sighted travelers. In *Proceedings of the 2021 CHI Conference on Human Factors in Computing Systems*, ACM, New York, NY, 1–16. DOI: 10.1145/3411764.3445638. 136

3. Ali Abdolrahmani, Ravi Kuber, and Stacy M. Branham. 2018. "Siri Talks at You": An empirical investigation of voice-activated personal assistant (VAPA) usage by individuals who are blind. *Proceedings of the 20th International ACM SIGACCESS Conference on Computers and Accessibility*, ACM, 249–258. DOI: 10.1145/3234695.3236344. 13, 46

4. Ali Abdolrahmani, Kevin M. Storer, Antony Rishin Mukkath Roy, Ravi Kuber, and Stacy M. Branham. 2020. Blind leading the sighted: drawing design insights from blind users toward more productivity-oriented voice interfaces. *ACM Transactions on Accessible Computing* 12, 4: 18:1-18:35. DOI: 10.1145/3368426. 107

5. Loide K. S. Abiatal and Grant R. Howard. 2019. Constructivist assistive technology in a mathematics classroom for the deaf: Going digital at a rural Namibian primary school. *Proceedings of the South African Institute of Computer Scientists and Information Technologists 2019*, ACM, 1–9. DOI: 10.1145/3351108.3351136. 97

6. Lúcia Abreu, Ana Cristina Pires, and Tiago Guerreiro. 2020. TACTOPI: A playful approach to promote computational thinking for visually impaired children. *The 22nd International ACM SIGACCESS Conference on Computers and Accessibility*, ACM, 1–3. DOI: 10.1145/3373625.3418003. 95

7. Sarah Alba, Victoria Austin, Catherine Holloway, and Rainer Kattal. 2021. New economics of assistive technology: A call for a missions approach. UCL Institute for Innovation and Public Purpose. Retrieved February 15, 2021 from https://www.ucl.ac.uk/bartlett/public-purpose/publications/2021/jan/new-economics-assistive-technology-call-missions-approach. 119

8.   Alice Sheppard. *Alice Sheppard Is Moving The Conversation Beyond Loss and Adversity*. Retrieved October 28, 2021 from https://www.dancemagazine.com/disability-dance-2574024089.html. 42

9.   Badriya AlSadrani, Mohammed Alzyoudi, Negmeldin Alsheikh, and Elazab Elazab Elshazly. 2020. The digital divide in inclusive classrooms. *International Journal of Learning, Teaching and Educational Research* 19, 3. 92

10. Patricia Ananga. 2020. Pedagogical considerations of e-learning in education for development in the face of COVID-19. *International Journal of Technology in Education and Science* 4, 4: 310–321. DOI: 10.46328/ijtes.v4i4.123. 101

11. Jessica S. Ancker, Holly O. Witteman, Baria Hafeez, Thierry Provencher, Mary Van de Graaf, and Esther Wei. 2015. "You get reminded you're a sick person": Personal data tracking and patients with multiple chronic conditions. *Journal of Medical Internet Research* 17, 8: e4209. DOI: 10.2196/jmir.4209. 121

12. Ryoichi Ando, Isao Uebayashi, Hayato Sato, et al. 2021. Research on the transcendence of bodily differences, using sport and human augmentation medium. *Augmented Humans Conference 2021*, ACM, 31–39. DOI: 10.1145/3458709.3458981. 42

13. Lisa Anthony, YooJin Kim, and Leah Findlater. 2013. Analyzing user-generated Youtube videos to understand touchscreen use by people with motor impairments. *Proceedings of the SIGCHI Conference on Human Factors in Computing Systems*, ACM, 1223–1232. DOI: 10.1145/2470654.2466158.

14. David Armstrong. 2017. Wicked problems in special and inclusive education. *Journal of Research in Special Educational Needs* 17, 4: 229–236. DOI: 10.1111/1471-3802.12402. 31

15. Ikram Asghar, Shuang Cang, and Hongnian Yu. 2019. Impact evaluation of assistive technology support for the people with dementia. *Assistive Technology* 31, 4: 180–192. DOI: 10.1080/10400435.2017.1411405. 7

16. AT2030. 2021. *Powering Inclusion: AI and AT*. The findings of an online expert roundtable|AT2030 Program. 137

17. Muhammad Atif, Iram Malik, Dalia Dawoud, Anwar Gilani, Naseer Ahmed, and Zaheer-Ud-Din Babar. 2019. Essential medicine list, policies, and the world health organization. *Encyclopedia of Pharmacy Practice and Clinical Pharmacy* 1: 239–249. 125

18. ATscale. 2020. *The Case for Investing in Assistive Technology*. 118

19. ATscale and AT2030. 2020. *Product Narrative: Digital*. 47, 68

20. ATscale and AT2030. 2020. *Product Narrative: Wheelchairs*. 68

21.   ATscale and AT2030. 2020. *Product Narrative: Prostheses.* 68

22.   ATscale and AT2030. 2020. *Product Narrative: Eyeglasses.* 68

23.   ATscale and AT2030. 2019. *Product Narrative: Hearing Aids.* 68, 131

24.   Victoria Austin, Kate Mattick, and Cathy Holloway. 2021. "This is the story of community leadership with political backing. (Pm1)" Critical junctures in paralympic legacy: framing the London 2012 disability inclusion model for new global challenges. *Sustainability* 13, 16: 9253. DOI: 10.3390/su13169253. 137

25.   A. Bailin. 2019. Clearing up some misconceptions about neurodiversity [Blog post]. *Scientific American*: Observations. 112

26.   Catherine M. Baker, Lauren R. Milne, and Richard E. Ladner. 2019. Understanding the impact of TVIs on technology use and selection by children with visual impairments. In *Proceedings of the 2019 CHI Conference on Human Factors in Computing Systems.* ACM, New York, NY, 1–13. DOI: 10.1145/3290605.3300654. 97

27.   E. P. Ballou. 2018. What the neurodiversity movement does-and doesn't offer. *Thinking Person's Guide to Autism.* 112

28.   Maryam Bandukda, Catherine Holloway, Aneesha Singh, and Nadia Berthouze. 2020. PLACES: A framework for supporting blind and partially sighted people in outdoor leisure activities. *The 22nd International ACM SIGACCESS Conference on Computers and Accessibility*, ACM, 1–13. DOI: 10.1145/3373625.3417001. 60, 137

29.   G. Barbareschi and D. Morgado Ramirez. 2020. Individuality over function: the role of technology in disability identity. ACM. 16

30.   Giulia Barbareschi, C. Aranda Jan, Michael Nique, F. Ramos Barajas, and Catherine Holloway. 2019. Mobile phones as assistive technologies: Gaps and opportunities. *The 22nd International ACM SIGACCESS Conference on Computers and Accessibility* 50: 1–13. 68, 75

31.   Giulia Barbareschi, Ben Oldfrey, Long Xin, Wyclife A. Wetende, Victoria P. Austin, Catherine Holloway, Grace N. Magomere, Carol Wanjira, and Joyce Olenja. 2020. Bridging the Divide: Exploring the use of digital and physical technology to aid mobility impaired people living in an informal settlement. *Proceedings of the 22nd International ACM SIGACCESS Conference on Computers and Accessibility* (ASSETS '20), ACM. DOI:10.1145/3373625.3417021. 10, 76, 77, 105

32.   Giulia Barbareschi, Mark T. Carew, Elizabeth Aderonke Johnson, Norah Kopi, and Catherine Holloway. 2021. "When they see a wheelchair, they've not even seen me"—Factors shaping the experience of disability stigma and discrimination in Kenya. *Inter-*

national Journal of Environmental Research and Public Health 18, 8: 4272. DOI: 10.3390/ijerph18084272. 10, 85

33. Giulia Barbareschi, Enrico Costanza, and Catherine Holloway. 2020. TIP-Toy: a tactile, open-source computational toolkit to support learning across visual abilities. *The 22nd International ACM SIGACCESS Conference on Computers and Accessibility*, ACM, 1–14. DOI: 10.1145/3373625.3417005. 76, 95

34. Giulia Barbareschi, Sibylle Daymond, Jake Honeywill, et al. 2020. Value beyond function: analyzing the perception of wheelchair innovations in Kenya. *The 22nd International ACM SIGACCESS Conference on Computers and Accessibility*, ACM, 1–14. DOI: 10.1145/3373625.3417017. 10, 49, 89

35. Giulia Barbareschi, Catherine Holloway, Katherine Arnold, et al. 2020. The social network: how people with visual impairment use mobile phones in Kibera, Kenya. *Proceedings of the 2020 CHI Conference on Human Factors in Computing Systems*, 1–15. DOI: 10.1145/3313831.3376658. 10, 75, 76, 77, 89, 137

36. Giulia Barbareschi, Rosie Richards, Matt Thornton, Tom Carlson, and Catherine Holloway. 2015. Statically vs. dynamically balanced gait: Analysis of a robotic exoskeleton compared with a human. Conference proceedings: *Annual International Conference of the IEEE Engineering in Medicine and Biology Society*. IEEE Engineering in Medicine and Biology Society, Annual Conference 2015; 6728–6731. DOI: 10.1109/EMBC.2015.7319937. 39

37. Giulia Barbareschi, Norah Shitawa Kopi, Ben Oldfrey, and Catherine Holloway. 2021. What difference does tech make? Conceptualizations of disability and assistive technology among Kenyan youth: Conceptualizations of disability and AT. *The 23rd International ACM SIGACCESS Conference on Computers and Accessibility*, 1–13. DOI: 10.1145/3441852.3471226. 85

38. Cynthia L. Bennett, Erin Brady, and Stacy M. Branham. 2018. Interdependence as a frame for assistive technology research and design. *Proceedings of the 20th International ACM SIGACCESS Conference on Computers and Accessibility*, ACM, 161–173. DOI: 10.1145/3234695.3236348. 22, 58

39. Cynthia L. Bennett, Keting Cen, Katherine M. Steele, and Daniela K. Rosner. 2016. An intimate laboratory? Prostheses as a tool for experimenting with identity and normalcy. *Proceedings of the 2016 CHI Conference on Human Factors in Computing Systems*, ACM, 1745–1756. DOI: 10.1145/2858036.2858564. 8, 128

40. Cynthia L. Bennett, Burren Peil, and Daniela K. Rosner. 2019. Biographical prototypes: Reimagining recognition and disability in design. *Proceedings of the 2019 on Designing Interactive Systems Conference*, 35–47. DOI: 10.1145/3322276.3322376. 8, 37

41. Cynthia L. Bennett and Daniela K. Rosner. 2019. The promise of empathy: Design, Disability, and knowing the "other". *CHI '19: Proceedings of the 2019 CHI Conference on Human Factors in Computing Systems*, 1–13. DOI: 10.1145/3290605.3300528. 9

42. Roger Bennett, Rohini Vijaygopal, and Rita Kottasz. 2020. Willingness of people who are blind to accept autonomous vehicles: An empirical investigation. *Transportation Research Part F: Traffic Psychology and Behaviour*, 69: 13–27. DOI: 10.1016/j.trf.2019.12.012. 143

43. Tom Bentley. 2012. *Learning Beyond The Classroom: Education For A Changing World*. Routledge. DOI: 10.4324/9780203201756. 93

44. Eric Bergman, Alistair Edwards, Deborah Kaplan, Greg Lowney, T. V. Raman, and Earl Johnson. 1996. Universal design: Everyone has special needs. *Conference Companion on Human Factors in Computing Systems*, ACM, 153–154. DOI: 10.1145/257089.257893. 4, 5

45. Tigmanshu Bhatnagar, Nicolai Marquardt, Mark A. Miodownik, and Catherine Holloway. 2021. Transforming a monolithic sheet of nitinol into a passive reconfigurable tactile pixel array display at braille resolution. *IEEE World Haptics Conference, WHC 2021*, Montreal, QC, Canada, July 6–9, 2021, IEEE, 409–414. DOI: 10.1109/WHC49131.2021.9517239. 35, 69

46. Tigmanshu Bhatnagar, Vikas Upadhyay, Anchal Sharma, P. V. M. Rao. 2021. Drawing erasable tactile diagrams on Tacilia. *Conference: 2021 IEEE World Haptics Conference (WHC)*, IEEE. 35

47. BIMA. 2019. BIMA Tech Inclusion and Diversity Report 2019. 113

48. P. Biswas, P. M. Langdon, J. Umadikar, S. Kittusami, and S. Prashant. 2014. How interface adaptation for physical impairment can help able bodied users in situational impairment. *Inclusive Designing*, Springer International Publishing, 49–58. DOI: 10.1007/978-3-319-05095-9_5. 4

49. Janaka Biyanwila. 2011. Poverty and disability in the Global South. *Third World Quarterly* (TWQ) 32, 8:1537–1540. http://www.jstor.org/stable/41300300. DOI: 10.1080/01436597.2011.604525. 21

50. Sofie Blakstad and Robert Allen. 2018. Leapfrogging banks in emerging markets. In S. Blakstad and R. Allen, eds., *FinTech Revolution: Universal Inclusion in the New Financial*

Ecosystem. Springer International Publishing, Cham, 121–132. DOI: 10.1007/978-3-319-76014-8_7. 86

51. Peter Blanck. 2020. Disability inclusive employment and the accommodation principle: emerging issues in research, policy, and law. *Journal of Occupational Rehabilitation* 30, 4: 505–510. DOI: 10.1007/s10926-020-09940-9. 106

52. Ann Blandford. 2019. HCI for health and wellbeing: Challenges and opportunities. *International Journal of Human-Computer Studies* 131: 41–51. DOI: 10.1016/j.ijhcs.2019.06.007. 53, 131

53. Ann E. Blandford. 2017. Engaging in information interaction. *Proceedings of the 2017 Conference on Conference Human Information Interaction and Retrieval*, ACM, 3. DOI: 10.1145/3020165.3038293. 53

54. Ann Blandford, Jo Gibbs, Nikki Newhouse, Olga Perski, Aneesha Singh, and Elizabeth Murray. 2018. Seven lessons for interdisciplinary research on interactive digital health interventions. *Digital Health* 4: 2055207618770325. DOI: 10.1177/2055207618770325. 38, 39, 121, 122

55. Ann Blandford, Janet Wesson, René Amalberti, Raed AlHazme, and Ragad Allwihan. 2020. Opportunities and challenges for telehealth within, and beyond, a pandemic. *The Lancet Global Health* 8, 11: e1364–e1365. DOI: 10.1016/S2214-109X(20)30362-4. 122, 125

56. Hans-Peter Blossfeld and Jutta Von Maurice. 2011. 2 Education as a lifelong process. *Zeitschrift für Erziehungswissenschaft* 14, 2: 19–34. DOI: 10.1007/s11618-011-0179-2. 93

57. BMC Public Health. Equity in academic publishing. *BMC Public Health*. Retrieved October 28, 2021 from https://bmcpublichealth.biomedcentral.com/equity-in-academic-publishing. 71

58. Kristen Bottema-Beutel, Steven K. Kapp, Jessica Nina Lester, Noah J. Sasson, and Brittany N. Hand. 2021. Avoiding ableist language: Suggestions for autism researchers. *Autism in Adulthood* 3, 1: 18–29. DOI: 10.1089/aut.2020.0014. 112

59. Emily C Bouck, Andrea Jasper, Laura Bassette, and Jordan Shurr. 2015. Mobile phone: Repurposed assistive technology for individuals with disabilities. In *Encyclopedia of Mobile Phone Behavior*. IGI Global, 1442–1455. DOI: 10.4018/978-1-4666-8239-9.ch114. 74

60. Rupert Bourne, Jaimie D. Steinmetz, Seth Flaxman, Rupert Bourne, Jaimie D. Steinmetz, Seth Flaxman, Paul Svitil Briant, Hugh R. Taylor, Serge Resnikoff, Robert James Casson, Amir Abdoli, Eman Abu-Gharbieh, Ashkan Afshin, Hamid Ahmadieh, Yonas Akalu, Alehegn Aderaw Alamneh, Wondu Alemayehu, Ahmed Samir Alfaar, Vahid Alipour,

Etsay Woldu Anbesu, Sofia Androudi, Jalal Arabloo, Aries Arditi, Malke Asaad, Eleni Bagli, Atif Amin Baig, Till Winfried Bärnighausen, Maurizio Battaglia Parodi, Akshaya Srikanth Bhagavathula, Nikha Bhardwaj, Pankaj Bhardwaj, Krittika Bhattacharyya, Ali Bijani, Mukharram Bikbov, Michele Bottone, Tasanee Braithwaite, Alain M. Bron, Zahid A. Butt, Ching-Yu Cheng, Dinh-Toi Chu, Maria Vittoria Cicinelli, João M. Coelho, Baye Dagnew, Xiaochen Dai, Reza Dana, Lalit Dandona, Rakhi Dandona, Monte A. Del Monte, Jenny P. Deva, Daniel Diaz, Shirin Djalalinia, Laura E. Dreer, Joshua R. Ehrlich, Leon B. Ellwein, Mohammad Hassan Emamian, Arthur G. Fernandes, Florian Fischer, David S. Friedman, João M. Furtado, Abhay Motiramji Gaidhane, Shilpa Gaidhane, Gus Gazzard, Berhe Gebremichael, Ronnie George, Ahmad Ghashghaee, Mahaveer Golechha, Samer Hamidi, Billy Randall Hammond, Mary Elizabeth R. Hartnett, Risky Kusuma Hartono, Simon I. Hay, Golnaz Heidari, Hung Chak Ho, Chi Linh Hoang, Mowafa Househ, Segun Emmanuel Ibitoye, Irena M. Ilic, Milena D. Ilic, April D. Ingram, Seyed Sina Naghibi Irvani, Ravi Prakash Jha, Rim Kahloun, Himal Kandel, Ayele Semachew Kasa, John H. Kempen, Maryam Keramati, Moncef Khairallah, Ejaz Ahmad Khan, Rohit C. Khanna, Mahalaqua Nazli Khatib, Judy E. Kim, Yun Jin Kim, Sezer Kisa, Adnan Kisa, Ai Koyanagi, Om P. Kurmi, Van Charles Lansingh, Janet L. Leasher, Nicolas Leveziel, Hans Limburg, Marek Majdan, Navid Manafi, Kaweh Mansouri, Colm McAlinden, Seyed Farzad Mohammadi, Abdollah Mohammadian-Hafshejani, Reza Mohammadpourhodki, Ali H. Mokdad, Delaram Moosavi, Alan R. Morse, Mehdi Naderi, Kovin S. Naidoo, Vinay Nangia, Cuong Tat Nguyen, Huong Lan Thi Nguyen, Kolawole Ogundimu, Andrew T. Olagunju, Samuel M. Ostroff, Songhomitra Panda-Jonas, Konrad Pesudovs, Tunde Peto, Zahiruddin Quazi Syed, Mohammad Hifz Ur Rahman, Pradeep Y. Ramulu, Salman Rawaf, David Laith Rawaf, Nickolas Reinig, Alan L. Robin, Luca Rossetti, Sare Safi, Amirhossein Sahebkar, Abdallah M Samy, Deepak Saxena, Janet B. Serle, Masood Ali Shaikh, Tueng T. Shen, Kenji Shibuya, Jae Il Shin, Juan Carlos Silva, Alexander Silvester, Jasvinder A. Singh, Deepika Singhal, Rita S. Sitorus, Eirini Skiadaresi, Vegard Skirbekk, Amin Soheili, Raúl A. R. C. Sousa, Emma Elizabeth Spurlock, Dwight Stambolian, Biruk Wogayehu Taddele, Eyayou Girma Tadesse, Nina Tahhan, Md Ismail Tareque, Fotis Topouzis, Bach Xuan Tran, Ravensara S. Travillian, Miltiadis K. Tsilimbaris, Rohit Varma, Gianni Virgili, Ya Xing Wang, Ningli Wang, Sheila K. West, Tien Y. Wong, Zoubida Zaidi, Kaleab Alemayehu Zewdie, Jost B. Jonas, and Theo Vos. 2021. Trends in prevalence of blindness and distance and near vision impairment over 30 years: an analysis for the Global Burden of Disease Study. *The Lancet Global Health* 9, 2: e130–e143. DOI: 10.1016/S2214-109X(20)30425-3. 34

61.   Danielle Bragg, Oscar Koller, Mary Bellard, Larwan Berke, Patrick Boudreault, Annelies Braffort, Naomi Caselli, Matt Huenerfauth, Hernisa Kacorri, Tessa Verhoef, Christian Vogler, and Meredith Ringel Morris. 2019. Sign language recognition, generation, and translation: An interdisciplinary perspective. *The 21st International ACM SIGACCESS Conference on Computers and Accessibility*, ACM, 16–31. 100

62.   Stacy M. Branham and Shaun K. Kane. 2015. Collaborative accessibility: How blind and sighted companions co-create accessible home spaces. *Proceedings of the 33rd Annual ACM Conference on Human Factors in Computing Systems*, ACM, 2373–2382. DOI: 10.1145/2702123.2702511. 8, 16

63.   Stacy M. Branham and Shaun K. Kane. 2015. The invisible work of accessibility: how blind employees manage accessibility in mixed-ability workplaces. *Proceedings of the 17th International ACM SIGACCESS Conference on Computers #38; Accessibility*, ACM, 163–171. DOI: 10.1145/2700648.2809864. 13, 106, 107

64.   Karen Brennan and Mitchel Resnick. 2012. New frameworks for studying and assessing the development of computational thinking. In *AERA* 2012 25. 95

65.   Brigitte Rohwerder. 2018. Disability stigma in developing countries. *K4D Helpdesk Report*. Brighton, UK: Institute of Development Studies. 79, 80

66.   Barry Brown, Susanne Bødker, and Kristina Höök. 2017. Does HCI scale? Scale hacking and the relevance of HCI. *Interactions* 24, 5: 28–33. DOI: 10.1145/3125387. 14, 17

67.   Carl Brown. 1992. Assistive technology computers and persons with disabilities. *Communications of the ACM* 35, 5: 36–45. DOI: 10.1145/129875.129877. 2

68.   Emeline Brulé and Gilles Bailly. 2021. "Beyond 3D printers": Understanding long-term digital fabrication practices for the education of visually impaired or blind youth. In *Proceedings of the 2021 CHI Conference on Human Factors in Computing Systems. ACM*, New York, NY, 1–15. DOI: 10.1145/3411764.3445403. 38

69.   Richard Buchanan. 1992. Wicked problems in design thinking. *Design Issues* 8, 2: 5–21. DOI: 10.2307/1511637. 30, 31

70.   Erin Buehler, Stacy Branham, Abdullah Ali, Jeremy J. Chang, Megan Kelly Hofmann, Amy Hurst, and Shaun K. Kane. 2015. Sharing is caring: Assistive technology designs on Thingiverse. *Proceedings of the 33rd Annual ACM Conference on Human Factors in Computing Systems*, ACM, 525–534. DOI: 10.1145/2702123.2702525. 52

71.   Erin Buehler, William Easley, Amy Poole, and Amy Hurst. 2016. Accessibility barriers to online education for young adults with intellectual disabilities. *Proceedings of the 13th International Web for All Conference*, ACM, 1–10. DOI: 10.1145/2899475.2899481. 94

72.	Eleanor R. Burgess, Alice Renwen Zhang, Jessica L. Feuston, Madhu C. Reddy, Sindhu Kiranmai Ernala, Munmun De Choudhury, Stephen Schueller, Adrian Aguilera, and Mary Czerwinski. 2020. Technology ecosystems: Rethinking resources for mental health. *Extended Abstracts of the 2020 CHI Conference on Human Factors in Computing Systems*, ACM, 1–8. DOI: 10.1145/3334480.3375166. 128, 129

73.	Simon M. Bury, Rachel Jellett, Jennifer R. Spoor, and Darren Hedley. 2020. "It defines who I am" or "it's something I have": What language do [autistic] Australian adults [on the Autism Spectrum] prefer? *Journal of Autism and Developmental Disorders*. xix, 19

74.	Janine Butler, Brian Trager, and Byron Behm. 2019. Exploration of automatic speech recognition for deaf and hard of hearing students in higher education classes. *The 21st International ACM SIGACCESS Conference on Computers and Accessibility*, ACM, 32–42. DOI: 10.1145/3308561.3353772. 100

75.	Jill Butler, Kritina Holden, and William Lidwell. 2003. *Universal Principles of Design*. Rockport publishers Gloucester, MA, 2010, 112–113. 14

76.	W. Buxton, R. Foulds, M. Rosen, L. Scadden, and F. Shein. 1986. Human interface design and the handicapped user. *Proceedings of the SIGCHI Conference on Human Factors in Computing Systems*, ACM, 291–297. DOI: 10.1145/22339.22386. 1, 2, 5

77.	C. Papoutsi, J. Wherton, S. Shaw, C. Morrison, and T. Greenhalgh. 2021. Putting the social back into sociotechnical: Case studies of co-design in digital health. *Journal of the American Medical Informatics Association* 28: 284–293. DOI: 10.1093/jamia/ocaa197. 121

78.	Clara Caldeira, Matthew Bietz, Marisol Vidauri, and Yunan Chen. 2017. Senior care for aging in place: Balancing assistance and independence. *Proceedings of the 2017 ACM Conference on Computer Supported Cooperative Work and Social Computing*, ACM, 1605–1617. DOI: 10.1145/2998181.2998206. 121

79.	Rafael A. Calvo, Karthik Dinakar, Rosalind Picard, and Pattie Maes. 2016. Computing in mental health. *Proceedings of the 2016 CHI Conference Extended Abstracts on Human Factors in Computing Systems*, ACM, 3438–3445. DOI: 10.1145/2851581.2856463. 128

80.	Rafael A. Calvo and Dorian Peters. 2014. *Positive Computing: Technology for Wellbeing and Human Potential*. MIT Press. 57, 131

81.	Tom Carlson. 2017. Toward everyday shared control of lower limb exoskeletons. In J. González-Vargas, J. Ibáñez, J.L. Contreras-Vidal, H. van der Kooij, and J.L. Pons, Eds., *Wearable Robotics: Challenges and Trends*. Springer International Publishing, 133–135. DOI: 10.1007/978-3-319-46532-6_22. 143

82. Stefan Carmien, Melissa Dawe, Gerhard Fischer, Andrew Gorman, Anja Kintsch, and James F. Sullivan Jr. 2005. Socio-technical environments supporting people with cognitive disabilities using public transportation. *ACM Transactions on Computer–Human Interaction* (TOCHI) 12, 2: 233–262. DOI: 10.1145/1067860.1067865. 13

83. Patrick Carrington, Amy Hurst, and Shaun K. Kane. 2014. Wearables and chairables: inclusive design of mobile input and output techniques for power wheelchair users. *Proceedings of the SIGCHI Conference on Human Factors in Computing Systems*, ACM, 3103–3112. DOI: 10.1145/2556288.2557237. 126

84. Wayne F. Cascio and Ramiro Montealegre. 2016. How technology is changing work and organizations. *Annual Review of Organizational Psychology and Organizational Behavior* 3: 349–375. DOI: 10.1146/annurev-orgpsych-041015-062352. 104

85. Catherine Holloway, Behzad Herari, Sarah Nicholson, and Stephen Hailes. 2016. Street rehab: Linking accessibility and rehabilitation. *Annual International Conference of the IEEE Engineering in Medicine and Biology Society*, 2016. EMBC. DOI: 10.1109/EMBC.2016.7591401. 130

86. Catherine Holloway, Behzad Heravi, Sarah Nicholson, Vijay Rao, Shankar Subbiah, Vicki Austin, Revathy Rugmini, Maria Kett, and Steve Hailes. 2017. Street rehab: Linking accessibility and rehabilitation in Delhi. *Annual International Conference of the IEEE Engineering in Medicine and Biology Society.* DOI: 10.1109/EMBC.2016.7591401. 15, 130

87. Youngjun Cho. 2021. Rethinking eye-blink: Assessing task difficulty through physiological representation of spontaneous blinking. In *Proceedings of the 2021 CHI Conference on Human Factors in Computing Systems*. ACM, New York, NY, 1–12. DOI: 10.1145/3411764.3445577. 43

88. Youngjun Cho, Nadia Bianchi-Berthouze, and Simon J. Julier. 2017. DeepBreath: Deep learning of breathing patterns for automatic stress recognition using low-cost thermal imaging in unconstrained settings. *Seventh International Conference on Affective Computing and Intelligent Interaction* (ACII), 456–463. 12, 138

889. Youngjun Cho, Simon J. Julier, and Nadia Bianchi-Berthouze. 2019. Instant stress: Detection of perceived mental stress through smartphone photoplethysmography and thermal imaging. *JMIR Mental Health* 6, 4: e10140. DOI: 10.2196/10140. 138

90. Shaan Chopra, Emma Dixon, Kausalya Ganesh, Alisha Pradhan, Mary L. Radnofsky, and Amanda Lazar. 2021. Designing for and with people with dementia using a human

rights-based approach. In *Extended Abstracts of the 2021 CHI Conference on Human Factors in Computing Systems.* ACM, New York, NY, 1–8. DOI: 10.1145/3411763.3443434. 37

91. Vera Chouinard. 2018. Living on the global peripheries of law: Disability human rights law in principle and in practice in the Global South. *Laws* 7, 1: 8. DOI: 10.3390/laws7010008. 80

92. Leigh Clark, Nadia Pantidi, Orla Cooney, Philip Doyle, Diego Garaialde, Justin Edwards, Brendan Spillane, Emer Gilmartin, Christine Murad, Cosin Munteanu, Vincent Wade, and Benjamin R, Cowan. 2019. What makes a good conversation? Challenges in designing truly conversational agents. In *Proceedings of the 2019 CHI Conference on Human Factors in Computing Systems.* ACM, New York, NY, 1–12. DOI: 10.1145/3290605.3300705. 136

93. John Clarke, Janet Newman, and Louise Westmarland. 2008. The antagonisms of choice: New labour and the reform of public services. *Social Policy and Society* 7, 2: 245–253. DOI: 10.1017/S1474746407004198. 51

94. Roger Collier. 2012. Person-first language: Noble intent but to what effect? *Canadian Medical Association Journal*, 184, 18: 1977–1978. DOI: 10.1503/cmaj.109-4319. 19

95. Roger Collier. 2012. Person-first language: Laudable cause, horrible prose. *CMAJ* 184, 18: E939–E940. DOI: 10.1503/cmaj.109-4338. 19

96. Bettye Rose Connell, Mike Jones, Ron Mace, Jim Mueller, Abir Mullick, Elaine Ostroff, Jon Sanford, Ed Steinfeld, Molly Story, and Gregg Vanderheiden. 1997. The principles of universal design. Retrieved January 11, 2005. 13

97. Sara Csillag, Zsuzsanna Gyori, and Carmen Svastics. 2019. Long and winding road? Barriers and supporting factors as perceived by entrepreneurs with disabilities. *Journal of Enterprising Communities: People and Places in the Global Economy* 13, 1/2: 42–63. DOI: 10.1108/JEC-11-2018-0097. 104

98. Jamie Danemayer, Emma M. Smith, V. Delgado Ramos, L. Battistella, Sarah Polack, and Catherine Holloway. 2021. Indicating assistive technology supply and demand. *Assistive Technology: The journal of the Rehabilitation Engineering and Assistive Technology Society of North America.* 130

99. Mary E. W. Dankbaar and Peter G. M. de Jong. 2014. Technology for learning: how it has changed education. *Perspectives on Medical Education* 3, 4: 257–259. DOI: 10.1007/s40037-014-0141-0. 94

100. Laura Dantonio, Stephann Makri, and Ann Blandford. 2012. Coming across academic social media content serendipitously. *Proceedings of the American Society for Information Science and Technology* 49, 1: 1–10. DOI: 10.1002/meet.14504901002. 53

101. Maitraye Das, John Tang, Kathryn E. Ringland, and Anne Marie Piper. 2021. Toward accessible remote work: Understanding work-from-home practices of neurodivergent professionals. *Proceedings of the ACM on Human-Computer Interaction* 5, CSCW1: 183:1-183:30. DOI: 10.1145/3449282. 107, 108

102. M. Dawe. 2004. Complexity, cost and customization: Uncovering barriers to adoption of assistive technology. Refereed Poster at ASSETS'04. 6

103. Hanne De Jaegher. 2013. Embodiment and sense-making in autism. *Frontiers in Integrative Neuroscience* 7: 15. DOI: 10.3389/fnint.2013.00015. 96

104. Sunil Deepak, Jayanth Kumar, Parthipan Ramasamy, and Giampiero Griffo. 2014. An emancipatory research on CBR and the barriers faced by persons with disabilities. *Disability and Rehabilitation* 36, 18: 1502–1507. DOI: 10.3109/09638288.2013.800914. 105

105. C. Demetriou, Bilge Uzun Ozer, and C. Essau. 2015. Self-Report Questionnaires. DOI: 10.1002/9781118625392.wbecp507. 129

106. Universal Design. 1997. The Principles of universal design. Recuperado de www. design. ncsu. edu/cud. 3

107. Deirdre Desmond, Natasha Layton, Jacob Bentley, Fleur Heleen Boot, Johan Borg, Bishnu Maya Dhungana, Pamela Gallagher, Lynn Gitlow, Rosemary Joan Gowran, Nora Groce, Katerina Mavrou, Trish Mackeogh, Rachael McDonald, Cecilia Pettersson, and Marcia J. Scherer. 2018. Assistive technology and people: a position paper from the first global research, innovation and education on assistive technology (GREAT) summit. *Disability and Rehabilitation: Assistive Technology* 13, 5: 437–444. DOI: 10.1080/17483107.2018.1471169. 14, 124

108. Supriya Dey, Y. Vidhya, Suprgya Bhushan, and Mounika Neerukonda. 2019. Creating an accessible technology ecosystem for learning science and math: A case of visually impaired children in indian schools. Retrieved on October 28, 2021 at http://vision-empowertrust.in/wp-content/themes/html5blank/research/INAIS%20Submission%20-%20Creating%20an%20Accessible%20Technology%20Ecosystem.docx.pdf. 54

109. Mark Díaz and Nicholas Diakopoulos. 2019. Whose walkability? challenges in algorithmically measuring subjective experience. *Proceedings of the ACM on Human-Computer Interaction* 3, CSCW: 1–22. DOI: 10.1145/3359228. 15

110. Tawanna R. Dillahunt, Jason Lam, Alex Lu, and Earnest Wheeler. 2018. Designing future employment applications for underserved job seekers: A speed dating study. *Proceedings of the 2018 Designing Interactive Systems Conference*, ACM, 33–44. DOI: 10.1145/3196709.3196770. 105

111. Michelle C. Dimitris, Matthew Gittings, and Nicholas B. King. 2021. How global is global health research? A large-scale analysis of trends in authorship. *BMJ Global Health* 6, 1: e003758. DOI: 10.1136/bmjgh-2020-003758. 71

112. James A. Doubler, Dudley S. Childress, and John S. Strysik. 1978. A microcomputer-based control and communication system for the severely disabled. *ACM SIGCAPH Computers and the Physically Handicapped* 24: 43–46. DOI: 10.1145/951796.951803. 1

113. Karn Dubey, Palash Gupta, Rachna Shriwas, Gayatri Gulvady, and Amit Sharma. 2019. Learnings from deploying a voice-based social platform for people with disability. 111–121. DOI: 10.1145/3314344.3332503. 75

114. Devon C. Duhaney and Laurel M. Garrick Duhaney. 2000. Assistive technology: Meeting the needs of learners with disabilities. *International Journal of Instructional Media* 27, 4: 393–401. 93

115. Evelyne Durocher, Rosalie H. Wang, Jerome Bickenbach, Daphne Schreiber, and Michael G. Wilson. 2019. "Just access"? Questions of equity in access and funding for assistive technology. *Ethics and Behavior* 29, 3: 172–191. DOI: 10.1080/10508422.2017.1396461. 81

116. Jared Duval, Ferran Altarriba Bertran, Siying Chen, et al. 2021. Chasing play on TikTok from populations with disabilities to inspire playful and inclusive technology design. *Proceedings of the 2021 CHI Conference on Human Factors in Computing Systems* 1–15. DOI: 10.1145/3411764.3445303. 17

117. Thomas Shelley Duval and Paul J. Silvia. 2004. Self-awareness, self-motives, and self-motivation. In R. A. Wright, J. Greenberg and S. S. Brehm, Sharon (Eds). *Motivational Analyses of Social Behavior: Building on Jack Brehm's Contributions to Psychology* 57. 44

118. Elizabeth Murray, Eric B. Hekler, Gerhard Andersson, Linda M. Collins, Aiden Doherty, Chris Hollis, Daniel E. Rivera, Robert West, and Jeremy C. Wyatt. 2016. Evaluating digital health interventions: Key questions and approaches.s. *American Journal of Preventive Medicine* 51: 843–851. DOI: 10.1016/j.amepre.2016.06.008. 121

119. Ikenna D. Ebuenyi, Emma M. Smith, Catherine Holloway, Rune Jensen, Lucía D'Arino, and Malcolm MacLachlan. 2020. COVID-19 as social disability: the opportunity of so-

cial empathy for empowerment. *BMJ Global Health* 5, 8: e003039. DOI: 10.1136/bmjgh-2020-003039. 64

120. Ikenna D. Ebuenyi, Emma M. Smith, Juba Kafumba, Monica Z. Jamali, Alister Munthali, and Malcolm MacLachlan. 2020. Implementation of the Assistive Product List (APL) in Malawi through development of appropriate policy and systems: an action research protocol. *BMJ Open* 10, 11: e040281. DOI: 10.1136/bmjopen-2020-040281. 83, 84

121. A. D. N. Edwards. 1988. The design of auditory interfaces for visually disabled users. *Proceedings of the SIGCHI Conference on Human Factors in Computing Systems*, ACM, 83–88. DOI: 10.1145/57167.57180. 2

122. Elizabeth Ellcessor. 2021. Three vignettes in pursuit of accessible pandemic teaching. *Communication, Culture and Critique* 14, 2: 324–327. DOI: 10.1093/ccc/tcab010. 102, 103

123. Rasha ElSaheli-Elhage. 2021. Access to students and parents and levels of preparedness of educators during the COVID-19 emergency transition to e-learning. *International Journal on Studies in Education* 3, 2: 61–69. DOI: 10.46328/ijonse.35. 101

124. Stefanie Enriquez-Geppert, René J. Huster, and Christoph S. Herrmann. 2017. EEG-neurofeedback as a tool to modulate cognition and behavior: A review tutorial. *Frontiers in Human Neuroscience* 11: 51. DOI: 10.3389/fnhum.2017.00051. 43

125. N. Erevelles. 2011. *Disability and Difference in Global Contexts: Enabling a Transformative Body Politic*. Springer. DOI: 10.1057/9781137001184. 73

126. Heather A. Faucett, Kate E, Ringland, Amanda L, L, Cullen, and Gillian R, Hayes. 2017. (In)Visibility in disability and assistive technology. *ACM Transactions on Accessible Computing* (TACCESS) 10, 4: 1–17. DOI: 10.1145/3132040. 16

127. Michael B First. 2014. Structured clinical interview for the DSM (SCID). *The Encyclopedia of Clinical Psychology* 1–6. DOI: 10.1002/9781118625392.wbecp351. 129

128. Jonathan Follett. 2014. *Designing for Emerging Technologies: Ux for Genomics, Robotics, and The Internet of Things*. O'Reilly Media, Inc. 58, 137

129. Frederic Fovet. 2018. Making it work! Addressing teacher resistance in systemic UDL implementation across schools. *Inclusive education: Practitioners Perspective*. Mumbai: School Inclusive Education Development Initiative. 97

130. Sarah Fox, Mariam Asad, Katherine Lo, Jill P. Dimond, Lynn S. Dombrowski, and Shaowen Bardzell. 2016. Exploring social justice, design, and HCI. *Proceedings of the*

2016 CHI Conference Extended Abstracts on Human Factors in Computing Systems, ACM, 3293–3300. DOI: 10.1145/2851581.2856465. 73

131.   Christopher Frauenberger. 2015. Disability and technology: A critical realist perspective. *Proceedings of the 17th International ACM SIGACCESS Conference on Computers #38; Accessibility*, ACM, 89–96. DOI: 10.1145/2700648.2809851. 8, 13

132.   Jon E. Froehlich, Anke M. Brock, Anat Caspi, João Guerreiro, Kotaro Hara, Reuben Kirkham, Johannes Schöning, and Benhamin Tannert. 2019. Grand challenges in accessible maps. *Interactions* 26, 2: 78–81. DOI: 10.1145/3301657. 15

133.   GDI Hub. Home|Innovation Action. Retrieved October 28, 2021 from https://www.innovationaction.org/. 52

134.   GDI Hub. Assistive Tech Impact Fund. Retrieved October 28, 2021 from https://www.atimpactfund.com/. 65

135.   GDI Hub. Home|AT2030 Program. Retrieved October 28, 2021 from https://at2030.org/. 66

136.   Morton Ann Gernsbacher. 2017. Editorial perspective: The use of person-first language in scholarly writing may accentuate stigma. *Journal of Child Psychology and Psychiatry, and Allied Disciplines* 58, 7: 859–861. DOI: 10.1111/jcpp.12706. xix, 19

137.   Anita Ghai, Vidhya Yella Reddy, and Swaminathan, Manohar. 2020. Assistive technology research and disability studies in the Global South: The need for synergy. *CHI 2020 Workshop: Nothing About Us Without Us. Investigating the Role of Critical Disability Studies in HCI*. 73

138.   Cole Gleason, Stephanie Valencia, Lynn Kirabo, Jason Wu, Anhong Guo, Elizabeth Jeanne Carter, Jeffrey Bigham, Cynthia Bennett, and Amy Pavel. 2020. Disability and the COVID-19 pandemic: Using Twitter to understand accessibility during rapid societal transition. *The 22nd International ACM SIGACCESS Conference on Computers and Accessibility*, ACM, 1–14. DOI: 10.1145/3373625.3417023. 101, 102

139.   Sarah Glencross, Jonathan Mason, Mary Katsikitis, and Kenneth Mark Greenwood. 2021. Internet use by people with intellectual disability: Exploring digital inequality-a systematic review. *Cyberpsychology, Behavior and Social Networking* 24, 8: 503–520. DOI: 10.1089/cyber.2020.0499. 92

140.   Ephraim P. Glinert and Bryant W. York. 2008. Computers and people with disabilities. *ACM Transactions on Accessible Computing* 1, 2: 7:1-7:7. DOI: 10.1145/1408760.1408761. 2

141. Global Disability Innovation Hub. Disabled Students Survey. Retrieved October 28, 2021 from https://cdn.disabilityinnovation.com/uploads/images/Disabled-Students-Survey_2021.pdf?1619429071. 98

142. Scott A. Golder and Michael W. Macy. 2011. Diurnal and seasonal mood vary with work, sleep, and daylength across diverse cultures. *Science* 333, 6051: 1878–1881. DOI: 10.1126/science.1202775. 128

143. Gregg Gonsalves and Gavin Yamey. 2021. The covid-19 vaccine patent waiver: a crucial step toward a "people's vaccine." *BMJ* 373. DOI: 10.1136/bmj.n1249. 89

144. Nanna Gorm and Irina A. Shklovski. 2016. Steps, choices and moral accounting: Observations from a step-counting campaign in the workplace. CSCW *Proceedings of the 19th ACM Conference on Computer-Supported Cooperative Work & Social Computing*. DOI: 10.1145/2818048.2819944. 121, 144

145. Shaun Grech. 2015. Decolonising Eurocentric disability studies: why colonialism matters in the disability and global South debate. *Social Identities* 21, 1: 6–21. DOI: 10.1080/13504630.2014.995347. 73, 80, 88

146. Shaun Grech and Karen Soldatic. 2016. *Disability in the Global South: The Critical Handbook*. Springer. DOI: 10.1007/978-3-319-42488-0. 80

147. Trisha Greenhalgh, Sara Shaw, Joe Wherton, Gemma Hughes, Jenni Lynch, Christine A'Court, Sue Hinder, Nick Fahy, Emma Byrne, Alexander Finlayson, Tom Sorell, Rob Procter and Rob Stones. 2016. SCALS: A fourth-generation study of assisted living technologies in their organizational, social, political and policy context. *BMJ Open* 6, 2: e010208. DOI: 10.1136/bmjopen-2015-010208.121

148. Keith Grint and Steve Woolgar. 2013. *The Machine at Work: Technology, Work and Organization*. John Wiley and Sons. 104

149. Nora Groce, Maria Kett, Raymond Lang, and Jean-Francois Trani. 2011. Disability and poverty: The need for a more nuanced understanding of implications for development policy and practice. *Third World Quarterly* 32, 8: 1493–1513. DOI: 10.1080/01436597.2011.604520. 75

150. William Grussenmeyer, Jesel Garcia, Eelke Folmer, and Fang Jiang. 2017. Evaluating the accessibility of the job search and interview process for people who are blind and visually impaired. *Proceedings of the 14th International Web for All Conference*, ACM, 1–4. DOI: 10.1145/3058555.3058570. 105

151. GSMA. 2019. Understanding the Mobile Disability Gap. Insights on Mobile Phone Access and Usage by Persons with Disabilities in Kenya and Bangladesh. 68

152. GSMA. 2020. Education For All in the Time of COVID-19: How EdTech can be Part of the Solution. 102

153. GSMA. Assistive Tech. Mobile for Development. Retrieved October 28, 2021 from https://www.gsma.com/mobilefordevelopment/assistive-tech/. 47

154. GSMA. Principles for Driving the Digital Inclusion of Persons with Disabilities. Mobile for Development. Retrieved October 28, 2021 from https://www.gsma.com/mobilefor-development/principles-for-driving-the-digital-inclusion-of-people-with-disabilities/. 47

155. Jon R. Gunderson. 1994. American with Disabilities Act (ADA): Human computer interaction for persons with disablities. *Conference Companion on Human Factors in Computing Systems*, ACM, 381–382. DOI: 10.1145/259963.260515. 2

156. Arpit Gupta. 2020. Accelerating remote work after COVID-19. 1–2. 107

157. H. Taylor and N. Locket. Forthcoming. Developmental dyslexia: Neurodevelopmental disorder or specialisation in explorative cognitive search? Forthcoming. 113

158. Foad Hamidi, Melanie Baljko, and Isabel Gómez. 2017. Using participatory design with proxies with children with limited communication. *Proceedings of the 19th International ACM SIGACCESS Conference on Computers and Accessibility*, ACM, 250–259. DOI: 10.1145/3132525.3132527. 13

159. Foad Hamidi, Melanie Baljko, Toni Kunic, and Ray Feraday. 2014. Do-it-yourself (diy) assistive technology: A communication board case study. *Computers Helping People with Special Needs*, Springer International Publishing, 287–294. DOI: 10.1007/978-3-319-08599-9_44. 127

160. Giles Hamilton-Fletcher, Marianna Obrist, Phil Watten, Michele Mengucci, and Jamie Ward. 2016. "I always wanted to see the night sky": Blind user preferences for sensory substitution devices. *Proceedings of the 2016 CHI Conference on Human Factors in Computing Systems*, ACM, 2162–2174. DOI: 10.1145/2858036.2858241. 43, 140

161. Aimi Hamraie. 2018. Mapping access: Digital humanities, disability justice, and socio-spatial practice. *American Quarterly* 70, 3: 455–482. DOI: 10.1353/aq.2018.0031. 16

162. Aimi Hamraie and Kelly Fritsch. 2019. Crip technoscience manifesto. *Catalyst: Feminism, Theory, Technoscience* 5, 1: 1–33. DOI: 10.28968/cftt.v5i1.29607. 16, 37

163. John Paulin Hansen, Astrid Kofod Trudslev, Sara Amdi Harild, Alexandre Alapetite, and Katsumi Minakata. 2019. Providing access to vr through a wheelchair. *Extended Abstracts of the 2019 CHI Conference on Human Factors in Computing Systems*, ACM, CS07:1-CS07:8. DOI: 10.1145//3290607.3299048. 142

164. Kotaro Hara and Jon E. Froehlich. 2015. Characterizing and visualizing physical world accessibility at scale using crowdsourcing, computer vision, and machine learning. *ACM SIGACCESS Accessibility and Computing* 113: 13–21. DOI: 10.1145/2850440.2850442. 15

165. Donna J. Haraway and Thyrza Goodeve. 2018. *Modest_Witness@ Second_Millennium. FemaleMan_Meets_OncoMouse: Feminism and Technoscience*. Routledge. 71

166. Arno Hartholt, Sharon Mozgai, and Albert "Skip" Rizzo. 2019. Virtual job interviewing practice for high-anxiety populations. *Proceedings of the 19th ACM International Conference on Intelligent Virtual Agents*, ACM, 238–240. DOI: 10.1145/3308532.3329417. 105

167. Bilal Hassan, Muhammad Shoaib Farooq, Adnan Abid, and Nabeel Sabir. 2016. Pakistan sign language: Computer vision analysis and recommendations. *VFAST Transactions on Software Engineering* 4, 1: 1–6. DOI: 10.21015/vtse.v9i1.386. 85

168. Mustafa Tevfik Hebebci, Yasemin Bertiz, and Selahattin Alan. 2020. Investigation of views of students and teachers on distance education practices during the coronavirus (COVID-19) pandemic. *International Journal of Technology in Education and Science* 4, 4: 267–282. DOI: 10.46328/ijtes.v4i4.113. 101

169. Richard Heeks. 2017. Decent work and the digital gig economy: a developing country perspective on employment impacts and standards in online outsourcing, crowdwork, etc. *Development Informatics Working Paper* 71. DOI: 10.2139/ssrn.3431033. 92

170. P. Hernández-Peña. 2019. Global Spending on Health: A World in Transition [Global Report 2019]. WHO/HIS/HGF/HFWorkingPaper/ 19.4. 117

171. Roxana Ramirez Herrera, Catherine Holloway, Dafne Zuleima Morgado Ramirez, Bingqing Zhang, and Youngjun Cho. 2020. Breathing biofeedback relaxation intervention for wheelchair users in city navigation. 2020 *42nd Annual International Conference of the IEEE Engineering in Medicine Biology Society* (EMBC), 4575–4578. DOI: 10.1109/EMBC44109.2020.9176144. 130

172. Jody Heymann, Michael Ashley Stein, and Gonzalo Moreno. 2013. *Disability and Equity at Work*. Oxford University Press. DOI: 10.1093/acprof:oso/9780199981212.001.0001. 91

173. Kieran Hicks and Kathrin Gerling. 2015. Exploring casual exergames with kids using wheelchairs. *Proceedings of the 2015 Annual Symposium on Computer-Human Interaction in Play*, ACM, 541–546. DOI: 10.1145/2793107.2810304. 103

174. Deborah Hill, Catherine Sarah Holloway, Dafne Zuleima Morgado Ramirez, Peter Smitham, and Yannis Pappas. 2017. What are user perspectives of exoskeleton technol-

ogy? A literature review. *International Journal of Technology Assessment in Health Care* 33, 2: 160–167. DOI: 10.1017/S0266462317000460. 38

175. Megan Hofmann, Julie Burke, Jon Pearlman, Goeran Fiedler, Andrea Hess, Jon Schull, Scott Hudson and Jennifer Mankoff. 2016. Clinical and maker perspectives on the design of assistive technology with rapid prototyping technologies. *Proceedings of the 18th International ACM SIGACCESS Conference on Computers and Accessibility*, ACM, 251–256. DOI: 10.1145/2982142.2982181. 127

176. Megan Hofmann, Jeffrey Harris, Scott E. Hudson, and Jennifer Mankoff. 2016. Helping hands: requirements for a prototyping methodology for upper-limb prosthetics users. *Proceedings of the 2016 CHI Conference on Human Factors in Computing Systems—CHI '16*, ACM Press, 1769–1780. DOI: 10.1145/2858036.2858340. 127

177. Megan Hofmann, Devva Kasnitz, Jennifer Mankoff, and Cynthia L Bennett. 2020. Living disability theory: Reflections on access, research, and design. *The 22nd International ACM SIGACCESS Conference on Computers and Accessibility*, ACM, 1–13. DOI: 10.1145/3373625.3416996. 8, 13, 18, 28, 32, 61

178. Catherine Holloway. 2019. Disability interaction (DIX): A manifesto. *ACM Interactions* 26, 2 (February 2019): 44–49. DOI: 10.1145/3310322. 19

179. Catherine Holloway, Victoria Austin, Giulia Barbareschi, and Ramos. 2018. Scoping research report on Assistive Technology. On the road for universal assistive technology coverage. Prepared by the GDI Hub and partners for the UK Department for International Development. Global Disability Innvoation Hub. 22, 40, 72

180. Catherine Holloway, Kathrin Gerling, Christopher Power, Katta Spiel, Giulia Barbareschi, Anna Cox, and Paul Cairns. 2019. Disability interactions in digital games: From accessibility to inclusion. *Extended Abstracts of the Annual Symposium on Computer-Human Interaction in Play Companion Extended Abstracts*, ACM, 835–839. DOI: 10.1145/3341215.3349587. 84 , 103

181. Holloway, Catherine, Morgado Ramirez Zuleima Dafne, Tigmanshu Bhatnager, et al. 2021. A review of innovation strategies and processes to improve access to AT: looking ahead to open innovation ecosystems. *Assistive Technology: The journal of the Rehabilitation Engineering and Assistive Technology Society of North America.* 52, 53, 65, 83

182. Mahsa Honary, Roisin McNaney, and Fiona Lobban. 2018. Designing video stories around the lived experience of severe mental illness. *Proceedings of the 10th Nordic Conference on Human-Computer Interaction*, ACM, 25–38. DOI: 10.1145/3240167.3240188. 118

183.   https://plus.google.com/+UNESCO. 2019. Futures literacy. UNESCO. Retrieved October 28, 2021 from https://en.unesco.org/futuresliteracy/about. 135

184.   Amy Hurst and Shaun Kane. 2013. Making "making" accessible. *Proceedings of the 12th International Conference on Interaction Design and Children*, ACM, 635–638. DOI: 10.1145/2485760.2485883. 127

185.   Amy Hurst and Jasmine Tobias. 2011. Empowering individuals with do-it-yourself assistive technology. *The Proceedings of the 13th International ACM SIGACCESS Conference on Computers and Accessibility*, ACM, 11–18. DOI: 10.1145/2049536.2049541. 37, 127

186.   Abdulrashid A. Iliya and Chidi Ononiwu. 2021. Mechanisms for mobile phone use in empowerment: A critical realist study of people with disabilities in Nigeria. *The Electronic Journal of Information Systems in Developing Countries* 87, 2: e12158. DOI: 10.1002/isd2.12158. 106

187.   Gesu India, Geetha Ramakrishna, Jyoti Bisht, and Manohar Swaminathan. 2019. Computational thinking as play: experiences of children who are blind or low vision in India. *The 21st International ACM SIGACCESS Conference on Computers and Accessibility*, ACM, 519–522. DOI: 10.1145/3308561.3354608. 96

188.   Gesu India, Geetha Ramakrishna, Joyojeet Pal, and Manohar Swaminathan. 2020. Conceptual learning through accessible play: Project Torino and computational thinking for blind children in India. *Proceedings of the 2020 International Conference on Information and Communication Technologies and Development*, ACM, 1–11. DOI: 10.1145/3392561.3394634. 87

189.   Gesu India, Vidhya Y, Aishwarya O, Niralendu Diwakar, Mohit Jain, Aditya Vashistha, and Manohar Swaminathan. 2021. Teachers' perceptions around digital games for children in low-resource schools for the blind. In *Proceedings of the 2021 CHI Conference on Human Factors in Computing Systems,* ACM, New York, NY, 1–17. DOI: 10.1145/3411764.3445194. 97, 98

190.   Lilly Irani, Janet Vertesi, Paul Dourish, Kavita Philip, and Rebecca E. Grinter. 2010. Postcolonial computing: a lens on design and development. Presented at the *Proceedings of the Sigchi Conference on Human Factors in Computing Systems*, pp. 1311–1320. 1311–1320. 76

191.   Udeme Samuel Jacob and Jace Pillay. 2020. Impact of virtual learning space in teaching learners with moderate intellectual disability. *Psychology and Education Journal* 57, 9: 1120–1126. 97

192. Nusrat Jahan, Giulia Barbareschi, Clara Aranda Jan, Naemur Rahman, Genna Jones, Victoria Patricia Austin, Charles Musungu Mutuku, and Catherine Holloway. 2020. Inclusion and independence: the impact of mobile technology on the lives of persons with disabilities in Kenya and Bangladesh. *2020 IEEE Global Humanitarian Technology Conference* (GHTC), 1–8. DOI: 10.1109/GHTC46280.2020.9342934. 75, 105, 106

193. Dhruv Jain, Venkatesh Potluri, and Ather Sharif. 2020. Navigating graduate school with a disability. *The 22nd International ACM SIGACCESS Conference on Computers and Accessibility*, ACM, 1–11. DOI: 10.1145/3373625.3416986. 94, 99, 100

194. Jeffrey James. 2013. The diffusion of IT in the historical context of innovations from developed countries. *Social Indicators Research* 111, 1: 175–184. DOI: 10.1007/s11205-011-9989-0. 74

195. Spencer L. James, Degu Abate, Kalkidan Hassen Abate, Solomon M. Abay, Christiana Abbafati, Nooshin Abbasi, Hedayat Abbastabar, Foad Abd-Allah, Jemal Abdela, Ahmet Abdelalim, et al. 2018. Global, regional, and national incidence, prevalence, and years lived with disability for 354 diseases and injuries for 195 countries and territories, 1990–2017: a systematic analysis for the Global Burden of Disease Study 2017. *The Lancet* 392, 10159: 1789–1858. DOI: 10.1016/S0140-6736(18)32279-7. 128

196. Collin Johnson and Benjamin Kuipers. 2018. Socially-aware navigation using topological maps and social norm learning. *Proceedings of the 2018 AAAI/ACM Conference on AI, Ethics, and Society*, ACM, 151–157. DOI: 10.1145/3278721.3278772. 143

197. Jasmine Jones and Joyojeet Pal. 2015. Counteracting dampeners: understanding technology-amplified capabilities of people with disabilities in Sierra Leone. In *Proceedings of the Seventh International Conference on Information and Communication Technologies and Development, ICTD '15*. ACM, New York, NY, pp. 1–10. DOI: 10.1145/2737856.2738025. 10

198. Joseph Nathaniel Kaye. 2001. *Symbolic Olfactory Display*. Massachusetts Institute of Technology. 140

199. Sushant Kafle, Becca Dingman, and Matt Huenerfauth. 2021. Deaf and hard-of-hearing users evaluating designs for highlighting key words in educational lecture videos. *ACM Transactions on Accessible Computing* 14, 4: 20:1-20:24. DOI: 10.1145/3470651. 100

200. Vaishnav Kameswaran, Jatin Gupta, Joyojeet Pal, Sile O'Modhrain, Tiffany C. Veinot, Robin Brewer, Aakanksha Parameshwar, Vidhya Y, and Jacki O'Neill. 2018. "We can go anywhere": Understanding independence through a case study of ride-hailing use

by people with visual impairments in metropolitan India. Proc. *ACM Human-Computer Interactions* 2, CSCW: 85:1-85:24. DOI: 10.1145/3274354. 59, 79

201. Steven K. Kapp, Kristen Gillespie-Lynch, Lauren E. Sherman, and Ted Hutman. 2013. Deficit, difference, or both? Autism and neurodiversity. *Developmental Psychology* 49, 1: 59–71. DOI: 10.1037/a0028353. 112

202. Devva Kasnitz and Russell Shuttleworth. 2001. Introduction: Anthropology in disability studies. *Disability Studies Quarterly* 21, 3. DOI: 10.18061/dsq.v21i3.289. 81

203. David Kennedy. 2003. The international human rights movement: Part of the problem? In *Human Rights*. Routledge. 80

204. Noel Kennedy, Rosemary Abbott, and Eugene S. Paykel. 2004. Longitudinal syndromal and sub-syndromal symptoms after severe depression: 10-year follow-up study. *The British Journal of Psychiatry* 184: 330–336. DOI: 10.1192/bjp.184.4.330. 45

205. L. P. J. Kenney, Robert Ssekitoleko, A. E. A Chadwell, Louise Ackers, Maggie Donovan Hall, Dafne Zuleima, Morgado Ramirezz, Cathrine Holloway, Paul Graham, Alan Cockcroft, Bernadette Deere, Steven McCormack, Akram Semwanga, Gizamba Mafabi Henry, and Kalibbala Mark Giggs. 2019. Prosthetics services in Uganda: a series of studies to inform the design of a low cost, but fit-for-purpose, body-powered prosthesis. Presented at the *Global Perspectives on Assistive Technology-Proceedings of the GReAT Consultation 2019*, WHO, pp. 414–426. 16

206. Lorcan Kenny, Caroline Hattersley, Bonnie Molins, Carole Buckley, Carol Povey, and Elizabeth Pellicano. 2016. Which terms should be used to describe autism? Perspectives from the UK autism community. *Autism* 20, 4: 442–462. DOI: 10.1177/1362361315588200. 19

207. Ronald C. Kessler, Patricia Berglund, Olga Demler, Robert Jin, Kathleen R. Merikangas, and Ellen E. Walters. 2005. Lifetime prevalence and age-of-onset distributions of dsm-iv disorders in the national comorbidity survey replication. *Archives of General Psychiatry* 62, 6: 593–602. DOI: 10.1001/archpsyc.62.6.593. 129

208. Os Keyes. 2020. Automating autism: Disability, discourse, and artificial intelligence. *The Journal of Sociotechnical Critique* 1, 1. DOI: 10.25779/89bj-j396. 139

209. Chapal Khasnabis, Catherine Holloway, and Malcolm MacLachlan. 2020. The digital and assistive technologies for ageing initiative: learning from the GATE initiative. *The Lancet Healthy Longevity* 1, 3: e94–e95. DOI: 10.1016/S2666-7568(20)30049-0. 120, 124, 125

210. Chapal Khasnabis, Zafar Mirza, and Malcolm MacLachlan. 2015. Opening the GATE to inclusion for people with disabilities. *Lancet* 386, 10010: 2229–2230. DOI: 10.1016/S0140-6736(15)01093-4. 22

211. Eunjung Kim. 2017. *Curative Violence: Rehabilitating Disability, Gender, and Sexuality in Modern Korea*. Duke University Press. 80

212. Lynn Kirabo, Elizabeth J. Carter, and Aaron Steinfeld. 2020. "You are asking me to pay for my legs" Exploring the experiences, perceptions, and aspirations of informal public transportation users in Kampala and Kigali. *ACM SIGCAS Conference on Computing and Sustainable Societies* 136–147. DOI: 10.1145/3378393.3402269. 10

213. Lynn Kirabo, Elizabeth Jeanne Carter, Devon Barry, and Aaron Steinfeld. 2021. Priorities, technology, & power: Co-designing an inclusive transit agenda in Kampala, Uganda. In *Proceedings of the 2021 CHI Conference on Human Factors in Computing Systems*. ACM, New York, NY, USA, 1–11. DOI: 10.1145/3411764.3445168. 10

214. Anne V. Kirby, Virginia A. Dickie, and Grace T. Baranek. 2015. Sensory experiences of children with autism spectrum disorder: In their own words. *Autism* 19, 3: 316–326. DOI: 10.1177/1362361314520756. 97

215. Sarah E. Kisanga and Dalton H. Kisanga. 2020. The role of assistive technology devices in fostering the participation and learning of students with visual impairment in higher education institutions in Tanzania. *Disability and Rehabilitation: Assistive Technology* 1–10. DOI: 10.1080/17483107.2020.1817989. 21

216. Predrag Klasnja, Sunny Consolvo, and Wanda Pratt. 2011. How to evaluate technologies for health behavior change in HCI research. Presented at the *Proceedings of the SIGCHI Conference on Human Factors in Computing Systems*, 3063–3072. DOI: 10.1145/1978942.1979396. 118, 119, 121

217. Frank Klassner. 1996. Artificial intelligence: Introduction. *XRDS: Crossroads, The ACM Magazine for Students* 3, 1: 2. DOI: 10.1145/332148.332149. 136

218. Varsha Koushik, Darren Guinness, and Shaun K. Kane. 2019. StoryBlocks: A tangible programming game to create accessible audio stories. In *Proceedings of the 2019 CHI Conference on Human Factors in Computing Systems*, ACM, New York, NY, 1–12. DOI: 10.1145/3290605.3300722. 95

219. Stacey Kuznetsov and Eric Paulos. 2010. Rise of the Expert Amateur: DIY projects, communities, and cultures. *Proceedings of the 6th Nordic Conference on Human-Computer Interaction: Extending Boundaries*, ACM, 295–304. DOI: 10.1145/1868914.1868950. 127

220. Kamal Lamichhane and Tomoo Okubo. 2014. The nexus between disability, education, and employment: Evidence from Nepal. *Oxford Development Studies* 42, 3: 439–453. DOI: 10.1080/13600818.2014.927843. 93

221. Jonathan Lazar, Abiodun Olalere, and Brian Wentz. 2012. Investigating the accessibility and usability of job application web sites for blind users. *Journal of Usability Studies* 7, 2: 68–87. 46, 104, 105

222. Kathy Leadbitter, Karen Leneh Buckle, Ceri Ellis, and Martijn Dekker. 2021. Autistic self-advocacy and the neurodiversity movement: Implications for autism early intervention research and practice. *Frontiers in Psychology* 12: 782. DOI: 10.3389/fpsyg.2021.635690. 45

223. Jean Lebel and Robert McLean. 2018. A better measure of research from the global south. *Nature* 559, 7712: 23–26. DOI: 10.1038/d41586-018-05581-4. 89

224. Zuzanna Lechelt, Yvonne Rogers, Nicolai Marquardt, and Venus Shum. 2016. Democratizing children's engagement with the internet of things through connectUs. *Proceedings of the 2016 ACM International Joint Conference on Pervasive and Ubiquitous Computing: Adjunct*, ACM, 133–136. DOI: 10.1145/2968219.2971435. 94

225. Zuzanna Lechelt, Yvonne Rogers, Nicola Yuill, Lena Nagl, Grazia Ragone, and Nicolai Marquardt. 2018. Inclusive computing in special needs classrooms: Designing for all. *Proceedings of the 2018 CHI Conference on Human Factors in Computing Systems*, ACM, 517:1-517:12. DOI: 10.1145/3173574.3174091. 94

226. Ronald Lee. 2003. The demographic transition: Three centuries of fundamental change. *Journal of Economic Perspectives* 17, 4: 167–190. DOI: 10.1257/089533003772034943. 119

227. K. Lim and C. Tan. 2014. Epilepsy stigma in Asia: the meaning and impact of stigma. *Neurology Asia* 19, 1. 80

228. Zilan Lin, Kai Kunze, Atsuro Ueki, and Masa Inakage. 2020. AromaCue—A scent toolkit to cope with stress using the 4-7-8 breathing method. *Proceedings of the Fourteenth International Conference on Tangible, Embedded, and Embodied Interaction*, ACM, 265–272. DOI: 10.1145/3374920.3374940. 140

229. Hanoch Livneh, Fong Chan, and Cahit Kaya. 2014. Stigma related to physical and sensory disabilities. In *The Stigma of Disease and Disability: Understanding Causes and Overcoming Injustices*. American Psychological Association, Washington, DC, US, 93–120. DOI: 10.1037/14297-006. 80

230.   J. Long. 1995. *Extraordinary Human-Computer Interaction: Interfaces for Users with Disabilities*. CUP Archive. 5, 6

231.   K.H. Low. 2011. Robot-assisted gait rehabilitation: From exoskeletons to gait systems. *Defense Science Research Conference and Expo* (DSR), 2011, 1–10. DOI: 10.1109/DSR.2011.6026886. 38

232.   Ewa Luger and Abigail Sellen. 2016. "Like having a really bad PA": The gulf between user expectation and experience of conversational agents. *Proceedings of the 2016 CHI Conference on Human Factors in Computing Systems*, ACM, 5286–5297. DOI: 10.1145/2858036.2858288. 136

233.   Daniel C. Lustig and David R. Strauser. 2007. Causal relationships between poverty and disability. *Rehabilitation Counseling Bulletin* 50, 4: 194–202. DOI: 10.1177/00343552070500040101. 21

234.   Alexander MacIntosh, Emily Lam, Vincent Vigneron, Nicolas Vignais, and Elaine Biddiss. 2019. Biofeedback interventions for individuals with cerebral palsy: A systematic review. *Disability and Rehabilitation* 41, 20: 2369–2391. DOI: 10.1080/09638288.2018.1468933. 43

235.   Alexander MacIntosh, Emily Lam, Vincent Vigneron, Nicolas Vignais, and Elaine Biddiss. 2019. Biofeedback interventions for individuals with cerebral palsy: A systematic review. *Disability and Rehabilitation* 41, 20: 2369–2391. DOI: 10.1080/09638288.2018.1468933. 43

236.   Kelly Mack, Emma McDonnell, Dhruv Jain, Lucy Lu Wang, Jon E. Froehlich, and Leah Findlater. 2021. What do we mean by "Accessibility Research"? A literature survey of accessibility papers in CHI and ASSETS from 1994 to 2019. In *Proceedings of the 2021 CHI Conference on Human Factors in Computing Systems*. ACM, New York, NY, 1–18. DOI: 10.1145/3411764.3445412. 1

237.   Kelly Mack, Emma McDonnell, Dhruv Jain, Lucy Lu Wang, Jon E. Froehlich, and Leah Findlater. 2021. What do we mean by "Accessibility Research"? A literature survey of accessibility papers in CHI and ASSETS from 1994 to 2019. *Proceedings of the 2021 CHI Conference on Human Factors in Computing Systems*, ACM, 1–18. DOI: 10.1145/3411764.3445412. 3, 28

238.   Malcolm MacLachlan, David Banes, Diane Bell, et al. 2018. Assistive technology policy: a position paper from the first global research, innovation, and education on assistive technology (GREAT) summit. *Disability and Rehabilitation: Assistive Technology* 13, 5: 454–466. DOI: 10.1080/17483107.2018.1468496. 24, 51, 82

239. Malcolm MacLachlan, Joanne McVeigh, Michael Cooke, et al. 2018. Intersections between systems thinking and market shaping for assistive technology: The SMART (Systems-Market for Assistive and Related Technologies) thinking matrix. *International Journal of Environmental Research and Public Health* 15, 12: 2627. DOI: 10.3390/ijerph15122627. 81, 82, 83

240. Malcolm MacLachlan and Marcia Scherer. 2018. Systems thinking for assistive technology: A commentary on the GREAT summit. *Disability and Rehabilitation: Assistive Technology* 0, 0: 1–5. DOI: 10.1080/17483107.2018.1472306. 23, 53, 125

241. Mirca Madianou. 2019. Technocolonialism: Digital innovation and data practices in the humanitarian response to refugee crises. *Social Media + Society* 5, 3: 2056305119863146. DOI: 10.1177/2056305119863146. 73

242. Galina Madjaroff and Helena Mentis. 2017. Narratives of older adults with mild cognitive impairment and their caregivers. *Proceedings of the 19th International ACM SIGACCESS Conference on Computers and Accessibility*, ACM, 140–149. DOI: 10.1145/3132525.3132554. 22

243. Abhijit Majumdar, Mahesh Shaw, and Sanjib Kumar Sinha. 2020. COVID-19 debunks the myth of socially sustainable supply chain: A case of the clothing industry in South Asian countries. *Sustainable Production and Consumption* 24: 150–155. DOI: 10.1016/j.spc.2020.07.001. 89

244. MakerNetAlliance. OpenKnow-Where. StandardsRepo. Retrieved October 28, 2021 from https://app.standardsrepo.com/MakerNetAlliance/OpenKnow-Where. 52

245. Stephann Makri, Ann Blandford, Mel Woods, Sarah Sharples, and Deborah Maxwell. 2014. "Making my own luck": Serendipity strategies and how to support them in digital information environments. *Journal of the Association for Information Science and Technology* 65, 11: 2179–2194. DOI: 10.1002/asi.23200. 53

246. Jennifer Mankoff. 2016. The wicked problem of making SIGCHI accessible. *Interactions* 23, 3: 6–7. DOI: 10.1145/2903528. 20, 31

247. Jennifer Mankoff, Gillian R. Hayes, and Devva Kasnitz. 2010. Disability studies as a source of critical inquiry for the field of assistive technology. *Proceedings of the 12th International ACM SIGACCESS Conference on Computers and Accessibility*, ACM, 3–10. DOI: 10.1145/1878803.1878807. 2, 8, 31

248. Marcia Rioux. 2021. Disability rights in education. *The SAGE Handbook of Special Education*. SAGE Publications Ltd. 91

249. Methusela Mishael Masanja, Marko Mwita Imori, and Ismail Juma Kaudunde. 2020. Factors associated with negative attitudes toward albinism and people with albinism: A case of households living with persons with albinism in Lake Zone, Tanzania. *Open Journal of Social Sciences* 8, 4: 523–537. DOI: 10.4236/jss.2020.84038. 80

250. Rebecca Matter, Mark Harniss, Tone Oderud, Johan Borg, and Arne H. Eide. 2017. Assistive technology in resource-limited environments: a scoping review. *Disability and Rehabilitation: Assistive Technology* 12, 2: 105–114. DOI: 10.1080/17483107.2016.1188170. 40

251. Michael Mauderer, Garreth W Tigwell, Benjamin M Gorman, and David R Flatla. 2017. Beyond accessibility: Lifting perceptual limitations for everyone. arXiv preprint arXiv:1709.08957. 4

252. Michael McCarthy. 2015. U.S. healthcare spending will reach 20% of GDP by 2024, says report. *BMJ* 351: h4204. DOI: 10.1136/bmj.h4204. 50

253. Cheryl McEwan and Ruth Butler. 2007. Disability and development: Different models, different places. *Geography Compass* 1, 3: 448–466. DOI: 10.1111/j.1749-8198.2007.00023.x. 79

254. David McGookin, Euan Robertson, and Stephen Brewster. 2010. Clutching at straws: using tangible interaction to provide non-visual access to graphs. In: *Proceedings of the SIGCHI Conference on Human Factors in Computing Systems, CHI '10*. ACM, Atlanta, Georgia, pp. 1715–1724. DOI: 10.1145/1753326.1753583. 23

255. Aoife McNicholl, Hannah Casey, Deirdre Desmond, and Pamela Gallagher. 2021. The impact of assistive technology use for students with disabilities in higher education: a systematic review. *Disability and Rehabilitation: Assistive Technology* 16, 2: 130–143. DOI: 10.1080/17483107.2019.1642395. 92

256. Helen Meekosha and Karen Soldatic. 2011. Human rights and the Global South: The case of disability. *Third World Quarterly* 32, 8: 1383–1397. DOI: 10.1080/01436597.2011.614800. 80 , 81

257. Zoë Meleo-Erwin, Betty Kollia, Joe Fera, Alyssa Jahren, and Corey Basch. 2021. Online support information for students with disabilities in colleges and universities during the COVID-19 pandemic. *Disability and Health Journal* 14, 1: 101013. DOI: 10.1016/j.dhjo.2020.101013. 101

258. Cristina Mesa Vieira, Oscar H. Franco, Carlos Gómez Restrepo, and Thomas Abel. 2020. COVID-19: The forgotten priorities of the pandemic. *Maturitas* 136: 38–41. DOI: 10.1016/j.maturitas.2020.04.004. 64

259.   Oussama Metatla and Clare Cullen. 2018. "Bursting the assistance bubble": Designing inclusive technology with children with mixed visual abilities. In *Proceedings of the 2018 CHI Conference on Human Factors in Computing Systems*. ACM, New York, NY, 1–14. DOI: 10.1145/3173574.3173920. 95

260.   Oussama Metatla, Anja Thieme, Emeline Brulé, Cynthia Bennett, Marcos Serrano, and Christophe Jouffrais. 2018. Toward classroom experiences inclusive of students with disabilities. *Interactions* 26, 1: 40–45. DOI: 10.1145/3289485. 94, 97

261.   Ashley Miller, Joan Malasig, Brenda Castro, Vicki L. Hanson, Hugo Nicolau, and Alessandra Brandão. 2017. The use of smart glasses for lecture comprehension by deaf and hard of hearing students. *Proceedings of the 2017 CHI Conference Extended Abstracts on Human Factors in Computing Systems*, ACM, 1909–1915. DOI: 10.1145/3027063.3053117. 13

262.   Katie Miller. 2020. *A Matter of Perspective: Discrimination, Bias, and Inequality in AI*. IGI Global. DOI: 10.4018/978-1-7998-3130-3.ch010. 139

263.   Damian E. M. Milton. 2012. On the ontological status of autism: the "double empathy problem." *Disability and Society* 27, 6: 883–887. DOI: 10.1080/09687599.2012.710008. 96

264.   Higinio Mora, Virgilio Gilart-Iglesias, Raquel Pérez-del Hoyo, and María Dolores Andújar-Montoya. 2017. A comprehensive system for monitoring urban accessibility in smart cities. *Sensors* (Basel, Switzerland) 17, 8. DOI: 10.3390/s17081834. 91

265.   D. Morgado-Ramirez, Giulia Barbareschi, Maggie Donovan-Hall, Mohammad Sobuh, ida' Elayyan, Brenda T. Nakandi, Robert Tamale Ssekitoleko, and Joyce Olenja. 2020. Disability design and innovation in computing research in low resource settings. *The International Acm Sigaccess Conference on Computers and Accessibility*. DOI: 10.1145/3373625.3417301. 10, 72, 76, 88

266.   Priya Morjaria and Andrew Bastawrous. 2017. Helpful developments and technologies for school eye health programs. *Community Eye Health* 30, 98: 34–36. 131

267.   Meredith Ringel Morris, Andrew Begel, and Ben Wiedermann. 2015. Understanding the challenges faced by neurodiverse software engineering employees: toward a more inclusive and productive technical workforce. *Proceedings of the 17th International ACM SIGACCESS Conference on Computers* #38, Accessibility, ACM, 173–184. DOI: 10.1145/2700648.2809841. 107

268.   Cecily Morrison, Edward Cutrell, Anupama Dhareshwar, Kevin Doherty, Anja Thieme, and Alex Taylor. 2017. Imagining artificial intelligence applications with people with visual disabilities using tactile ideation. *Proceedings of the 19th International ACM SIGACCESS*

Conference on Computers and Accessibility, ACM, 81–90. DOI: 10.1145/3132525.3132530. 137

269. Cecily Morrison, Nicolas Villar, Alex Hadwen-Bennett, Tim Regan, Daniel Cletheroe, Anja Thieme, and Sue Sentance. 2021. Physical programming for blind and low vision children at scale. *Human–Computer Interaction* 36, 5–6: 535–569. DOI: 10.1080/07370024.2019.1621175. 95, 96

270. Cecily Morrison, Nicolas Villar, Anja Thieme, Zahra Ashktorab, eloise Taysom, Oscar Salandin, Daniel Cletheroe, Greg Saul, Alan F. Blackwell, Darren Edge, Martin Grayson, and Haiyan Zhang. 2020. Torino: A tangible programming language inclusive of children with visual disabilities. *Human–Computer Interaction* 35, 3: 191–239. DOI: 10.1080/07370024.2018.1512413. 87, 94, 95

271. Ingunn Moser and John Law. 1999. Good passages, bad passages. *The Sociological Review* 47, S1: 196–219. DOI: 10.1111/j.1467-954X.1999.tb03489.x. 58

272. Motivation. The next generation of wheelchairs. Retrieved October 28, 2021 from https://www.motivation.org.uk/next-generation-wheelchairs. 48

273. Martez E. Mott, Radu-Daniel Vatavu, Shaun K. Kane, and Jacob O. Wobbrock. 2016. Smart Touch: Improving touch accuracy for people with motor impairments with template matching. *Proceedings of the 2016 CHI Conference on Human Factors in Computing Systems*, ACM, 1934–1946. DOI: 10.1145/2858036.2858390. 6

274. Goutam Mukherjee and Amalendu Samanta. 2005. Wheelchair charity: A useless benevolence in community-based rehabilitation. *Disability and Rehabilitation* 27, 10: 591–596. DOI: 10.1080/09638280400018387. 10

275. Emmanuel Mutisya and Masaru Yarime. 2011. Understanding the grassroots dynamics of slums in Nairobi: the dilemma of Kibera informal settlements. *International Transaction Journal of Engineering, Management & Applied Sciences & Technologies* 2, 2: 197–213. 76

276. Junichi Nabeshima, MHD Yamen Saraiji, and Kouta Minamizawa. 2019. Arque: artificial biomimicry-Inspired tail for extending innate body functions. *ACM SIGGRAPH 2019 Emerging Technologies*, ACM, 1–2. DOI: 10.1145/3305367.3327987. 144

277. Timothy Neate, Abi Roper, Stephanie Wilson, and Jane Marshall. 2019. *Empowering Expression for Users with Aphasia Through Constrained Creativity*. 1–12. 13

278. Kristin Neidlinger, Stephanie Koenderink, and Khiet P. Truong. 2021. Give the body a voice: Co-design with profound intellectual and multiple disabilities to create mul-

tisensory wearables. *Extended Abstracts of the 2021 CHI Conference on Human Factors in Computing Systems*, ACM, 1–6. DOI: 10.1145/3411763.3451797. 44

279. Isabel Neto, Wafa Johal, Marta Couto, Hugo Nicolau, Ana Paiva, and Arzu Guneysu. 2020. Using tabletop robots to promote inclusive classroom experiences. *Proceedings of the Interaction Design and Children Conference, ACM*, 281–292. DOI: 10.1145/3392063.3394439. 94

280. Rita Newton, Marcus Ormerod, Elizabeth Burton, Lynne Mitchell, and Catharine Ward-Thompson. 2010. Increasing independence for older people through good street design. *Journal of Integrated Care* 18, 24. DOI: 10.5042/jic.2010.0246. 19

281. Janet Njelesani, Goli Hashemi, Cathy Cameron, Deb Cameron, Danielle Richard, and Penny Parnes. 2018. From the day they are born: a qualitative study exploring violence against children with disabilities in West Africa. *BMC Public Health* 18, 1: 1–7. DOI: 10.1186/s12889-018-5057-x. 80

282. Christopher Noessel. 2017. *Designing Agentive Technology: AI that Works for People*. Rosenfeld Media. 135

283. Christopher S. Norrie, Annalu Waller, and Elizabeth F. S. Hannah. 2021. Establishing context: AAC device adoption and support in a special-education setting. *ACM Transactions on Computer-Human Interaction* 28, 2: 13:1-13:30. DOI: 10.1145/3446205. 97

284. Office for National Statistics. 2019. *Disability and Employment*, UK: 2019. 92

285. Ben Oldfrey, Giulia Barbareschi, Priya Morjaria, Tamara Giltsoff, Jessica Massie, Mark Miodownik, and Catherine Holloway. 2021. Could assistive technology provision models help pave the way for more environmentally sustainable models of product design, manufacture and service in a post-covid world? *Sustainability* 13, 19: 10867. DOI: 10.3390/su131910867. 145

286. Miranda Olff. 2015. Mobile mental health: a challenging research agenda. *European Journal of Psychotraumatology* 6: 10.3402/ejpt.v6.27882. DOI: 10.3402/ejpt.v6.27882. 128

287. Brian O'Rourke, Wija Oortwijn, Tara Schuller, and the International Joint Task Group. 2020. The new definition of health technology assessment: A milestone in international collaboration. *International Journal of Technology Assessment in Health Care* 36, 3: 187–190. DOI: 10.1017/S0266462320000215. 117

288. Edgar Pacheco. 2021. Digital technologies in the context of university transition and disability: theoretical and empirical advances. Retrieved October 28, 2021 at: https://philpapers.org/rec/PACDTI. DOI: 10.31235/osf.io/vu5ch. 100

289.   Joyojeet Pal, Priyank Chandra, Terence O'Neill, Maura Youngman, Jasmine Jones, Hi Hye Song, William Strayer, and Ludmila Ferrari. 2016. An accessibility infrastructure for the Global South. *Proceedings of the Eighth International Conference on Information and Communication Technologies and Development*, ACM, 24:1-24:11. DOI: 10.1145/2909609.2909666. 10, 58, 78, 79

290.   Joyojeet Pal and Meera Lakshmanan. 2012. Assistive technology and the employment of people with vision impairments in India. *Proceedings of the Fifth International Conference on Information and Communication Technologies and Development*, ACM, 307–317. DOI: 10.1145/2160673.2160711. 79, 106

291.   Joyojeet Pal and Meera Lakshmanan. 2015. Mobile devices and weak ties: a study of vision impairments and workplace access in Bangalore. *Disability and Rehabilitation: Assistive Technology* 10, 4: 323–331. DOI: 10.3109/17483107.2014.974224. 105

292.   Joyojeet Pal, Anandhi Viswanathan, Priyank Chandra, Anisha Nazareth, Vaishnav Kameswaran, Hariharan Subramonyam, Aditya Johri, Mark S. Ackerman, and Sile O'Modhrain. 2017. Agency in assistive technology adoption: Visual impairment and smartphone use in Bangalore. *Proceedings of the 2017 CHI Conference on Human Factors in Computing Systems*, ACM, 5929–5940. DOI: 10.1145/3025453.3025895. 59

293.   Joyojeet Pal, Anandhi Viswanathan, and Ji-Hye Song. 2016. Smartphone adoption drivers and challenges in urban living: Cases from Seoul and Bangalore. *Proceedings of the 8th Indian Conference on Human Computer Interaction*, ACM, 24–34. DOI: 10.1145/3014362.3014364. 18, 74

294.   T Louise-Bender Pape, J Kim, and B Weiner. 2002. The shaping of individual meanings assigned to assistive technology: a review of personal factors. *Disability and Rehabilitation* 24, 1–3: 5–20. DOI: 10.1080/09638280110066235. 7

295.   Ioannis Theoklitos Paraskevopoulos, Emmanouil Tsekleves, Alyson Warland, and Cherry Kilbride. 2016. Virtual Reality-based holistic framework:a tool for participatory development of customised playful therapy sessions for motor rehabilitation. In *IEEE*, ESP. DOI: 10.1109/VS-GAMES.2016.7590378. 44

296.   Penny Parnes, Debra Cameron, Nancy Christie, Lynn Cockburn, Goli Hashemi, and Karen Yoshida. 2009. Disability in low-income countries: Issues and implications. *Disability and Rehabilitation* 31, 14: 1170–1180. DOI: 10.1080/09638280902773778. 79

297.   Balaji Parthasarathy, Supriya Dey, and Pranjali Gupta. 2021. Overcoming wicked problems and institutional voids for social innovation: University-NGO partnerships in the

Global South. *Technological Forecasting and Social Change* 173: 121104. DOI: 10.1016/j. techfore.2021.121104. 54

298. A. Patricia Aguilera-Hermida. 2020. College students' use and acceptance of emergency online learning due to COVID-19. *International Journal of Educational Research Open* 1: 100011. DOI: 10.1016/j.ijedro.2020.100011. 101

299. Pitambar Paudel. 2020. Online Education: Benefits, Challenges and Strategies During and After COVID-19 in Higher Education. *International Journal on Studies in Education* 3, 70–85. DOI: 10.46328/ijonse.32. 101

300. Sachin R. Pendse, Naveena Karusala, Divya Siddarth, Pattie Gonsalves, Seema Mehrotra, John A Naslund, Mamta Sood, Neha Kumar, and Amit Sharma. 2019. Mental health in the global south: challenges and opportunities in HCI for development. *Proceedings of the 2nd ACM SIGCAS Conference on Computing and Sustainable Societies*, ACM, 22–36. DOI: 10.1145/3314344.3332483. 128, 129

301. Vyjeyanthi S. Periyakoil. 2007. Taming wicked problems in modern health care systems. *Journal of Palliative Medicine* 10, 3: 658–659. DOI: 10.1089/jpm.2007.9955. 31

302. Hans Persson, Henrik Åhman, Alexander Arvei Yngling, and Jan Gulliksen. 2015. Universal design, inclusive design, accessible design, design for all: different concepts—one goal? On the concept of accessibility—historical, methodological and philosophical aspects. *Universal Access in the Information Society* 14, 4: 505–526. DOI: 10.1007/s10209-014-0358-z. 3, 6

303. Jackie Pichette, Sarah Brumwell, and Jessica Rizk. 2020. *Improving the Accessibility of Remote Higher Education: Lessons from the Pandemic and Recommendations*. Higher Education Quality Council of Ontario. 101

304. Robert P. Pierce and James J. Stevermer. 2020. Disparities in use of telehealth at the onset of the COVID-19 public health emergency. *Journal of Telemedicine and Telecare*: 1357633X20963893. DOI: 10.1177/1357633X20963893. 122

305. A. Pires, Filipa Rocha, António Neto, Hugo Simão, H. Nicolau, and Tiago Guerreiro. 2020. Exploring accessible programming with educators and visually impaired children. In: *Proceedings of the Interaction Design and Children Conference, IDC '20*. ACM, New York, NY, pp. 148–160. DOI: 10.1145/3392063.3394437.94

306. Sheila Pontis, Ann Blandford, Elke Greifeneder, Hesham Attalla, and David Neal. 2017. Keeping up to date: An academic researcher's information journey. *Journal of the Association for Information Science and Technology* 68, 1: 22–35. DOI: 10.1002/asi.23623. 53

307. Halley P Profita, Abigale Stangl, Laura Matuszewska, Sigrunn Sky, and Shaun K Kane. 2016. Nothing to hide: Aesthetic customization of hearing AIDS and cochlear implants in an online community. In: *Proceedings of the 18th International ACM SIGACCESS Conference on Computers and Accessibility, ASSETS '16*. ACM, Reno, Nevada, pp. 219–227. DOI: 10.1145/2982142.2982159. 7

308. Halley P. Profita, Abigale Stangl, Laura Matuszewska, Sigrunn Sky, Raja Kushalnagar, and Shaun K Kane. 2018. "Wear it loud" how and why hearing aid and cochlear implant users customize their devices. *ACM Transactions on Accessible Computing* (TACCESS) 11, 3: 1–32. DOI: 10.1145/3214382. 8

309. Jasbir K. Puar. 2009. Prognosis time: Toward a geopolitics of affect, debility and capacity. *Women and Performance: A Journal of Feminist Theory* 19, 2: 161–172. DOI: 10.1080/07407700903034147. 73

310. Muhammad Aminur Rahaman, Mahmood Jasim, Md. Haider Ali, and Md. Hasanuzzaman. 2014. Real-time computer vision-based Bengali Sign Language recognition. *2014 17th International Conference on Computer and Information Technology* (ICCIT), 192–197. DOI: 10.1109/ICCITECHN.2014.7073150. 85

311. Amon Rapp, Federica Cena, Claudio Mattutino, Guido Boella, Claudio Schifanella, Roberto Keller, and Stefania Brighenti. 2019. Designing an urban support for autism. *Proceedings of the 21st International Conference on Human-Computer Interaction with Mobile Devices and Services* 1–6. DOI: 10.1145/3338286.3344390. 13

312. Minna Räsänen and James M Nyce. 2006. A new role for anthropology? rewriting" context" and" analysis" in HCI research. In: *Proceedings of the 4th Nordic Conference on Human-Computer Interaction: Changing Roles, NordiCHI '06*. ACM, New York, NY, pp. 175–184. DOI: 10.1145/1182475.118249. 74

313. Emily Read, Cora Woolsey, Chris A. McGibbon, and Colleen O'Connell. 2020. Physiotherapists' experiences using the ekso bionic exoskeleton with patients in a neurological rehabilitation hospital: A qualitative study. *Rehabilitation Research and Practice* 2020: e2939573. DOI: 10.1155/2020/2939573. 91

314. Marti Lynn Riemer-Reiss. 1997. *Factors Associated with Assistive Technology Discontinuance Among Individuals with Disabilities*. University of Northern Colorado. 7

315. Brigitte Ringbauer, Matthias Peissner, and Maria Gemou. 2007. From "design for all" toward "design for one"–A modular user interface approach, *International Conference on Universal Access in Human-Computer Interaction*, Springer, 517–526. DOI: 10.1007/978-3-540-73279-2_58. 36

316. Kathryn E. Ringland, Jennifer Nicholas, Rachel Kornfield, Emily G. Lattie, David C. Mohr, and Madhu Reddy. 2019. Understanding mental ill-health as psychosocial disability: Implications for assistive technology. *The 21st International ACM SIGACCESS Conference on Computers and Accessibility*, ACM, 156–170. DOI: 10.1145/3308561.3353785. 45

317. Horst W. J. Rittel and Melvin M. Webber. 1973. Dilemmas in a general theory of planning. *Policy Sciences* 4, 2: 155–169. DOI: 10.1007/BF01405730. 21, 30

318. Hayley Robinson, Bruce A. MacDonald, Ngaire Kerse, and Elizabeth Broadbent. 2013. Suitability of healthcare robots for a dementia unit and suggested improvements. *Journal of the American Medical Directors Association* 14, 1: 34–40. DOI: 10.1016/j. jamda.2012.09.006. 143

319. Raquel Robinson, Katelyn Wiley, Amir Rezaeivahdati, Madison Klarkowski, and Regan L Mandryk. 2020. "Let's get physiological, physiological!" A systematic review of affective gaming. In *Proceedings of the Annual Symposium on Computer-Human Interaction in Play, CHI PLAY'20*. ACM, New York, NY, pp. 132–147. DOI: 10.1145/3410404.3414227. 44

320. Yvonne Rogers. 2012. *HCI Theory: Classical, Modern, and Contemporary*. Morgan & Claypool Publishers. DOI: 10.2200/S00418ED1V01Y201205HCI014. 62

321. Yvonne Rogers, Kay Connelly, Lenore Tedesco, William Hazlewood, Andrew Kurtz, Robert E. Hall, Josh Hursey, and Tammy Toscos. 2007. Why it's worth the hassle: The value of in-situ studies when designing Ubicomp. *UbiComp 2007: Ubiquitous Computing*, Springer, 336–353. DOI: 10.1007/978-3-540-74853-3_20. 33

322. Yvonne Rogers and Gary Marsden. 2013. Does he take sugar? Moving beyond the rhetoric of compassion. *Interactions* 20, 4: 48–57. DOI: 10.1145/2486227.2486238. 60

323. Yvonne Rogers and Paul Marshall. 2017. *Research in the Wild*. Synthesis Lectures on Human-Centered Informatics 10, 3: i–97. DOI: 10.2200/S00764ED1V01Y201703HCI037. 33, 34

324. Yvonne Rogers, Venus Shum, Nic Marquardt, Susan Lechelt, Rose Johnson, Howard Baker, and Matt Davies. 2017. From the BBC micro to micro:bit and beyond: a British innovation. *Interactions* 24, 2: 74–77. DOI: 10.1145/3029601. 94

325. Yvonne Rogers, Nicola Yuill, and Paul Marshall. 2013. Contrasting lab-based and in-the-wild studies for evaluating multi-user technologies. In *The SAGE Handbook of Digital Technology Research*. SAGE Publications Inc., 359–373. DOI: 10.4135/9781446282229. n24. 33

326. Crystal Rolfe and Benjamin Gardner. 2016. Experiences of hearing loss and views toward interventions to promote uptake of rehabilitation support among UK adults. *International Journal of Audiology* 55, 11: 666–673. DOI: 10.1080/14992027.2016.1200146. 119

327. Hillary K. Rono, Andrew Bastawrous, David Macleod, Emmanuel Wanjala, Gian Luca Di Tanna, Helen A. Weiss, and Matthew J. Burton. 2018. Smartphone-based screening for visual impairment in Kenyan school children: a cluster randomised controlled trial. *The Lancet Global Health* 6, 8: e924–e932. DOI: 10.1016/s2214-109x(18)30244-4. 131

328. Daniel Rosenberg. 2016. Educating for HCI at scale. *Interactions* 23, 4: 72–75. DOI: 10.1145/2931081. 13, 14

329. Harilyn Rousso. 2008. Role models, mentors and muses for women with disabilities. *Impact: Feature Issue on Employment and Women with Disabilities* 21, 1: 8–9. 93

330. Shanna Russ and Foad Hamidi. 2021. Online learning accessibility during the COVID-19 pandemic. In *Proceedings of the 18th International Web for All Conference, W4A '21.* ACM, New York, NY, pp. 1–7. DOI: 10.1145/3430263.3452445. 101

331. Dan Saffer. 2010. *Designing for Interaction.* New Riders Berkeley. 36, 37, 39

332. Panjaj Kumar Sah. 2013. Assistive technology competencies: Need, outlook, and prospects with reference to special educators for children with visual impairment. *American Journal of Disability* 200, 15: 22–35. 97

333. Nithya Sambasivan and Thomas Smyth. 2010. The human infrastructure of ICTD. *Proceedings of the 4th ACM/IEEE International Conference on Information and Communication Technologies and Development*, ACM, 40:1-40:9. DOI: 10.1145/2369220.2369258. 58, 60

334. Theodosios Sapounidis and Stavros Demetriadis. 2013. Tangible versus graphical user interfaces for robot programming: exploring cross-age children's preferences. *Personal and Ubiquitous Computing* 17, 8: 1775–1786. DOI: 10.1007/s00779-013-0641-7. 94

335. Sarah Albala, Catherine Holloway, Malcolm MacLachlan, Vivki Austin, David Banes, Rose Bandukda, Rainer Kattel, Marian Mazzucato, and Julian Walker. 2019. Capturing and creating value in the assistive technologies landscape through a mission-oriented approach: a new research and policy agenda. AT2030 Working Paper Series 1. 118

336. Candice Satchwell and Gail Davidge. 2018. The mismeasure of a young man: an alternative reading of autism through a co-constructed fictional story. *Qualitative Research in Psychology* 15, 2–3: 336–351. DOI: 10.1080/14780887.2018.1430208. 97

337. S. L. Saunders and B. Nedelec. 2014. What work means to people with work disability: a scoping review. *Journal of Occupational Rehabilitation* 24, 1: 100–110. DOI: 10.1007/s10926-013-9436-y. 80, 91

338. Cornelia Schneider. 2017. Teachers' perceptions of disabilities on the island of Roatán, Honduras. *Disability, CBR and Inclusive Development* 28, 2: 5–22. DOI: 10.5463/dcid.v28i2.573.

339. Lisa Schur, Kyongji Han, Andrea Kim, Mason Ameri, Peter Blanck, and Douglas Kruse. 2017. Disability at Work: A Look Back and Forward. *Journal of Occupational Rehabilitation* 27, 4: 482–497. DOI: 10.1007/s10926-017-9739-5. 104

340. Tom Shakespeare. 2006. The social model of disability. *The Disability Studies Reader* 2: 197–204. 80, 81

341. Stuart C. Shapiro. 2003. Artificial intelligence (AI). In *Encyclopedia of Computer Science*. John Wiley and Sons Ltd., GBR, 89–93. 136

342. Helen Sharp, Jennifer Preece, and Yvonne Rogers. 2019. *Interaction Design: Beyond Human-Computer Interaction*. John Wiley and Sons. 46

343. Lichao Shen, Yamen Saraji, Kai Steven Kunze, and Kouta Minamizawa. 2018. Unconstrained neck: Omnidirectional observation from an extra robotic neck. *Proceedings of the 9th Augmented Human International Conference, AH 2018*, ACM, a38. DOI: 10.1145/3174910.3174955. 144

344. Alice Sheppard. 2021. *Kinetic Light*. Retrieved October 28, 2021 from https://alicesheppard.com/disabilitydanceworks/kinetic-light/. 42

345. M. Sherry. 2007. Chapter 1. In *(Post) Colonising Disability*. Wagadu, 21–26. 80

346. Ashley Shew. 2020. Ableism, technoableism, and future AI. *IEEE Technology and Society Magazine* 39, 1: 40–85. DOI: 10.1109/MTS.2020.2967492. 32

347. Ashley Shew. 2020. Let COVID-19 expand awareness of disability tech. *Nature* 581, 7806: 9–9. DOI: 10.1038/d41586-020-01312-w. 102

348. Kristen Shinohara, Michael McQuaid, and Nayeri Jacobo. 2020. Access differential and inequitable access: Inaccessibility for doctoral students in computing. *The 22nd International ACM SIGACCESS Conference on Computers and Accessibility*, ACM, 1–12. DOI: 10.1145/3373625.3416989. 99

349. Kristen Shinohara and Josh Tenenberg. 2009. A blind person's interactions with technology. *Communications of the ACM* 52, 8: 58–66. DOI: 10.1145/1536616.1536636. 7

350. Kristen Shinohara and Jacob O. Wobbrock. 2011. In the shadow of misperception: Assistive technology use and social interactions. *Proceedings of the SIGCHI Conference on Human Factors in Computing Systems*, ACM, 705–714. DOI: 10.1145/1978942.1979044. 7, 8, 22

351. Kristen Shinohara and Jacob O. Wobbrock. 2016. Self-conscious or self-confident? A diary study conceptualizing the social accessibility of assistive technology. *ACM Transactions on Accessible Computing* 8, 2: 5:1-5:31. DOI: 10.1145/2827857. 7

352. Ben Shneiderman. 2016. *The New ABCs of Research: Achieving Breakthrough Collaborations*. Oxford University Press. DOI: 10.1093/acprof:oso/9780198758839.001.0001. 32, 33, 58

353. Robert Sielski, Winfried Rief, and Julia Anna Glombiewski. 2017. Efficacy of biofeedback in chronic back pain: a meta-analysis. *International Journal of Behavioral Medicine* 24, 1: 25–41. DOI: 10.1007/s12529-016-9572-9. 43

354. Judy Singer. 2017. *Neurodiversity: The Birth of an Idea*. Self published on July 3, 2016 by Judy Singer. 112

355. Jeon Small, Pamela Schallau, Karen Brown, and Richard Appleyard. 2005. Web accessibility for people with cognitive disabilities. *CHI '05 Extended Abstracts on Human Factors in Computing Systems*, ACM, 1793–1796. DOI: 10.1145/1056808.1057024. 46

356. Gabrielle Smethurst, Helen M. Bourke-Taylor, Claire Cotter, and Fiona Beauchamp. 2021. Controlled choice, not choice and control: Families' reflections after one year using the National Disability Insurance Scheme. *Australian Occupational Therapy Journal* 68, 3: 205–216. DOI: 10.1111/1440-1630.12715. 51

357. C. Smith, H. Dickinson, Sophie Yates, and Massimiliano Bertuol. 2020. Not even remotely fair: Experiences of students with disability during COVID-19. Teaching and Learning in COVID-19 Times Study. https://apo.org.au/sites/default/files/resource-files/2020-07/apo-nid307154.pdf. 101

358. Emma M. Smith, Rosemary Joan Gowran, Hasheem Mannan, Brian Donnelly, Liliana Alvarez, Diane Bell, Silvana Contepomi, Liezel Ennion, Evert Jan Hoogerwerf, Tracey Howe, Yih Kuen Jan, Jenne Kazwiza, Natasha Layton, Ritchard Ledgerd, Malcolm MacLachlan, Giulia Oggero, Cecilia Pettersson, Thais Pousada, Elsje Scheffler, and Sam Wu. 2018. Enabling appropriate personnel skill-mix for progressive realization of equitable access to assistive technology. *Disability and Rehabilitation: Assistive Technology* 13, 5: 445–453. DOI: 10.1080/17483107.2018.1470683. 82

359. Emma M. Smith, Maria Luisa Toro Hernandez, Ikenna D. Ebuenyi, and Elena V. Syurina. 2020. Assistive technology use and provision during COVID-19: Results from a rapid global survey. *International Journal of Health Policy and Management*. DOI: 10.34172/ijhpm.2020.210. 64, 122, 123

360. Matthew Sparkes. What is a metaverse and why is everyone talking about it? *New Scientist*. Retrieved August 18, 2021 from https://www.newscientist.com/article/2286778-what-is-a-metaverse-and-why-is-everyone-talking-about-it/. DOI: 10.1016/S0262-4079(21)01450-0. 142

361. Katta Spiel, Christopher Frauenberger, Eva Hornecker, and Geraldine Fitzpatrick. 2017. When empathy is not enough: Assessing the experiences of autistic children with technologies. *Proceedings of the 2017 CHI Conference on Human Factors in Computing Systems* 2853–2864. DOI: 10.1145/3025453.3025785. 9

362. Katta Spiel, Christopher Frauenberger, Os Keyes, and Geraldine Fitzpatrick. 2019. Agency of autistic children in technology research—A critical literature review. *ACM Transactions on Computer-Human Interaction* 26, 6: 38:1-38:40. DOI: 10.1145/3344919. 1, 96

363. Katta Spiel and Kathrin Gerling. 2021. The Purpose of Play: How HCI games research fails neurodivergent populations. *ACM Transactions on Computer-Human Interaction* 28, 2: 11:1-11:40. DOI: 10.1145/3432245. 1

364. Katta Spiel, Kathrin Gerling, Cynthia L Bennett, Emeline Brulé, Rua Mae Williams, Jennifer Rode, and Jennifer Mankoff. 2020. Nothing about us without us: Investigating the role of critical disability studies in HCI. *CHI '20: CHI Conference on Human Factors in Computing Systems* 1–8. DOI: 10.1145/3334480.3375150. 8, 31

365. Katta Spiel, Laura Malinverni, Judith Good, and Christopher Frauenberger. 2017. Participatory evaluation with autistic children. *Proceedings of the 2017 CHI Conference on Human Factors in Computing Systems*, ACM, 5755–5766. DOI: 10.1145/3025453.3025851. 97

366. Emily J. Steel. 2019. The duplicity of choice and empowerment: disability rights diluted in Australia's policies on assistive technology. *Societies* 9, 2: 39. DOI: 10.3390/soc9020039. 50, 51

367. Emily J. Steel, Natasha Ann Layton, Michele M. Foster, and Sally Bennett. 2016. Challenges of user-centered assistive technology provision in Australia: shopping without a prescription. *Disability and Rehabilitation: Assistive Technology* 11, 3: 235–240. DOI: 10.3109/17483107.2014.941953. 50

368. Rebekah Steele and Marjorie Derven. 2015. Diversity and Inclusion and innovation: a virtuous cycle. *Industrial and Commercial Training*. DOI: 10.1108/ICT-09-2014-0063. 50

369. Constantine Stephanidis and Gavriel Salvendy. 1998. Toward an information society for all: An international research and development agenda. *International Journal of Human–Computer Interaction* 10, 2: 107–134. DOI: 10.1207/s15327590ijhc1002_2. 3

370. Jean-François Stich, Monideepa Tarafdar, and Cary L. Cooper. 2018. Electronic communication in the workplace: boon or bane? *Journal of Organizational Effectiveness: People and Performance* 5, 1: 98–106. DOI: 10.1108/JOEPP-05-2017-0046. 104

371. Emma Stone. 1999. *Disability and Development: Learning from Action and Research on Disability in the Majority World.* Disability Press. 79

372. Christine Duden Street, Robert Koff, Harvey Fields, Lisa Kuehne, Larry Handlin, Michael Getty, and David R. Parker. 2012. Expanding access to STEM for at-risk Learners: A new application of universal design for instruction. *Journal of Postsecondary Education and Disability* 25, 4: 363–375. 94

373. S Sujatha, Ganesh M Bapat, and Swostik Sourav Dash. 2021. GRID: a model for the development of assistive devices in developing countries. *Disability and rehabilitation Assistive Technology* 16, 3: 317–323. DOI: 10.1080/17483107.2019.1673838. 46, 132

374. Sharifa Sultana and Syed Ishtiaque Ahmed. 2019. Witchcraft and HCI: Morality, modernity, and postcolonial computing in rural Bangladesh. In *Proceedings of the 2019 CHI Conference on Human Factors in Computing Systems, CHI '19.* ACM, Glasgow, Scotland UK, pp. 1–15. DOI: 10.1145/3290605.3300586. 76

375. T. Sund. 2017. Assistive technology in Norway—a part of a larger system. Oslo, Norwegian Labour and Welfare Administration. 51

376. T. Sund. 2017. The Norwegian model of assistive technology provision. In *Global Perspectives on Assistive Technology: Proceedings of the GReAT Consultation.* World Health Organization. 51

377. Vidya Sundar, John O'Neill, Andrew J. Houtenville, Kimberly G. Phillips, Tracy Keirns, Andrew Smith, and Elaine E. Katz. 2018. Striving to work and overcoming barriers: Employment strategies and successes of people with disabilities. *Journal of Vocational Rehabilitation* 48, 1: 93–109. DOI: 10.3233/JVR-170918. 104

378. Manohar Swaminathan and Joyojeet Pal. 2020. Ludic design for accessibility in the Global South. *Assistive Technology and the Developing World,* M. Stein and J. Lazar (Eds.). Oxford University Press. Preprint at https://www. microsoft. com/en-us/research/publication/ludic-design-for-accessibility. 87

379. Saiganesh Swaminathan, Kotaro Hara, and Jeffrey P. Bigham. 2017. The crowd work accessibility problem. *Proceedings of the 14th International Web for All Conference*, ACM, 1–4. DOI: 10.1145/3058555.3058569. 92

380. Kazue Takayanagi, Takahiro Kirita, and Takanori Shibata. 2014. Comparison of verbal and emotional responses of elderly people with mild/moderate dementia and those with severe dementia in responses to Seal Robot, PARO. *Frontiers in Aging Neuroscience* 6: 257. DOI: 10.3389/fnagi.2014.00257. 143

381. Talila A. Lewis. 2020. Ableism 2020: An Updated Definition. Retrieved October 28, 2021 from http://www.talilalewis.com/1/post/2020/01/ableism-2020-an-updated-definition.html. 32

382. John Tang. 2021. Understanding the telework experience of people with disabilities. *Proceedings of the ACM on Human-Computer Interaction* 5, CSCW1: 30:1-30:27. DOI: 10.1145/3449104. 108, 109

383. Tanni Grey-Thompson. 2018. @Sarah_racewear Yes. I'm not keen on person with a disability. Makes it sound like I have a choice. I'm not a person with welshness. @Tanni_GT. Retrieved October 27, 2021 from https://twitter.com/Tanni_GT/status/996293106713669632. xix

384. S. Taraporevala. 2016. STEM education for blind and low vision students the socio-technical challenge: The Indian perspective. *The 3rd International Workshop on Digitization and E-Inclusion in Mathematics and Science* 2016 (DEIMS2016). 54

385. Tate. Futurism—Art Term. Tate. Retrieved August 12, 2021 from https://www.tate.org.uk/art/art-terms/f/futurism. 135

386. Helen Taylor, Brice Fernandes, and Sarah Wraight. 2021. The evolution of complementary cognition: Humans cooperatively adapt and evolve through a system of collective cognitive search. *Cambridge Archaeological Journal* 1–17. DOI: 10.1017/S0959774321000329. 112, 113

387. Emma Tebbutt, Rebecca Brodmann, Johan Borg, Malcolm MacLachlan, Chapal Khasnabis, and Robert Horvath. 2016. Assistive products and the sustainable development goals (SDGs). *Globalization and Health* 12: 79. DOI: 10.1186/s12992-016-0220-6. 91

388. Marko Teräs, Juha Suoranta, Hanna Teräs, and Mark Curcher. 2020. Post-Covid-19 education and education technology "solutionism": A seller's market. *Postdigital Science and Education* 2, 3: 863–878. DOI: 10.1007/s42438-020-00164-x. 102

389. Anja Thieme, Cynthia L. Bennett, Cecily Morrison, Edward Cutrell, and Alex S. Taylor. 2018. "I can do everything but see!" How people with vision impairments negotiate their

abilities in social contexts. *Proceedings of the 2018 CHI Conference on Human Factors in Computing Systems*, ACM, Paper 203. DOI: 10.1145/3173574.3173777. 8

390. Anja Thieme, Cecily Morrison, Nicolas Villar, Martin Grayson, and Siân Lindley. 2017. Enabling collaboration in learning computer programing inclusive of children with vision impairments. *Proceedings of the 2017 Conference on Designing Interactive Systems, ACM*, 739–752. DOI: 10.1145/3064663.3064689. 95

391. Linda P. Thurston, Cindy Shuman, B. Jan Middendorf, and Cassandra Johnson. 2017. Postsecondary STEM education for students with disabilities: Lessons learned from a decade of NSF Funding. *Journal of Postsecondary Education and Disability* 30, 1: 49–60. 94

392. Tomas Diez. *Fab City: The Mass Distribution of (Almost) Everything*. Institute for Advanced Architechture of Catalonia. 64

393. Transport Research Laboratory. streetaudit—PERS—TRL Software. Retrieved October 28, 2021 from https://trlsoftware.com/products/road-safety/street-auditing/streetaudit-pers/. 15

394. Thea Turner, Pernilla Qvarfordt, Jacob T. Biehl, Gene Golovchinsky, and Maribeth Back. 2010. Exploring the workplace communication ecology. *Proceedings of the SIGCHI Conference on Human Factors in Computing Systems*, ACM, 841–850. DOI: 10.1145/1753326.1753449. 104

395. Ivan Turok and Jackie Borel-Saladin. 2018. The theory and reality of urban slums: Pathways-out-of-poverty or cul-de-sacs? *Urban Studies* 55, 4: 767–789. DOI: 10.1177/0042098016671109. 76

396. UK Government. 2021. National Disability Strategy. Retrieved October 25, 2021 from https://www.gov.uk/government/publications/national-disability-strategy. 92

397. UNESCO. 2021. UNESCO Science Report: the race against time for smarter development—UNESCO Digital Library. 71

398. UNESCO Institute for Statistics. 2018. Education and Disability: Analysis of Data from 49 Countries. 91, 92

399. UNESCO. 2020. Global Education Monitoring Report 2020: Inclusion and Education: All Means All. 91

400. Stephen Uzor, Jason T. Jacques, John J Dudley, and Per Ola Kristensson. 2021. Investigating the accessibility of crowdwork tasks on Mechanical Turk. In *Proceedings of the 2021 CHI Conference on Human Factors in Computing Systems*. ACM, New York, NY, 1–14. DOI: 10.1145/3411764.3445291. 92

401. Gretchen L. Van Meer and Charles D. Sigwart. 1992. The impact of the Americans with Disabilities Act of 1990. *ACM SIGCAPH Computers and the Physically Handicapped* 45: 3–14. DOI: 10.1145/141433.141435. 2

402. G. C. Vanderheiden, D. F. Lamers, A. M. Volk, and C. D. Geisler. 1973. A communications device for the severely handicapped. *Proceedings of the ACM Annual Conference, ACM*, 396–397. DOI: 10.1145/800192.805743. 1

403. Gregg C. Vanderheiden. 1993. Making software more accessible for people with disabilities: a white paper on the design of software application programs to increase their accessibility for people with disabilities. *ACM SIGCAPH Computers and the Physically Handicapped* 47: 2–32. DOI: 10.1145/155824.155826. 2

404. Aditya Vashistha, Erin Brady, William Thies, and Edward Cutrell. 2014. Educational content creation and sharing by low-income visually impaired people in India. *Proceedings of the Fifth ACM Symposium on Computing for Development*, ACM, 63–72. DOI: 10.1145/2674377.2674385. 100

405. Aditya Vashistha, Edward Cutrell, Gaetano Borriello, and William Thies. 2015. Sangeet swara: A community-moderated voice forum in rural India. In *Proceedings of the 33rd Annual ACM Conference on Human Factors in Computing Systems, CHI '15*. ACM, New York, NY, pp. 417–426. DOI: 10.1145/2702123.2702191. 75

406. Aditya Vashistha, Edward Cutrell, Nicola Dell, and Richard Anderson. 2015. Social media platforms for low-income blind people in India. *Proceedings of the 17th International ACM SIGACCESS Conference on Computers and Accessibility*, ACM, 259–272. DOI: 10.1145/2700648.2809858. 11

407. Aditya Vashistha, Pooja Sethi, and Richard Anderson. 2018. BSpeak: An accessible voice-based crowdsourcing marketplace for low-income blind people. *Proceedings of the 2018 CHI Conference on Human Factors in Computing Systems*, ACM, 57:1-57:13. DOI: 10.1145/3173574.3173631. 92

408. Carlos Velasco and Marianna Obrist. 2020. *Multisensory Experiences: Where the Senses Meet Technology*. Oxford University Press. DOI: 10.1093/oso/9780198849629.001.0001. 42, 43

409. Gerbrand Verburg, Debbie Field, Francois St. Pierre, and Stephen Naumann. 1986. Toward universality of access: Interfacing physically disabled students to the icon educational microcomputer. *SIGCHI Bulletin* 18, 4: 75–80. DOI: 10.1145/1165387.30863. 2

410. Nina Vindegaard and Michael Eriksen Benros. 2020. COVID-19 pandemic and mental health consequences: Systematic review of the current evidence. *Brain, Behavior, and Immunity* 89: 531–542. DOI: 10.1016/j.bbi.2020.05.048. 129

411. Jonathan Waddington, Conor Linehan, Kathrin Gerling, Kieran Hicks, and Timothy L Hodgson. 2015. Participatory design of therapeutic video games for young people with neurological vision impairment. *Proceedings of the 33rd Annual ACM Conference on Human Factors in Computing Systems, CHI '15*. Association for Computing Machinery, New York, NY, pp. 3533–3542. DOI: 10.1145/2702123.2702261.103

412. Patrice L. Tamar Weiss, Emily A. Keshner, and Mindy F. Levin. 2014. *Virtual Reality for Physical and Motor Rehabilitation*. Springer Publishing Company, Incorporated. 42

413. Zikai Alex Wen, Erica Silverstein, Yuhang Zhao, Anjelika Lynne Amog, Katherine Garnett, and Shiri Azenkot. 2020. Teacher views of math e-learning tools for students with specific learning disabilities. *The 22nd International ACM SIGACCESS Conference on Computers and Accessibility*, ACM, 1–13. DOI: 10.1145/3373625.3417029. 97

414. Meredith Whittaker, Meryl Alper, Cynthia L. Bennett, Sara Hendren, Liz Kaziunas, Mara Mills, Meredith Ringel Morris, Joy Rankin, Emily Rogers, Marcel Salas, and Sarah Myers West. 2019. Disability, bias, and AI. For Work / Against Work. Retrieved October 28, 2021 from https://onwork.edu.au/bibitem/2019-Whittaker,Meredith-Alper,Meryl-etal-Disability,bias,and+AI/. 139

415. WHO. 1994. *A User's Guide to the Self Reporting Questionnaire (SRQ)*. Retrieved from http://apps.who.int/iris/bitstream/10665/61113/1/WHO_MNH_PSF_94.8.pdf. 129

416. WHO. 2016. *Priority Assistive Products List*. World Health Organization. 124

417. WHO. 2017. *Global Priority Research Agenda for Improving Access to High-Quality Affordable Assistive Technology*. World Health Organization. 22

418. WHO. 2019. *Mental Health in Emergencies*. Retrieved October 28, 2021 from https://www.who.int/news-room/fact-sheets/detail/mental-health-in-emergencies. 128

419. WHO. 2021. WHO Fact Sheet on Assistive Technology. Retrieved October 28, 2021 from https://www.who.int/news-room/fact-sheets/detail/assistive-technology. 22

420. Danielle Wilde and Patrizia Marti. 2018. Exploring aesthetic enhancement of wearable technologies for deaf women. *Proceedings of the 2018 Designing Interactive Systems Conference* 201–213. DOI: 10.1145/3196709.3196777. 13

421. Michele A. Williams, Amy Hurst, and Shaun K. Kane. 2013. "Pray before you step out" describing personal and situational blind navigation behaviors. *Proceedings of the 15th*

International ACM SIGACCESS Conference on Computers and Accessibility, ASSETS '13. ACM, New York, NY, p. 28:1–28:8. DOI: 10.1145/2513383.2513449. 22

422. Rhys James Williams, Catherine Holloway, and Mark Miodownik. 2016. The ultimate wearable: Connecting prosthetic limbs to the IoPH. *Proceedings of the 2016 ACM International Joint Conference on Pervasive and Ubiquitous Computing: Adjunct*, ACM, 1079–1083. DOI: 10.1145/2968219.2972711. 126

423. Rhys James Williams, Atsushi Takashima, Toru Ogata, and Catherine Holloway. 2019. A pilot study toward long-term thermal comfort research for lower-limb prosthesis wearers. *Prosthetics and Orthotics International* 43, 1: 47–54. DOI: 10.1177/0309364618791604. 127

424. Rua M. Williams. 2020. Falsified incompetence and other lies the positivists told me. *Canadian Journal of Disability Studies* 9, 5: 214–244. DOI: 10.15353/cjds.v9i5.696. 32

425. Rua M. Williams and Juan E. Gilbert. 2019. Cyborg perspectives on computing research reform. *Extended Abstracts of the 2019 CHI Conference on Human Factors in Computing Systems, CHI EA '19*. ACM, New York, NY, pp. 1–11. DOI: 10.1145/3290607.3310421. 9, 19

426. Rua M. Williams and Juan E. Gilbert. 2019. "Nothing about us without us" transforming participatory research and ethics in human systems engineering. In *Advancing Diversity, Inclusion, and Social Justice Through Human Systems Engineering*. CRC Press. DOI: 10.1201/9780429425905-9. 63

427. Rua M. Williams, Kathryn Ringland, Amelia Gibson, Mahender Mandala, Arne Maibaum, and Tiago Guerreiro. 2021. Articulations toward a crip HCI. *Interactions* 28, 3: 28–37. DOI: 10.1145/3458453. 9

428. Rua M. Williams, Simone Smarr, Diandra Prioleau, and Juan E. Gilbert. 2021. Oh no, not another trolley! On the need for a co-liberative consciousness in CS pedagogy. *IEEE Transactions on Technology and Society*: 1–1. DOI: 10.1109/TTS.2021.3084913. 139

429. Rua Mae Williams. 2019. Metaeugenics and metaresistance: From manufacturing the "includeable body" to walking away from the broom closet. *Canadian Journal of Children's Rights/Revue Canadienne des Droits des Enfant*s 6, 1: 60–77. DOI: 10.22215/cjcr. v6i1.1976. 56, 57, 63, 66

430. Stephen Winn and Ian Hay. 2009. Transition from school for youths with a disability: issues and challenges. *Disability and Society* 24, 1: 103–115. DOI: 10.1080/09687590802535725. 98

431. WIPO. 2021. WIPO Technology Trends 2021: Assistive Technology. World, Geneva: World Intellectual Property Organization. 64

432. Luc de Witte, Emily Steel, Shivani Gupta, Vinicius Delgado Ramos, and Uta Roentgen. 2018. Assistive technology provision: toward an international framework for assuring availability and accessibility of affordable high-quality assistive technology. *Disability and Rehabilitation: Assistive Technology* 13, 5: 467–472. DOI: 10.1080/17483107.2018.1470264. 83

433. Jacob O. Wobbrock, Krzysztof Z. Gajos, Shaun K. Kane, and Gregg C. Vanderheiden. 2018. Ability-based design. *Communications of the ACM* 61, 6: 62–71. DOI: 10.1145/3148051. 4, 5, 6, 13, 36, 57

434. Marisol Wong-Villacres, Adriana Alvarado Garcia, and Javier Tibau. 2020. Reflections from the classroom and beyond: Imagining a decolonized HCI education. *Extended Abstracts of the 2020 CHI Conference on Human Factors in Computing Systems*, ACM, 1–14. DOI: 10.1145/3334480.3381808. 73

435. Lisa Wood, Billie Giles-Corti, and Max Bulsara. 2005. The pet connection: pets as a conduit for social capital? *Social Science and Medicine* (1982) 61, 6: 1159–1173. DOI: 10.1016/j.socscimed.2005.01.017. 140

436. World Bank. 2020. Pivoting to Inclusion: Leveraging Lessons from the COVID-19 Crisis for Learners with Disabilities. 102

437. Lucy Yardley, Bonnie J. Spring, Heleen Riper, Leanne G. Morrison, David H. Crane, Kristina Curtis, Gina C. Merchant, Felix Nughton, and Ann Blandford. 2016. Understanding and promoting effective engagement with digital behavior change interventions. *American Journal of Preventive Medicine* 51, 5: 833–842. DOI: 10.1016/j.amepre.2016.06.015. 121

438. Anon Ymous, Katta Spiel, Os Keyes, Rua M. Williams, Judith Good, Eva Hornecker, and Cynthia L. Bennett. 2020. "I am just terrified of my future"; Epistemic violence in disability related technology research. *Extended Abstracts of the 2020 CHI Conference on Human Factors in Computing Systems*, ACM, 1–16. DOI: 10.1145/3334480.3381828. 9, 28

439. Bin Yu, Mathias Funk, Jun Hu, Qi Wang, and Loe Feijs. 2018. Biofeedback for everyday stress management: A systematic review. *Frontiers in ICT* 5: 23. DOI: 10.3389/fict.2018.00023. 43

440.   Bingqing Zhang, Catherine Holloway, T. Carlson, and R. Ramirez Herrera. 2019. Shared-control in wheelchairs–building interaction bridges. *CHI'19 workshop: Weaving the Threads of Vehicle Automation.* 143

441.   Bingqing Zhang, Catherine Holloway, and Tom Carlson. 2020. A hierarchical design for shared-control wheelchair navigation in dynamic environments. *2020 IEEE International Conference on Systems, Man, and Cybernetics* (SMC), 4439–4446. 41, 143

442.   Yuhang Zhao, Michele Hu, Shafeka Hashash, and Shiri Azenkot. 2017. Understanding low vision people's visual perception on commercial augmented reality glasses. *Proceedings of the 2017 CHI Conference on Human Factors in Computing Systems, CHI '17.* ACM, New York, NY, pp. 4170–4181. DOI: 10.1145/3025453.3025949. 22

443.   Dingding Zheng, Laura Lugaresi, Masa Inakage, George Chernyshov, Kai Kunze, and Benjamin Tag. 2017. Wearable aura: An interactive projection on personal space to enhance communication. *Proceedings of The 2017 ACM International Joint Conference on Pervasive and Ubiquitous Computing and Proceedings of the 2017 ACM International Symposium on Wearable Computers* (Ubicomp/Iswc '17 Adjunct). DOI: 10.1145/3123024.3123161. 140 , 141

444.   Hui Zheng and Vivian Genaro Motti. 2018. Assisting students with intellectual and developmental disabilities in inclusive education with smartwatches. *Proceedings of the 2018 CHI Conference on Human Factors in Computing Systems*, ACM, 350:1-350:12. DOI: 10.1145/3173574.3173924. 94

445.   Alyssa Hillary Zisk and Elizabeth Dalton. 2019. Augmentative and alternative communication for speaking autistic adults: Overview and recommendations. *Autism in Adulthood* 1, 2: 93–100. DOI: 10.1089/aut.2018.0007. 105

446.   Annuska Zolyomi, Anushree Shukla, and Jaime Snyder. 2017. Technology-mediated sight: A case study of early adopters of a low vision assistive technology. *Proceedings of the 19th International ACM SIGACCESS Conference on Computers and Accessibility, ASSETS '17.* ACM, New York, NY, pp. 220–229. DOI: 10.1145/3132525.3132552. 22 , 108

447.   Kathryn Zyskowski, Meredith Ringel Morris, Jeffrey P. Bigham, Mary L. Gray, and Shaun K. Kane. 2015. Accessible crowdwork? Understanding the value in and challenge of microtask employment for people with disabilities. *Proceedings of the 18th ACM Conference on Computer Supported Cooperative Work and Social Computing*, ACM, 1682–1693. DOI: 10.1145/2675133.2675158. 92

448.   2020. International Day of Persons with Disabilities: How disability affects labour market outcomes. *ILOSTAT.* Retrieved October 28, 2021 from https://ilostat.ilo.org/in-

ternational-day-of-persons-with-disabilities-how-disability-affects-labour-market-out-comes/. 92, 106

449. WHO|World report on disability. Retrieved January 23, 2019 from https://www.who.int/disabilities/world_report/2011/report/en/. 9, 14

450. TikTok suppressed disabled users' videos—BBC News. Retrieved October 28, 2021 from https://www.bbc.com/news/technology-50645345. 17

451. Disabled Creators on TikTok Go Beyond "Inspiration Porn"|Allure. Retrieved October 28, 2021 from https://www.allure.com/story/disabled-creators-on-tiktok. 17

452. TikTok Creators with Disabilities Find Community on the App. Verywell Health. Retrieved October 28, 2021 from https://www.verywellhealth.com/tiktok-community-disability-pride-month-5193467. 17

453. What are Wicked Problems? The Interaction Design Foundation. Retrieved August 8, 2021 from https://www.interaction-design.org/literature/topics/wicked-problems. 30, 31

454. Goal 4|Department of Economic and Social Affairs. Retrieved October 17, 2021 from https://sdgs.un.org/goals/goal4. 34

455. Argus II: the life-changing retinitis pigmentosa treatment. Second Sight. Retrieved October 28, 2021 from https://secondsight.com/discover-argus/. 43

456. Assistive Technology Strategy|NDIS. Retrieved October 25, 2021 from https://www.ndis.gov.au/about-us/strategies/assistive-technology-strategy. 50

457. Global patterns in the publishing of academic knowledge: Global North, global South—Fran M Collyer, 2018. Retrieved October 28, 2021 from https://journals.sagepub.com/doi/abs/10.1177/0011392116680020?journalCode=csia. DOI: 10.1177/0011392116680020. 72

458. Game accessibility guidelines|A straightforward reference for inclusive game design. Retrieved October 28, 2021 from https://gameaccessibilityguidelines.com/. 103

459. Virginia Morash-Macneil, Friggita Johnson, and Joseph B. Ryan, 2018. *A Systematic Review of Assistive Technology for Individuals with Intellectual Disability in the Workplace*—Retrieved October 28, 2021 from https://journals.sagepub.com/doi/abs/10.1177/0162643417729166?journalCode=jsta. DOI: 10.1177/0162643417729166. 104

460. #WeThe15—A movement for an inclusive world. Retrieved October 28, 2021 from https://www.wethe15.org/. 113

461. Neurodiversity Hiring|Global Diversity and Inclusion at Microsoft. Retrieved October 25, 2021 from https://www.microsoft.com/en-us/diversity/inside-microsoft/cross-disability/neurodiversityhiring. 114, 115

462. WHO|Seventy-first World Health Assembly adopts resolution on assistive technology. WHO. Retrieved April 29, 2019 from http://www.who.int/phi/implementation/assistive_technology/71stWHA-adopts-resolution-on-assistive-technology/en/. 124

463. WHO|Guidelines on the provision of manual wheelchairs in less-resourced settings. WHO. Retrieved July 24, 2017 from http://www.who.int/disabilities/publications/technology/wheelchairguidelines/en/. 124

464. Seeing AI|Talking camera app for those with a visual impairment. Retrieved October 28, 2021 from https://www.microsoft.com/en-gb/ai/seeing-ai. 137

465. Abascal, J., 2002. Human-computer interaction in assistive technology: from "Patchwork" to "Universal Design". Presented at the *IEEE International Conference on Systems, Man and Cybernetics*, IEEE, pp. 6-pp. DOI: 10.1109/ICSMC.2002.1176076. 4

466. Chesbrough, H., Vanhaverbeke, andW., West, J., 2014. *New Frontiers in Open Innovation*. Oxford University Press. DOI: 10.1093/acprof:oso/9780199682461.001.0001. 57

467. Loch, C.H., DeMeyer, A., and Pich, M., 2011. *Managing the Unknown: A New Approach to Managing High Uncertainty and Risk in Projects*. John Wiley & Sons. 57

468. Peters, D., Ahmadpour, N., and Calvo, R. A. (2020). Tools for wellbeing-supportive design: Features, characteristics, and prototypes. *Multimodal Technologies and Interaction*, 4(3), 40. DOI: 10.3390/mti4030040. 57

469. Riva, G., Baños, R.M., Botella, C., Wiederhold, B.K., and Gaggioli, A., 2012. Positive technology: using interactive technologies to promote positive functioning. *Cyberpsychology, Behavior, and Social Networking* 15, 69–77. DOI: 10.1089/cyber.2011.0139. 57

470. Hassenzahl, M., 2010. Experience design: Technology for all the right reasons. Synthesis Lectures on Human-Centered Informatics 3, 1–95. DOI: 10.2200/S00261ED1V01Y-201003HCI008. 57

471. Desmet, P.M. and Pohlmeyer, A.E., 2013. Positive design: An introduction to design for subjective well-being. *International Journal of Design* 7. 57

472. Barbareschi, G., Swaminathan, M., Pimenta Freire, A., Holloway, and C., 2021. Challenges and strategies for accessibility research in the Global South: A panel discussion. In *X Latin American Conference on Human Computer Interaction, CLIHC 2021*. Association for Computing Machinery, New York, NY, USA, pp. 1–5. DOI: 10.1145/3488392.3488412. 89

473.   Bainbridge, L. (1983). Ironies of automation. In *Analysis, Design and Evaluation of Man–Machine Systems* (pp. 129–135). Pergamon. DOI: 10.1016/B978-0-08-029348-6.50026-9. 142

Authors' Biographies

Cathy Holloway (she/her/hers) is a Professor of Interaction Design & Innovation at University College London's Interaction Centre, as well as a co-founder and the Academic Director of the Global Disability Innovation Hub (GDI Hub). Cathy co-directs the World Health Organization's (WHO) only Collaborating Centre on Assistive Technology at UCL. She graduated from the National University of Ireland, Galway in Industrial Engineering (design stream) before embarking on a brief career as an R&D Engineer with Medtronic. She left Ireland to pursue her career in assistive technology and disability at University College London (UCL). This began with a Ph.D. that explored the biomechanics of wheelchair propulsion. During her Ph.D., years she hung out in equal measures at the Royal National Orthopaedic Hospital, the Accessibility Research Group, and Science and Technology Studies. During this time, she developed her interest in the intersectionality of technology, disability, and poverty—and ultimately power within societies. Cathy went on to run the UCL Pedestrian Accessibility Movement Environment Laboratory and learned a lot about UCL, academia, port, and life from her mentor and boss Prof Nick Tyler CBE. In 2016, she transferred her academic post from Accessibility Engineering to UCLIC as she began the journey to start the Global Disability Innovation Hub (GDI Hub) with her co-founders and friends Victoria Austin and Iain McKinnon. UCLIC is the base from which Cathy has found her vision and purpose, and the GDI Hub journey has allowed Cathy to realize her childhood dream to work in all areas of the globe and with people who are marginalized. She feels grateful and privileged each day for the opportunities she is afforded in her roles at UCL. Cathy's research will continue to try and advance the possible with technology while searching for social justice. Currently, this is achieved though her formal roles with the World Health Organization, in her teaching and research, and by mentoring and leading a wonderful team.

Giulia Barbareschi (she/her/hers) is a Research Fellow in Disability and Assistive Technology Innovation at the Keio School of Media Design in Yokohama and the Global Disability Innovation Hub in London. She received her Ph.D. in 2018 from University College London, a Specialist Diploma in Medical Device Science from the National University of Galway in 2014, and a B.Sc. in Physiotherapy from the University of Genoa in 2008. From 2018 to 2021 she was a research fellow at the UCL Interaction Centre. Her research interest centers on the design, development, and evaluation of new and existing technologies to empower people with disabilities living in different parts of the world. This has included work on exploring the use of mobile phones by people with disabilities, developing and evaluating assistive technologies for mobility such as wheelchairs and lower limbs prosthetics, understanding how orientation and mobility skills support navigation for individuals with visual impairments, and evaluating the use of accessible technologies for improving access to inclusive education. A recent focus has been on how assistive technology influences self and external perceptions of disability across different cultures. Throughout her career Giulia has collaborated with several academic institutions across the world, start-ups and private ventures, NGOs, DPOs, and UN agencies.

Printed in the United States
by Baker & Taylor Publisher Services